THE NORTH EAST ELEMENTARY EDUCATION

THE NORTH EAST ELEMENTARY EDUCATION

Jayashree Roy

GYAN PUBLISHING HOUSE
New Delhi - 110002

THE NORTH EAST ELEMENTARY EDUCATION

Jayashree Roy

ISBN : 9788121208529

Published in 2015 in India by
Gyan Publishing House
23, Ansari Road, Daryaganj,
New Delhi - 110002
Phones : 23261060, 23282060 Fax : 23285914
e-mail : books@gyanbooks.com
website : gyanbooks.com

Contents

Acknowledgements 9

List of Tables 11

Introduction 17
A Brief Resume of Elementary Education Policy from the Nineteenth Century to 1992; The North-East Region; The Mizo and Naga Movements.

1. **A Background to the Development of Elementary Education in the North Eastern Region of India** 55
The Region; Colonial Policy; The Role of the Missions in Education.

2. **Elementary Schooling Facilities in the Region** 71
Primary Section; Growth of Primary and Upper Primary Schools; School Buildings; Ancillary Facilities; Furniture and Mats for Students; Furniture for Teachers; Black Boards; Teachers; Finance of Elementary Education 1975-76-1993-1994.

3. **Female Literacy and Elementary Education for Girls** 109
Literacy and the Tribal Dimension; Inter-district disparity - a Reflection of Tribal Groupings; Inter-District Disparities in Literacy 1981 and 1991; State and District-wise Position of Female Literacy and Enrolment of Girls; District-wise Percentage of Girls to Total Enrolment in Class I-V in 1986-87 in SC/ST Categories; Girl Enrolment and Dropouts from the Elementary Level.

4. **Decentralization of Education** 137
Powers and Functions of the District Council; District Council and State Government; District Councils and Their

Functioning; Evolution of the Role of Local Authorities in Primary Education in India; Education under Local Bodies in the North East.

5. **Case Study: Mizoram - A Description of the State** 157
Historical Background; Physical Setting; Economy; Demographic Characteristics; Education; Teachers' Training.

6. **Quality of Lower Primary Schools in LADC in Mizoram** 181
Academic Inputs; Teaching Staff; Inspection and Supervision; Curricular Innovations; Conclusion; Autonomy and Infrastructural Facilities; Curricular Innovations; Pupil Evaluation; Teacher Accountability; Community Participation; Sharing of Responsibility.

7. **Case Study II: Nagaland - A Description of the State** 197
Distribution of Marginal Workers and Non-Workers of Scheduled Tribes by the Activity and Level of Education in percentages in Nagaland; Literacy; Characteristics of Elementary Education; Teachers' Training; Structure and Administration of School Education; Financing of Elementary Education; Kohima District; Study Sample; Quality of Lower Primary Schoolsin the North Eastern Region of India.

Appendices 233

Bibliography 279

Index 289

Acknowledgements

I owe the completion of this thesis mainly to the constant guidance, patience and encouragement which I received from my supervisors, Professor Aparna Basu and Professor Sumit Sarkar without whose help the work would not have been completed. To my present institute of work namely, the National Institute of Educational Planning and Administration. To Professor B.P. Khandelwal I owe my gratitude for allowing me to do extensive field work as part of my work schedule, thereby enabling me to revisit the seven states several times to collect first hand information. To my ex-directors, Professor Satya Bhusan, Professor Kuldeep Mathur and my ex-department Head, Late Mr. M.M. Kapoor I owe my special thanks for making me take up the educational concerns of the North Eastern Region of India. Dr. N.V. Verghese, Dr. Pramila Menon, Dr. A.C. Mehta and Dr. Zaidi, my colleagues have always been a source of inspiration My thanks are also due to Prof. Pradip Kumar the Present Director. My special thanks go to Mr. Satbir Bhardwaz and Mr. Satish Kumar for typing the manuscript. My other colleagues like Ramblia, Sheila, Sushma and Sobha have shown their patience when at times I had felt I could not finish the given task. My thanks are also due to Mr. Irfan Ahmed and Mr. Arvind K. Sinha for helping me analyze the data and to my family members Prof. Rani Roy and Sridhar Chakraborty for keeping the work going. Ms. Nirmal Malhotra, Consultant NIEPA library has always helped me collect recent material on the subject. To all I also owe my thanks. And finally I would be failing in my duty if I did not acknowledge the help of Mr. F. Lallura, Director, School Education, Government of Mizoram for explaining in detail the situation in the North East and particularly Mizoram for the past thirteen years, His insight into the rapid development of education in the state and variables involved was of immense importance in understanding a complex phenomenon.

Jayashree Roy

List of Tables

1.1.	North Eastern Region Basic	55
2.1.	Growth Rate in Primary Schools	77
2.2.	Growth Rate on Middle Schools	78
2.3.	Total Number of Recognised Primary and Middle Schools in North-East 1993, 2001-2002	78
2.4.	Statewise Primary School According to Type of Buildings 1986	79
2.4.1.	Statewise Primary School According to Type of Buildings 1993	79
2.5.	Middle School According to Types of Buildings 1986	80
2.5.1.	Middle School According to Types of Buildings 1993	80
2.6.	Statewise Primary Schools Having Ancillary Facilities in North East 1986	81
2.6.1.	Statewise Primary Schools Having Ancillary Facilities in North East 1993	81
2.7.	Statewise Upper Primary Schools Having Ancillary Facilities in North East 1986	82
2.7.1.	Statewise Upper Primary Schools Having Ancillary Facilities in North East 1993	82
2.8.	Percentage Increase in Number of Primary School Teacher	86
2.9.	Percentage Increase in Number of Middle School Teachers	87
2.10.	Percentage of Female Teachers in Primary Schools	87
2.11.	Percentage of Female Teachers in Upper Primary Schools	87

2.12.	Statewise Pupil-Teacher Ratio at Primary and Upper Primary Stages in North East 1986	89
2.12.1.	Statewise Pupil-Teacher Ratio at Primary and Upper Primary Stages in North East 1993	89
2.13.	Percentage of Teachers in Position in Primary Schools in 1986	90
2.13.1.	Percentage of Teachers in Position in Primary Schools in 1993	90
2.14.	Percentage of Trained Primary School Teachers	91
2.15.	Percentage of Trained Middle School Teachers	91
2.16.	Qualifications of Primary School Teachers in Percentage	93
2.16.1.	Qualifications of Primary School Teachers in Percentage (1993)	94
2.17.	Qualifications of Middle School Teachers in Percentage	94
2.17.1.	Qualifications of Primary Middle School Teachers in Percentage (1993)	94
2.18.	State-wise Village with Non-Formal Education Centres and Enrolment, 1978	95
2.18.1.	Number of Villages with Centre at	95
2.19.	Non-Formal Education Centres and Enrolment 1986	95-96
2.19.1.	Non-Formal Education Centres and Enrolment, 1993	96
2.20.	Arunachal Pradesh : Data on Finance on Elementary Education	98
2.21.	Assam : Data on Finance on Elementary Education 1975-76 –1993-94	99
2.22.	Manipur : Data on Finance on Elementary Education 1975-76 – 1993-94	100
2.23.	Meghalaya : Data on Finance on Elementary Education 1975-76 – 1993-94	101
2.24.	Mizoram : Data on Finance on Elementary Education 1975-76 – 1993-94	102
2.25.	Nagaland : Data on Finance on Elementary Education 1975-76 – 1993-94	103
2.26.	Tripura : Data on Finance on Elementary Education 1975-76 – 1993-94	104

2.27. State-wise Data on Finance on Elementary Education 1994-95 –2001-02 BE 105-106

3.1. Economic Classification of Population 1991 110

3.1.1. Total Workers (main+marginal) and their categories-India, North Eastern States: 2001 111

3.2. Elementary Education 112

3.3. Growth Rate on Literacy in Percentage 113

3.4. Districtwise Levels of Educational Development 1981 115-117

3.5. District-wise Levels of Educational Development 1991 118-122

3.6. List of State-wise Distribution of Backward Districts with low age specific (6-11 years) enrolment ratio for Girls in Rural areas, 1986 123

3.6.1. Classification of Districts according to Total Literacy Levels 124

3.6.2. Classification of Districts according to Female Literacy Levels 125

3.7. Literacy by SC, ST in North-Eastern States 128

3.8. Growth Rate on Enrolment at Primary Level Total and Girls in Percentage 129-130

3.9. Growth Rate in Middle School Enrolment Total and Girls in Percentage 130

3.10. North Eastern States : Enrolment and Dropout Rates at Primary Schools 1986, 1993 131

3.11. North Eastern States: Enrolment and Dropout Rates at Middle Schools 1986, 1993 132

5.1. Districts, Educational Blocks, Inhabited Villages and Habitations 159

5.2. Percentage of main workers in Cultivation, Agricultural Labour, Household Industry and Other Work to Total main workers for Mizoram and India: 1971 to 1991 161

5.3. Percentage of Different Categories of Workers to Total Main Workers for Males and Females Mizoram, 1981 and 1991 163

5.4. Selected Demographic Indicators 164

5.5. Literacy Rates in Mizoram : 1961-1991 165

5.6.	District-wise Break up of Literates as percentage of Total Population	165
5.6.1.	District-wise Literacy Rates, Mizoram	166
5.7.	Enrolment Ratio in Classes I-V and VI-VIII of Schools for General Education : Mizoram and India, 1994-95 and 2001-02	167
5.8.	Completion Rates of Schooling at the Primary Level in the North East 1993	167
5.9.	Elementary Schooling Facilities per sq. km; in Mizoram, 1993	168
5.10.	Number of Teachers, Percentage Trained and Teacher Pupil Ratio as on 30th September, 1993	168
5.11.	Sub-division-wise Number of Teachers by Sex in Mizoram	169
5.12.	Subdivision-wise Enrolment in Primary Schools by Management, 1993	171
5.13.	Subdivision-wise Teachers in Primary Schools by Management, Training and Sex-wise	173
5.14.	Subdivision-wise Enrolment in Middle Schools by Management	174
5.15.	Subdivision-wise Training of Middle School Teachers by Management and Sex	175
5.16.	Qualification of Government Primary School Teachers, 1992	177
5.17.	Lai Autonomous District Council Education Budget 1995-96.	178
6.1.	Physical Facilities provided by Lai Autonomous District Council	182
6.2.	Provision of Academic Facilities	183
6.3.	Staff Strength in Sample Schools, 1995	185
6.4.	Use of Teaching Aids	185
7.1.	District-wise Breakup of Male/Female Literacy in Percentage in Nagaland	200
7.1.1.	District-wise Literacy Rates, North East	200
7.2.	Percentage of Illiterate ST with their Total Rural/Urban Population in Nagaland	201

7.3. Sector-wise Distribution of Workforce in Nagaland in Percentages 201-202
7.4. Marginal Workers 202-203
7.5. Non Workers 203
7.6. Kohima District : Schedule Tribe Workers 204
7.7. Kohima District : Non-Workers 204-205
7.8. Literate, Workers, Main Workers, Scheduled Tribe Population in the District Kohima 206
7.9. Selected Demographic Indicators 208
7.10. Nagaland Districts, Educational Blocks, Inhabited Villages and Habitations 209
7.11. Literacy Rate in Nagaland in Percentage : 1961-2001 210
7.12. District-wise Literate Nagaland Population by Sexes 211
7.13. Government Primary and Middle Schools in Nagaland 213
7.14. District-wise Teacher-Pupil Ratio in Government Schools in Nagaland in 1993 214
7.15. Number of Students in Educational Institutions in Nagaland 214-215
7.15.1. Number of Educational Institutions, Nagaland 215
7.16. Number of Teachers in Educational Institutions in Nagaland 216
7.16.1. Number of Teachers in Educational Institutions in Nagaland 217
7.17. Enrolment of Children in Schools in the Kohima District by Stages in 1993 222

Introduction

Universalisation of Elementary Education and its quality has been a major concern for all developing countries after the Second World War. However, unlike China and a few countries of South East Asia, India still has to enroll, retain and give quality education to all its children between the ages 6 to 14 years. It is not that this sector was neglected in the pre-independence period, but that primary and middle school curriculum which was often irrelevant to the socio-economic needs of school children failed to attract the children to schools. A colonial bias in curriculum, with emphasis on English and bookish knowledge of social studies, maths, and environmental sciences had little to do with the participation of economically deprived children employed in agricultural, industrial and household labour. Nor did the curriculum teach these children anything needed by their local environment. This "alien" education, therefore, failed to retain children in schools after Class I. Though as far as regions in India are concerned, the North East has a higher level of completion rates of primary school children, nevertheless it has also pockets of backwardness among illiterate tribes living in remote areas. A history of the development of elementary education in India with reference to the North East may throw some light on the causes of success or failure of universal elementary education policy.

In this book I have tried to trace the origin of modern education in the North East, analyze the growth of elementary schooling facilities, study the position of female literacy and girls' education in the context of educationally forward and backward tribes in districts, the effects of decentralization and the role of local bodies in primary education through case studies of Mizoram and Nagaland and finally to see as to how far the ethnic, or political movements of the region have either encouraged the growth of education or have adversely effected it.

A Brief Resume of Elementary Education Policy from the Nineteenth Century to 1992

At the beginning of the nineteenth century, several types of indigenous schools existed, the "schools of learning" included the Pathshalas for the Hindus and Madrassa for the Muslims. Although they were separate schools, they had several important features in common, for instance, both received pecuniary assistance from rulers, chieftains and opulent or religious citizens. Both were staffed by learned teachers, some of whom were authors of repute, but most of whom received very low remuneration. In both, instruction was mostly given gratis and no regular fees were charged. Both were medieval in character, imparting classical language as the medium of instruction (Sanskrit in one case and Arabic or Persian in the other). In both cases the teachers were rewarded either by grants of land made by rulers, by occasional voluntary presents from pupils and members of the public, by allowances paid by wealthy citizens and by payments in the form of food, clothes and other articles. Some of the teachers who taught gratis also provided their pupils food and lodging.

Generally speaking, the schools had no special buildings of their own. Where these existed, they were built either by the teachers themselves or at the expense of the parents or friends or by subscription from the people. In most cases, however the schools were held in the local temple or the mosque and not infrequently in the houses of local magnates or patrons or the teacher themselves. The students entered school at a fairly early age and studied as long as they desired, often for as long as twelve years or more. The state however, had nothing to do with the day-to-day functioning of these schools.[1]

The Hindu schools of learning were conducted almost exclusively by Brahmins and the majority of the students came from the same caste. In the Persian and Arabic schools, teachers were generally Muslims, and a Hindu teacher was a rare phenomenon. However, several Hindus attended Persian schools conducted by Muslims because Persian was then the court language.

There also existed what is known as "Indigenous Elementary Schools", which was the main agency for the spread of mass education. It was a humbler but far more useful institution where instruction was limited to the three 'Rs.' although it catered to the requirements of other upper castes, it had no endowments either from the state or from the public. Its teachers were ordinary, and, very often knew little more than what they imparted. These teachers also received less money than the teacher in the "schools of learning", except in those cases where the teachers were maintained by a rich person. Their earnings consisted of small collections or occasional presents from parents of children who attended the schools. Sometimes the teachers followed some other profession or trade for their own survival.

The indigenous schools were hardly adequately equipped. They had no buildings and classes were held in the house of the teacher or the patron of the school, often in a local temple and not infrequently under a tree. There were no printed books and the slates or pens used by pupils were of such quality as could be easily made in the locality. The instruction hours could also be adjusted to local requirements. The size of the school was small, the number of pupils varied from one or two to ten or fifteen. Consequently there were no class hours or period of admission. The student could join the school at any time and study at his/her own pace. The student was also free to leave the school as and when he/she had obtained the desired knowledge.[2] In the bigger schools, the senior pupils were appointed to teach their juniors. This model was adopted by Dr. Bell, the Presidency Chaplain at Madras, and later extended to England in the form of what became known as the monitorial or Madras system. The curriculum consisted of reading, writing, arithmetic and accounts. There was no fee in the modern sense, but each parent of the child attending school, made some payment to the teacher either in cash or in kind.

One of the chief merits of the 'indigenous system' of elementary schools was its capacity to adapt itself to the local environment. Their main defect was the exclusion of girls and Harijan pupils. Another was the lack of training of its teachers. However, by the beginning of the nineteenth century, the indigenous system of education was fast decaying, because of the inability of Indians to support education owing to their poor economic conditions.

Adams report indicated that Indian national system of education could be built upon the foundations of indigenous schools. He had maintained that to whatever extent such institutions may exist, and in whatever condition they may be found, they present the only true and sure foundations upon which any scheme of general or national education ought to be established.

The East India Company accepted the responsibility for the education of Indians only in 1813 when the Charter Act stipulated that rupees one lakh should be set aside for education.

After 1765 when the Company became a political power in India, the educational policy underwent a change. The Company felt that it must do something for the education of the Indian people instead of directing its attention exclusively to European and Anglo-Indian children. Politically too, it was a successor to Hindu and Muslim rulers after the Battle of Plassey. Initially it sought to establish Madrassas and Pathsalas by giving pecuniary grants to learned Pandits and Maulavis and by endowing institutions of higher religious studies. The Company wanted to educate sons of influential Indians for higher posts to make them eligible in the government and thereby win the confidence of the upper classes and consolidate its rule in India. The Company in its desire to establish higher centres of learning for both the Hindus and the Muslims started the Calcutta Madrassah (1775) by Warren Hastings and the Benaras Sanskrit College (1791), by Jonathan Duncan, the Resident.

Side by side with the Company's efforts to educate natives, a number of missionaries organised other educational activities. As pioneers of private enterprise in education the contribution of the missionaries is significant. For the North East India the Danish missionaries were of no significance as their work was confined to Madras. The work of the Serampore missionaries in Bengal both at Serampore and Chinsura were done under the protection of the Dutch settlements. Dr. Carey, a representative of the Baptist Missionary Society in 1793 worked among the Bengalis in Malda and Calcutta. In 1799, two other missionaries—Ward and Marshman arrived in Calcutta, with the original objective to join Carey in his work in North Bengal, but the East India Company did not permit them to do so, hence they settled down in Serampore. All these three came to be known as the Serampore Trio.

The Serampore Trio did not come to any serious conflict with the Company's officials. There was a slow growth of missionary enterprise prior to 1813, when the Company became the official political power in India, it became conscious of the political importance of maintaining strict religions neutrality and this realization made it abandon all their earlier efforts to "teach Christianity".[3] Incidents like the Sepoy Mutiny at Vellore had made the Company (by 1800), keep the missionaries out of its territories. In the same way, the adoption of the Orientalist policy in education, between 1781 and 1791, deprived the mission schools of sympathy and support of the Company which they had enjoyed thus far. Charles Grant in his "Observations on the state of society among the Asiatic subjects of Great Britain, particularly with respect to morals.

and the means of improving it", pointed out that Hindus were generally concerned with themselves and were apathetic towards others. He suggested that English language should be adopted as a medium of instruction and that the situation in India would improve only if Indians were first educated and then converted to Christianity. They were to be taught Western knowledge and enlightenment.

In the meanwhile two things happened simultaneously. While the missionaries agitated in England for a change in the Company's educational policy, the officials of the Company in India wanted to spread Oriental education beyond the Calcutta Madrassah and Benaras Sanskrit College. The Orientalists wanted larger funds to revive and improve classical learning. Lord Minto, Governor-General of India, from 1806 to 1813, personally an admirer of Oriental literature, felt that, that kind of study would enrich Indians. It was against this background that the Charter Act of 1813 was passed. It discussed as to whether the missionaries should be allowed to go to India and work in the territory of the Company for the spread of education and for teaching of Christianity, and whether the Company should accept the responsibility for education of the Indian people. The Act clearly stated that although the missionaries were free to preach within the Company's territory, the Company was ultimately responsible for educating Indians. Henceforth, missionaries arrived in large numbers in India and a comparatively large amount of money was secured by the Company for educational activities among the Indians.

The period between 1813 and 1854, the year of Wood's Despatch, was one of consolidation of British power in India; hence education was not a major concern. It was also a period in which Indians were eager to imbibe western liberal scientific education. The importance of English language was also growing at that time. On February 2, 1835, Lord Macaulay came out with his Minutes advocating Western learning and English language. He felt that it was England's duty to teach Indians Western knowledge through English. Macaulay won the support of Lord Bentinck and Lord Auckland. In 1844, the Government announced its policy of giving every encouragement to educated westernised Indians by employing them in Government service.

From 1833 to 1853, the Government concentrated on the spread of western knowledge, securing properly trained servants for public administration of the country. It also believed that education of the upper classes of society would contribute to the development of a governing class in India. Education would gradually filter down to the masses and, that this upper class natives would ultimately educate the lower classes in their mother tongues. This was also a period of religious neutrality. It was a time when the relationship between the Company's officials and the missionaries was very cordial, and hence the missionaries contributed largely to the spread of western education. Three types of modern schools were developed, namely, (a) mission schools with their insistence on Bible teaching; (b) secular schools conducted by Indian social reformers which were more popular among the natives, and (c) government schools which were also secular. A large number of British non-officials, mainly businessmen, also assisted in the spread of western education. David Hare (1775-1842), a humble watchmaker and jeweller from Calcutta, started the Hindu Vidyalaya or College with the object of providing good English education to the sons of Hindu gentlemen. This became in 1854 the Presidency College. It emphasized secularism. Among the enlightened Indians of that period was Raja Ram Mohan Roy (1772-1833); but neither David Hare nor Ram Mohan had any impact on the North East India which was left to missionaries as elaborated in Chapter I of the Book.

In 1854 Charles Wood, the then President of the Board of Control, in his Education Despatch suggested new schemes. The first step was to create Departments of Public Instruction in each of the five provinces, namely Bengal, Madras, Bombay, the North-Western Province and Punjab. They were placed under Director of Public Instruction assisted by an adequate number of Inspecting Officers. The Despatch also dealt with university education, but for school education the network of graded schools was an important issue. Below the University and affiliated colleges came the high schools where instruction was either given in English or in a modern Indian language. At the very bottom stood the indigenous primary schools. The Despatch thus rejected the "Downward Filtration Theory" and recommended that modern Indian languages were to be the medium of instruction at the secondary schools. The inclusion of indigenous schools was of importance as the Despatch thought of a national system of education. A grant-in-aid system was also recommended for the Provincial Government which was to be framed according to their own needs.[4]

The Despatch did commend the work of missionary schools which were to be given government grant-in-aid. Teachers training became important and the necessity of providing suitable school books in Indian languages was realized.

The need to establish schools of industry along with vocational colleges was an attempt to link education with employment.

The general feature of the Victorian era (1854-1902) was one of tranquility. In general the Indians were also somewhat sympathetic towards the British rule, though by 1902 national sentiments and movements once again challenged the British dominance. With the establishment of the Indian National Congress in 1885, with leaders like Dadabhai Naoroji, criticism about the un-British character of the Indian administration began to surface. What was important for India as well as for the North East was that the centre of education had shifted from London to Calcutta. It was also a period of financial stringency with the result that education could not avail of liberal grants. However, private Indian enterprise in this field grew and special taxes were collected for education. Primary schools of the modern type also grew in numbers. In the North East, education of the tribes also grew.

As far as primary education is concerned the Despatch of 1859 recommended that the Department of Education should rely mainly on government schools for the spread of mass education. It was argued that elementary education should spread as widely as possible through schools directly controlled by the government. Ultimately each province was allowed to develop along its own lines. In Bengal, the system of primary education had been built entirely upon the indigenous school system. The Despatch of 1859 also suggested that local taxes should be imposed to meet the cost of mass education. Accordingly local taxes were imposed in all provinces to meet local expenditure including education. In rural areas, the land revenue provided the basic expenses. The local taxes in rural areas took the form of a cess on land revenue, except for Bengal where the existence of Lord Cornwallis' Permanent Settlement provided a different model. In the urban areas, the tax on houses was imposed and collected through municipalities. Although a local cess on land revenue was introduced in Assam in 1879, no cess on land revenue was imposed in Bengal even up to 1882. The Despatch of 1859 gave importance to the training of teachers for primary education. In Bengal, large government grants and adoption of the agency of indigenous schools helped the province to achieve considerable expansion of elementary schools.

The Indian Education Commission of 1882 referred to the spread of elementary education. As far as policy was concerned it stated that:

(i) Primary education be regarded as the instruction of the masses through vernacular in such subjects as will fit them for their position in life and not be necessarily regarded as leading up to the university.

(ii) Selection of persons to fill the lowest offices under government would give preference to candidates who can read and write.

(iii) The State should devote itself to the spread of elementary education.

(iv) Primary education be extended in backward districts, especially to those areas which were inhabited by the "aboriginal races"(tribes) by extending grants-in-aid to those who were willing to maintain them.

Primary education became the responsibility of the districts and municipal boards.

Further, that indigenous schools deserved encouragement and incorporation in the official system. Instruction in primary schools should be adapted to the environment and should be simplified and practical subjects such as Indian methods of arithmetic and accounts should be introduced. Managers should be free to choose the textbooks and utmost flexibility given to reading hours of the day and seasons of the year. Instruction should be made through the mother tongue. The Commission also recommended that a specific fund be created for primary education. The accounts of primary education fund in municipal areas should be separated from those of rural areas. Local funds had to be utilized mainly for primary education.

Lord Ripon accepted the recommendations of the Commission and hence the concept of local self-government was adopted. It does not mean that there was a devolution of authority in administration and decentralization of financial resources but a recognition that popular education was the means by which alone progressive communities could cope with the increasing problem of government. Primary education was declared to be an obligatory duty of local bodies.

The main achievements of the period 1854 to 1902 were the construction of school buildings; improvement of teacher training and qualification of teachers; admission of girls and pupils of low-castes; use of printed books, adoption of new methods of teaching and improvement of the curriculum to include kindergarten, drawing, object lessons, geography, history, singing, recreation, hygiene, agricultural, science, second language, physical exercises and manual work.

The period after the Victorian era (1902-21) was characterized by certain features, namely, involvement of larger finances; more active role of the State in education; vigorous attempts at qualitative improvement in all types of educational institutions; unprecedented expansion in almost all branches of education as well as the growth of militant nationalism. As far as finances were concerned the stable relationship between the central and provincial governments contributed to the growth of education. Central funds flowed in abundance due to the increase in world trade and commerce to which India was also a partner. The earliest of these grants was sanctioned by Lord Curzon. Between 1902 and 1918-19 the grants amounted to Rs.500 lakhs as non-recurring and Rs.300 lakhs as recurring. Larger finances were also available for education due to the improved condition of provincial governments. The local boards and municipalities also prospered during this period adding to their ability to assist in financing education. The other sources of increased finance were available under heads like endowments, donations, subscriptions, etc. Thus the total expenditure on education from both private and public sources which was only Rs. 401 lakhs in 1901-02 became Rs.1,837 lakhs in 1921-22.

Prior to Lord Curzon, the State only limited itself to providing grant-in-aid to private institutions. But now it was held that the State had a duty to maintain a few institutions of every type as models. A more vigilant policy of inspection and supervision of private schools was now adopted. Factors both in England and India were responsible for the State's commitment to education. In England the Balfour Act of 1902 was enacted to control private enterprise in elementary education and also improve its quality. In India too, the rise of native intelligentsia and political consciousness demanded greater responsibility of the State to improve the quality of Indian education. The fact that Western education was held largely responsible for the growth of nationalism led the British government to exercise greater control over private schools. The control of the State over private schools came to be resented by the nationalists. In 1921, under the system of dyarchy introduced by the Montagu-Chelmsford Reforms, the control of the Education Departments in the provinces was transferred to the Indian ministers.

As far as qualitative improvement was concerned, Lord Curzon, instead of accepting the principle of compulsory education at the elementary level wanted quality improvement. However, there was unprecedented expansion of elementary education between 1901-02 and 1921-22. In 1901-02 there were 97,854 primary schools and by 1921-22 that grew to 1,55,017. The number of primary school students also expanded from 32,04,336 in 1901-02 to 61,09,752 in 1921-22. This expansion was largely due to the social and political awakening among the Indians. Whereas quality improvement was due to official enterprise, quantitative expansion was due to Indian initiative. Lord Curzon introduced the kindergarten methods and object methods in primary schools.

In order to make primary education compulsory G.K. Gokhale, a nationalist leader, introduced a Bill in the Imperial Legislative Assembly, quoting the Compulsory Education Acts of England, 1870 and 1876 and the Irish Education Act of 1892. But the Bill was rejected by the government on the ground that financial constraint and administrative difficulties would not allow its implementation. Gokhale's work was taken up at the provincial level by Shri Vithalbai J. Patel in Bombay, and was extended to the Bombay Municipality between 1905 and 1922 where emphasis was given to the training of teachers and this was accepted as the State's responsibility. Thus, 38 per cent of the primary school teachers in Bombay were trained by 1922. The salary of a primary school teacher also grew from Rs. 8 to Rs. 33 per month. The primary school curriculum underwent a change to include subjects like School Gardening and Nature Study. Some improvement was also done to school buildings and equipment.

The most significant feature of this period was the growth of the idea of a "national education". So far, western education and teaching of English had been emphasized in primary schools, now the demand was for Indian management, introduction of a spirit of sacrifice on the part of the founders and teachers of institutions, provision of Indian religious education, lower fees and emphasis on classical and modern Indian languages. The demand was for "Swadeshi" education. It was felt that inculcation of love and reverence to the motherland should be an integral part of education. Mahatma Gandhi's Wardha Scheme of Basic Education became popular as it taught craft as central to the process of learning. The craft taught in basic schools was based upon local needs and hence Gandhiji attempted to link education with the world of work, making it more vocational and related to the agricultural activities of the country. Primary education, according to Gandhi also had to be financially self-sufficient by the sale of crafts taught in schools.

Under 'Dyarchy' (1921-37) there was a rapid development of mass education. Compulsory Education Acts were passed in Punjab, United Provinces, Bengal, Bihar and Orissa in 1919; Bombay, Central Provinces and Madras in 1920, Assam in 1926 and in rural Bengal in 1930, but it had no impact in Mizoram and Nagaland. The provincial governments transferred power to local bodies and local self-government institutions had to provide for primary education in their areas. The local authorities were free to enforce primary education at their own wishes, but an educational cess was imposed in order to meet the expenses of primary education. However, the government assisted the local authorities with finances. The age of compulsory education varied from province to province between 6 and 10, 7 to 11, and 6 to 11 years of age. The Acts made provision to penalise the parents who did not send their children to school. During this period the Muslims made attempts to spread education, untouchability was condemned, and hence a greater number of lower castes participated in primary education.

Provincial autonomy came into existence in 1937. Primary education was made compulsory and in Bombay it was extended to several municipal areas and in all the villages with a population of 1,000 or more. Opening of schools in school-less villages, sanctioning of additional grants to local bodies, opening of additional girls' schools, and sanctioning of additional posts for teachers in existing schools were the main features of the education scene between 1937-47. Gandhiji's Basic education was accepted throughout the country and tried out. North-East India, however, remained unaffected by this, especially the tribal states of Nagaland and Mizoram. As far as deployment of primary teachers were concerned there was to be one teacher for every 30 pupils in pre-basic school and for every 25 pupils in junior basic schools. The minimum qualification for a teacher was to be the High School Certificate followed by a training of two years.

After Independence the First (1951-55) and the Third (1961-65) Five Year Plans laid emphasis on the expansion of primary education, but compulsory education was only made a fundamental right for the child in 2001. The salary of a primary school teacher rose from Rs. 380 a year in 1946-47 to Rs. 800 a year in 1960-61. More teacher training institutes were established.

The period between 1947 and 1961 was characterized by the partnership between the Central Government and the States in sharing the responsibility to educate. The local bodies continued to play an important role in primary education. Overall the two major concerns of elementary education were quantitative expansion of education activities and quality improvement in terms of teachers' qualification, syllabus, teaching methods and textbooks.[5] Basic education was adopted as the national pattern of education. Enrolment of school children was also a major concern in this period and between 1946-47 and 1965-66 there was 250 per cent increase in enrolment of children in the primary stage and 378 per cent in the middle schools. As far as teachers' qualifications were concerned, matriculation was a must for the primary stage and graduation for the middle stage. Thus, by 1960-61 there was 36.3 per cent increase in the number of matriculate teachers. The percentage of trained teachers also increased. The salaries of primary and middle school teachers increased to Rs.873 and Rs.1,585. Schemes like the midday meals were introduced in schools.

Prior to the attainment of the status of UTs and Statehood, hill areas such as the Garo, Khasi and Jaintia hills (now Meghalaya), Lushai (now Mizoram) and Mikir Hills comprising of 13,12,939 (1961 census) population were a part of Assam. Primary education grew and by 1960-61 there were 15,979 institutions with 10,46,530 scholars.[6] Basic education also grew in Assam for which teachers were sent to Delhi, Jamia Millia, Wardha and Sevagram for training. For the hill areas comprising of Scheduled Tribes, the Sixth Schedule was introduced giving the Districts Councils autonomy in planning and management of primary education. Special grants were given for the construction of school buildings, hostels, teachers' quarters and scholarships to the tribal groups by the Central Government and 97 per cent of the ST population benefited from these.

After Independence, the Constitution of India in its Article 45 (Part IV) under the Directive Principles of State Policy made provision for 'Free and Compulsory Education for Children'. It said that 'The State shall endeavour to provide, within a period of ten years from the commencement of this constitution, for free and compulsory education for all children until they complete the age of fourteen years.' This emphasis on compulsory and free education was largely responsible for quantitative expansion of educational facilities between 1950 and 1980. Further, under Articles 15 and 17 under Fundamental Rights: Prohibition of Discrimination on Grounds of Religion, Race, Caste, Sex or Place of Birth, protection of the educational interests of the weaker sections of the Indian community, socially and educationally backward classes of citizens and Scheduled Castes and Schedules Tribes was given special importance.

Education was to be secular, but by Article 30 (1) all minorities, whether based on religion or language had the right to establish and administer educational institutions according to their choice. Hence throughout the North-East three types of primary and upper primary schools grew namely, government, aided and private schools. In the Concurrent List Entry No. 25, education was made the joint responsibility of the State and Central Government and hence numerous centrally sponsored schemes were provided to the states for quality improvement of primary schools such as the Operation Black Board, Mid-day meals scheme, Non-formal Education, Hindi teacher for the middle school for non-Hindi speaking areas.

In the First Five Year Plan (1951-56), emphasis was given to the Gandhian model of Basic Education which incorporated a rural based craft into the curriculum of elementary education. However, the Kothari Commission better known as the Indian Education Commission 1964-66, introduced 'Work Experience' to mean something wider than rural craft from the middle school onwards. It also stressed on the three-language formula which entailed the mother tongue or regional language, English as a link language and Hindi, or an Indian classical language or European language in schools. The students of primary schools had to be taught either in the mother tongue or regional language and in two languages at the upper primary stage such as the mother tongue and the official or semi-official language. It is due to this language policy that English became important in the North Eastern States. The Commission by laying emphasis on health education also helped the Central Government to introduce measures like free medical check-ups for students and free vaccination.

In order to uplift the weaker sections of society the Central Government started supplying the states with free textbooks and stipends which some of the North Eastern Scheduled Castes and Scheduled Tribe children benefited from. Residential tribal schools and staff quarters were sponsored for remote areas, which taken together enhanced the expansion of educational facilities in elementary schools. In 1986, the Central Government had come up with yet another package to boost the elementary sector of education for the Scheduled Castes and Scheduled Tribes, in its Programme of Action, in stating that not only all these category of students need to be enrolled and retained up to Class VIII, but they have to perform satisfactorily. Several other incentive schemes were also introduced such as pre-metric scholarship in addition to uniforms, books, and stationery. Moreover, constant micro-planning, which is, planning at the grass-root level, was also emphasized for ensuring enrolment, retention and successful completion of courses. The document stressed on the need to employ teachers from Scheduled Castes and Schedule Tribes. The preparation of primers for Classes I-II in tribal languages was considered a necessity. Infrastructural facilities in educational institutions were one of its concerns.[7]

In 1992, the Government of India came up with some other policy initiatives. The drop out rates for the years 1987-88 for the Scheduled Castes and Scheduled Tribes in India being high for Class I-VIII (68.81 for SC and 80.01 for ST), in addition to the post-metric scholarship, grant-in-aid to voluntary organizations was given in order to encourage them to open schools in remote areas. Further, book banks, coaching and allied schemes were encouraged. Educational complexes were set up for low literacy areas. For the tribal areas it was suggested that educational plan be implemented in an integrated manner – pre-school education (through Balwadis), non-formal education, elementary education and adult education. Decentralization and giving responsibility to local bodies to look after primary education was considered very important.[8]

The North-East Region

Historically speaking the North-East region comprising of Arunachal Pradesh, Assam, Manipur, Meghalaya, Mizoram and Nagaland and Tripura remained in relative isolation from changes in the colonial policy on elementary education. Even, when the British arrived in Assam, in the nineteenth century, most of Assam's population could hardly read or write. The Ahoms had kept education confined to the priestly class and the aristocracy learnt Sanskrit literature in 'Tols' taught by Brahmins.[9] Western impact in the hill areas of Assam, such as in present day Meghalaya, Mizoram and Nagaland and in the hill areas of Manipur, was felt because of the presence of Christian missionaries. The large number of converts in these regions took to learning the Bible in a few tribal languages and hence literacy and learning of the three 'R's took place resulting in what many social scientists feel was "detribalization". Though allowing the indigenous system of education to prevail, the British started educating Assamese youth with the hope that they would be able to occupy junior administrative posts, although Bengalis were retained in higher government positions. In 1835 the first English school was set up at Gauhati followed by the one in Sibsagar in 1840.[10]

In fact there was no noticeable progress of education in the region by the colonial rulers before the Charter Act of 1833, as David Scott, the agent to the Governor-General for the whole eastern frontier, favoured oriental learning rather than western education. He feared that undue attention to western learning would hurt local sentiments.[11] Hence indigenous schools were given grants and their pass-outs were even absorbed in government jobs.

The prejudice against female education in Assam, hindered the growth of separate schools for girls.[12] It was because of this dismal condition of girls, that, in 1917, the Calcutta University Commission recommended "Purdah" schools. Grants began to flow for girls' education and a number of scholarships were introduced for enhancing the qualification of women teachers. Provisions were also made for training of junior and senior vernacular teachers in Silchar and Nowgong. As a result of these government efforts and the growth of the idea that female education would contribute towards getting a good bridegroom, female literacy grew from 0.59 per cent in 1861 to 19.63 per cent in 1961 for the entire state of Assam. However, in 1904-05 the percentage of girls attending school in Lushai Hills (70) and Naga Hills (1.41) was better. The matriarchical and matrilineal character of the Khasi and Jaintia hills, where girls participation in socio-economic affairs prevailed, the demand for girls' education was more and in the same year, that is, 15.28 per cent. However, this demand for female education in that area, now Meghalaya state, decreased substantially as can be seen in Chapter III of this thesis.

Since by 1961 as many as 97.33 per cent of Mizos had embraced Christianity, the gap between male and female education was less in Mizo Hills. In fact this trend was seen as early as in 1939-40 where the percentage of girl students was 4.2 as against .8 in Naga hills.

In general, the British followed a policy of non-interference in tribal areas of Nagaland and Mizoram. They felt that it was not worth their while to meddle with the feuds and fights among tribal leaders but at the same time in 1851, Lord Dalhousie in his Minute of February 20th, had stated that the tribals would be encouraged to trade as long as they remained peaceful with the British.[13]

As discussed in Chapter I, a combination of missionary and Government efforts enhanced the literacy levels of the hill areas of Assam. In the Mizo hills, where most of the population was Christian, literacy percentage grew steadily came from 1931 onwards. Though Christianity first to Khasi and Jaintia Hills, in 1820 (Now Meghalaya), nevertheless, its growth became slow when compared with Mizo Hills. According to1961 data, of the rural areas of Mizo Hills there were 512 primary schools with 30,604 students, 90 junior basic schools with 9,346 students and 93 middle schools with 6,657 students.[14] These figures show that the percentage of Mizo population in primary schools was high (i.e., 5+ years of age). The average teacher-pupil ratio was also favourable 46:1. In the Mizo hills where 49.78 of its population was literate by 1961, parents wanted their children to participate in elementary education. The creation of their native language or Mizo tongue helped the different ethnic groups to unite, thereby asserting their own identity.

In 1963, the Assam government had initiated a special scheme for the educational development of Mizo Hills in which 200 additional posts of primary school teachers were sanctioned. This certainly helped the growth of elementary education in the area, as compared with the United Khasi and Jaintia Hills. In fact, the economic condition of the Khasi and Jaintia as well as that of Assam's Muslim population was so poor that the children worked in fields and could not even help in household work. These economic conditions explain the educational backwardness of these areas when compared with Mizo Hills, where children were enrolled in schools.

Another factor behind the growth of literacy and participation of children at the elementary level is the growth of the 'Mizo' tongue or a language derived from Lushai, but used by all groups of people. Ethnic minorities living in the Mizo Hills such as Chakma Kuki, Lakher (now Mara) and Pawi (now Lai) speak the Lushai or Mizo language. Even as early as in 1961 census, out of 10,000 rural population 7,878 spoke Mizo and 8,702 urban Mizos spoke the same. Chapter I traces the historical development of elementary education in the north-eastern region from colonial times till 1947 in detail.

One of the special characteristics of this region is the rise of ethnic or separatist movements which have had an effect either positive, as in the case of Mizoram or negative as in the case of Nagaland on the development of elementary education from the 1960s to 1980s. The isolation of the region encouraged the development of incredibly complex sub-systems, and of people who were largely unaffected by the mainstream Indian culture for centuries. While retaining their traditional life style the tribes of the hill regions remained for years busy with inter-feudal warfare.[15] The region's economy varied from place to place, and although 'slash and burn' method of agriculture prevailed in backward areas, yet modern types of terrace farming, use of advanced implements in farming, were also begun. However, there were very few industries except for tea, oil and a hydro-electric projects and local handicrafts in wood, bamboo and weaving of cloth.

During the 1950's there grew a conspicuous peripheral protest and dissent mobilization against the regional and national power centres. This is evident in the movements initiated by Naga Confederation of tribes. One of its features was to combine and unite various sub-groups. distributed among the different administrative units to form one coherent unit. In the case of the territories occupied by the Naga confederation of tribes (present day Arunachal Pradesh) the cry was for a separate and distinct territorial status. There was a demand for the recognition of respective language/ dialects as medium of communication in education.[16]

The North-Eastern Frontier Tract, renamed North-Eastern Frontier Agency in 1954, came under the jurisdiction of the Ministry of External Affairs. In 1965 its administrative jurisdiction was transferred to Ministry of Home Affairs and by 1972 it became a Union Territory, which in 1987 was called the State of Arunachal Pradesh.

In 1954-58 the Naga Hills and the Tuensang Frontier Districts were a part of Assam, which in 1963 was renamed as the State of Nagaland. In 1960 there was all round opposition to the language bill in the hill regions of Assam and hence the Administrative Re-organisation Commission in its report in 1971 recommended the reorgnization of states. The districts of Garo, Khasi and Jaintia were separated, and in 1972 they formed the state of Meghalaya. In the same year the Union Territories of princely states of Manipur and Tripura were also given full statehoods. The Lushai hills were renamed as Mizoram and became a Union Territory, and by 1987 it was given full statehood.

"The type of regionalism that developed in the region was a form that challenged the inevitability of integration and assimilation into the national mainstream".[17] The hill areas were kept away from development and maintained their traditional systems of economy with minimum communication facilities. These ethnic groups were confined to their respective territorial limits. The majority Mizo group of tribes also began to express their demands for autonomy and separation from Assam state in the 1950s and 1960s. Details of whose development, along with the Naga separatist movement will be dealt with later.

Several causes have been attributed to the rise of insurgency movements in the north-east. According to Dr. B. Dutta Roy 'the insurgency in the north-east India is the result of the total lack of agriculture, industrial and other developmental works. There is a perception gap between the government and the people of the region. . . .' The region is also to him, and other scholars, a victim of easy money poured by the centre which 'has affected the ethics and social structure of the people instead of sustained development.[18] Today insurgency is often seen as an 'armed rebellion by a section of people against a legally constituted government which also demands political, economic and social change led by a disciplined and highly motivated cadre of leaders who on the one hand strives to mobilize and motivate the masses and on the other tries to erode the authority of the government'[19]. however, its roots were far deeper embedded in the body politics of Assam government, before 1950.

While citing the economic underdevelopment of the region, Sukhendu Mazumdar also attributes the causes of insurgency to population growth, unemployed youth and influx of Bangladeshis and other population from Indian states. In fact, he along with many other scholars has referred to the involvement of Pakistan, Myanmar, China and Bangladesh where insurgent outfits take shelter and are trained in military and guerilla warfare.[20] Influx of Bengali Hindus and Muslims, as a result of the addition of Sylhet district to Assam in 1874, had created both language and identity problem[21] which a century later, resulted in the "anti-outsiders" or and "vai" (Mizorams) movement. To the Mizo, the domination of professions such as medicine, engineering, law and higher government jobs by the "vais" led to an anti-Bengali or rather anti-Sylheti feelings from the 1970s. As a result of this the demand for education became stronger - so that Mizos could throw out these outsiders and manage their own affairs by employing only Mizos. Thus, the tribal identity became a major factor behind the insurgent or ethnic movements in this region. This was also due to the fact that after obtaining statehood, there were many more government jobs available for the native Mizos. Deori Omen points out that since independence development of other regions had kept the North-East totally out of the picture. However, in 1972, the creation of separate states and UTs, gave these north-eastern tribal states a sense of their own identity. Thus, progress in education, health services, supply of essential commodities began to flow.[22] Prof. Roy Burman holds that the lack of productive investment coupled with the 'geopolitical consideration of foreign powers due to its strategic location' that had led to the failure of the Indian government's policy to 'link up resource mobilization and developmental investments, like horticulture, were the facts that led to the frustration of educated local youths who joined separatist movements. In particular, in Nagaland the problem of manpower planning and reconciliating the career-interests of the local youth is responsible.[23]

L.S. Gassah feels that many of the political parties of the North-East arose as pressure groups with the aim to achieve social and economic goals and welfare of the people. Though traditionally the tribals needed to preserve their customs, traditions, the customary laws, language and religion as distinct identities, yet at a later stage, which was the beginning of the twentieth century, they acted as pressure groups to voice the exploitation of their tribal or colonial masters.[24] In the case of Mizoram, the feeling against the exploitation by the "Lals" or tribal chieftains was certainly one of the major features of the rise of Mizo regionalism.

In fact, Gassah, while tracing the development of the political parties in the North-East, says that while some of the parties managed to survive, others went underground or even disappeared. Those who formed their regional base, like the Mizo National Front, Assam Gana Parishad and Naga National Council, remained distinct, not joining with

Indian national parties like the Congress. Autonomy was always demanded by them as a right to exercise their freedom in choosing their own parties and programmes.

In fact that ethnicity, culture and politics are closely related comes out quite clearly in M.M. Agarwal's book which refers to the movements of Phizo in Nagaland, Laldenga in Mizoram and to the students' movements in Meghalaya.[25] Nationalism among the tribals and Assamese, as has been pointed out, could also be due to the lack of science education and the natural fear that the area would be dominated by better-educated central bureaucrats and the Marwari and Punjabi traders.[26] Hoksie Sema, one of the more prominent Naga leaders, and Chief Minister after Nagaland attained statehood, said that in Nagaland "it was a struggle between cessionists views on the one hand and national integration on the other.[27] He further said, 'politics that widens the mental horizon and ensures peace and progress and promotes the welfare of the people must be preferred over politics of hatred and bloodshed'. To him the modern Naga 'is slowly becoming alienated. He has no roots either in his home, his village, or his society. His education is not even remotely related to his culture, environment and the traditional value system . . . which is reflected in the frustration of the youth.' To him education of the state had to be made employment oriented with more emphasis on technical and vocational institutions, to inculcate pride in the ethics of work leading to self-confidence and self-reliance engaged in productive activities.[28] This then being one of the major causes for the Naga youth joining different insurgent groups; the case of Mizoram however is somewhat different.

In the 1980's inspired by Phizo and the Naga separatist movement, the Mizo leader Laldenga declared that 'Historians claim that we, the Mizo people are Mongoloids originating from time immemorial, from the southern part of China and migrating towards the present habitat between India and Burma through the Shan State of Burma in the 15th century' – Nehru had said that 'the tribal areas are defined as being those along the frontiers of India, which were neither of India, nor of Burma, or of an Indian state, nor of any foreign power'.[29] When in the 1960s, the Indian Government undertook the 'Regrouping of movement of the Mizo National Front as well as accelerated economic development in the district,'[30] it helped the developmental projects. From interiors the villages were shifted to the main roads and were named as PPVs or "Protected and Progressive Villages" mainly on the Silchar-Aizawl highway. Hence the district administration could do a lot for the development of these villages together with the educational efforts of voluntary organizations such as the Young Mizo Association, which ran its offices in the new villages as well as the Mahila Samity and Women's Welfare Organization.

The district authorities provided rice, wheat, salt, kerosene and other essential commodities from Assam. They assisted the people shift from 'Jhumming' to terrace cultivation, develop piggery, poultry and cottage industries as subsidiary occupations. Almost sixty-five per cent of the Mizo people benefited from this; as a consequence, there was a great scope of educated youth to get employed.[31] From a self-sufficient economy in which the Mizo built their own houses, procured rice and vegetables from their own 'jhum' and hunted for meat, there grew an economic change in the programme called "Grow More Food" (1957-58). Irrigation projects were started and some conservation measures were initiated. During 1970s when Mizoram was declared as a Union Territory agriculture was given the topmost priority. Under the Fifth Five Year Plan (1974-79) Mizoram's outlay was 1,567 for agriculture, 390 for irrigation and power, 312 for industry and mining 1,163 for transport and communication, 1,043 for social services including education and 84 for miscellaneous, in lakhs of rupees.[32]

This regrouping of the villages, by shifting their location from hill tops to roadsides enhanced the growth rate on enrollment and participation of primary school children in 1952-53 by 20.3 per cent, with not much difference between boys and girls (19.4 boys and 21.6 girls). Further, from 1968 to 1971, there was an annual percentage growth rate of 10.8.[33]

The demand for education and its link with employment was revealed in Mizoram as early as in the 1970s, quite contrary to the case of Nagaland. The total number of posts in the agricultural programme grew from 4 in 1972 to 17 in 1973 for Class I Officers; 31 to 36 for Class II Officers; 347 to 660 for Class III officers and from 217 to 351 for Class IV officers. This was despite the existence of numerous political parties in the state, none of whom interfered with the development of education and government sector in employment during the time when the state was made Union Territory.

After 1971, the Budget estimates for industries increased from 767 to 4,554 thousands rupees in 1974-75 with Class I and II created for the industrial sector. Although, unlike increased agricultural production between 1960-61 and 1972-73, growth in the industrial sectors was extremely slow in the seventies. Roads developed and with it the number of vehicles increased from 14 in 1951 to 1,824 in 1974. By 1966, a small airstrip was also constructed, not too far from Aizawal town. Each village had its own pharmacy and often primary schools were upgraded to middle schools. In the Directorate of Education in 1975 there were 23 Class I posts; 51 Class II; 2,215 Class III and 240 Class IV. By 1974 voluntary agencies like the Mahila Samity and Women's Welfare Agency had stated 60 village libraries, though mostly in Aizawl district (57). Thus, by 1980 the number of government Employees grew to 18,058, that is, 265 for Group 'A'; 692 for Group 'B'; 10,131, for Group 'C' and 6,970 for Goup'D'. Due to this increase in the availability of jobs on the service sector the female participation as 'main workers' basically involved in agriculture had also reduced.

Whereas in 1971, there were as much as 45.61 per cent main female workers, it had reduced to 41.21 in 1981.[34] According to 1981 census series 31, in Mizoram only 72.11 per cent of the states' main workers were engaged in agriculture. Agricultural labour was only 2.56 per cent. In 1980, the marginal workers in the urban areas was as high as 60 per cent indicating the growing urbanization in the state. Main workers engaged in household industry was merely 1.28 per cent and other workers were 24.05 per cent.

As pointed by researchers on Mizoram, that because of the UT status and the obtaining of statehood, urbanization took place in a rapid way. The state allocated liberal resources due to which there was an expansion of basic facilities such as roadways, electric power, water supply, educational institutions, hospitals and dispensaries all of which helped the state to be linked with other parts of the country.[35] This encouraged mobility of the local people and expanded the demand for education, as Mizos needed to communicate with the outside world.[36] Commercialization of the Mizo economy and the growth of industry and trade made the different political parties unite together in their sole demand for educational development, regardless of their changing political stands. A feature which Nagaland never had since the 1960s. In fact, by the 1980s among the tribal population in Indian Administrative and Allied Services from the North-East, the Mizos dominate in almost all fields.[37]

The growth of young age population from the 1960s had created financial and infrastructural problems of education and hence rose the need to link education to manpower needs of the economy.[38] As pointed out by Guha Roy, educational policy may discourage youth from entering the work force at an early age. This point was reflected in an interview with a Naga marine engineer at Kohima in 1990 by the investigator in which the former voiced his frustration at not obtaining a job in

Nagaland, after pursuing his higher studies in South India. The fact, that in Mizoram there is employment for most educated youths and not in Nagaland had become very obvious in interviews that were carried out with the employed or unemployed youths of both these states.[39] That the Naga service sector had not grown as fast as that of Mizoram so as to absorb the Naga educated youth, is spelled out clearly in later Chapters of the book where case studies are dealt with.

The roots of insurgency or a separatist movement among the tribals could be traced back to the British days when they were kept out of touch with the main currents of political development in the rest of India, the introduction of western values and a feeling of alienation spread by Christian missionaries. The money economy introduced and imposed on the tribal society upset the traditional agrarian practices. And since no economic inputs were undertaken in order to re-adjust these tribals into a new economic order, frustration grew. They were, therefore, 'restless people, uprooted from their traditional moorings and striving for social, economic and political equilibrium'.[40] In fact, the Indian Constitution by reorganizing the tribal states made the Lushai Hills, Naga Hills and North Cachar Hills 'Excluded Areas' without any representation in the Provincial Legislature of Assam but administered by the Deputy Commissioner of Assam. The Constituent Assembly set up under the Chairmanship of Gopinath Bcrdoloi, the premier of Assam, recommended the establishment of administration in hill areas based on the concept of regional autonomy in all matters affecting their customs, laws of inheritance, administration of justice, land, forests, etc. which ultimately took the form of the Sixth Schedule of the Constitution. The Sixth Schedule aimed at providing the tribals with a simple and inexpensive administration of their own, though they were to function as a part of Assam without threatening the unity and integrity of the state. Thus, six autonomous districts were created in Assam. These were: United Khasi and Jaintia Hills, Garo Hills, Lushai Hills, Naga Hills, North Cachar Hills and Mikir Hills with a District Council in each of them with 24 members, three-fourths of whom to be elected on adult franchise. There was only one autonomous region: the Pawi-lakher Region which after Mizoram attained statehood has been split up into the Chakma, Mara and Lai Autonomous District Councils in the Chhimtuipui administrative district of Mizoram. Manipur and Tripura, being Princely States, remained Part 'C' states and NEFA retained as a Frontier Agency later known as the UT and the State of Arunachal Pradesh. The Part 'C' states under the direct administration of the Chief Commissioner, and under the Government of India had little in common with the District Council which was accountable to the State/Provincial Legislature.

Following the feeling of misgivings and distrust for the Assam government by people in the hill areas, the Government of India set up the States Reorganization Commission in 1955. This Commission did not advocate any change in the status quo, despite the economic neglect of the hill areas by the Assam Government. Despite several Commissions, the resentment of the hill people grew leading to the creation of Nagaland in December1963, and Mizo District in 1954, and State in 1987 when the Mizo consciousness of statehood grew. As Horam points out, in the early 50s and 60s it was believed that there was nothing wrong with this region and that people with 'Swollen egos' demanded special attention. Further that the area had no special needs and hence their difficulties were nothing special than to of other parts of India. The people nursed imaginary grudges.[41]

The fact that even after 1950 the Central funds never reached the target groups is reflected in insufficient roadways, drinking water, erratic power supply, lack of irrigation and other indicators of underdevelopment in the hill states of the Northeast. There was a sense of insecurity among the people who felt that they will remain 'aliens' in their own country and despite the rise of insurgency movements the 'common man' was often sandwiched between government forces and insurgents resulting in the violation of human rights by the killings of innocent people.

In the 1950s there grew a demand for a separate hill state comprising of Manipur, Tripura, Cachar and Lushai Hills. In 1954, the States Reorganization Commission which visited Assam was boycotted by the Nagas and the demand for independence grew. However, the Hill State idea continued and acquired a concrete shape when Khasi and Jaintia Hills, the Garo Hills, the Mikir Hills and the Mizo Hills held a conference in Aizawl (the Aijal) and demanded a separate state in the hill districts of Assam. A new political party named Eastern India Tribal Union (EITU) was thus born in 1955, with the charge that Assam Government had shown apathy towards the hill people. Thus, Jawaharlal Nehru visited Shillong in 1957 to restore the confidence of these people after which three prominent members of EITU, Capt. Williamson Sangma (Garo Hills) Larsing Khyriem (Khasi and Jaintia Hills), and Lalmawia (Mizo Hills) were appointed as Minister, Deputy Minister and Parliamentary Secretary in the Assam Government. Nagas however demanded a separate statehood. The Assam Official Language Bill in 1961 made Assamese the official language of the state and led to protests among hill leaders, leading to the resignation of the Assam government. All the political parties existing in the hill districts in 1960, got together and formed the All Party Hill Leaders' Conference (APHLC) demanding that all hill districts should be separate from Assam. However, the Assam Government did not pay any attention to these demands.

While in Nagaland, Mizoram and Manipur the ethnic discontent was openly secessionist, in other places it was different. As for example, in the Northeast there were three distinct regions: Assam valley, Purbanchal and Meghalaya – Mikir region. The Purbanchal covering an area of 94,800 km., consisted of Nagaland, Manipur, Tripura, Mizo Hills, Cachar district and a fifth of Haflong Tesit of Assam state and a part of Arunachal Pradesh. Attempts of tribals like Nagas, Mizos, Tripuris and others to seek independence through foreign aid were attributed to the racial factor.[42] Geo-political forces have been responsible for splitting the tribals and non-tribals psychologically as well. While the Pakistani and Chinese involvement in insurgency movements are public knowledge, the testimony of an erstwhile secret agent, John Smith, reveals that the CIA had extended help to the underground Naga movement in the 50s, along with the KGB. The issue of foreign involvement gets further complicated in 1965 when the Pakistanis attempted to open a second front by offering help (through East Pakistan) to Mizo National Front.[43]

Saroj Chakraborty, while advocating against the secessionists movements, feels that they 'would undermine the democratic right of India, secede border regions themselves which would eventually fall into bondage to international imperialism, maintained that 'ethnic integration and democratic alliance between our nationalities' would be required to put an 'end to the estrangement and isolations of the border regions.[44] He wrote, the 'Central Government must become no less near and dear to the masses of the border regions' and suggested several measures through which the Central Government can bridge the gap between mainstream Indian life and that of border areas.

The Mizo and Naga Movements

The Mizo and the Naga separatist movements started with many common traits but took different turns due to the historical development of their societies. As pointed out by researchers both were anti-Assamese movements and the assertion of their tribal identities, their Christian religion with 'God' as their saviours. The church or religion being a part and parcel of their societies, allowed for a close nexus between the aspirations of the political parties and that of the local churches. For both, the Hindu character of India after 1947 left the tribals bereft of any socio-economic development. In fact, they longed for an extension of British rule and their existence as separate states within the British Commonwealth, rather than become a part of Assam till 1960s. However, in Mizoram, Mizo regionalism or ethnic identity is different from that of the Nagas. As stated earlier, the different tribes living in the geographical unit of Mizo Hills were first of all "Mizos" and "Christians" and then a part of the numerous political parties that existed in their territory. To them there was one aim which was becoming a separate state having its own language, legislature and the practice of customary laws. The slow absorption of ethnic minorities such as the Brus,Riang,Chakmas, Maras and Lais as a part of the 'Mizo consciousness due to the spread of Christianity had helped to unite them together in attaining statehood in 1987.

As far as Nagaland was concerned, the personality cult of their leaders mattered more than that of a Naga identity. With the existence of almost 16 tribes, including subtribes. there was no language in common and the Naga political leadership remained confined to their tribal identities such as Sema, Ao, Angami, Thangkhul etc. Moreover, territorially, their leaders wanted a greater Nagaland comprising all Nagas, inhabiting areas beyond present day Nagaland, such as parts of Assam, Manipur and Arunachal Pradesh. More than their Mizo counterparts, who also have a sizeable Mizo population living in Manipur and across the border to Myanmar, the Naga leaders wanted an 'autonomous' status away from the Indian Union. In education, the fragmented leadership of the Naga separatist movement hindered their progress and this is true even today when the state, busy with infighting among different political factions, has failed to avail of many educational benefits from the Central Government's pool for development funds; especially from bodies like the North-Eastern Council. Because of the very fact that even after a decade of attaining statehood, the Nagas are suspicious of the Centre, they abstain from taking a share of the North Eastern Council's fund flow to the different states. The Council which was formed by the Planning Commission in 1971 as an Advisory body for all the seven states had as much as Rs.33 lakhs for the Fourth Plan period 1969-74. This grew to 575 crores in the Seventh Plan period in the 1980s.[45]

There is a paucity of literature on the origin of the Mizo and the clan-distinction is more or less absent in them, in contrast to the Nagas, except for the Lai, Chakma, Brus Riangs and Maras. In fact the process of socialization and modernization have almost wiped out these distinctions, although these groups are less and varied in literacy as compared to the "Lushai", the prominent Mizo group. Though the clan dialects have much in common, yet these are not always totally "assimilated" with the "Mizo tongue" or Mizo Language.[46] (Mizo tongue is often referred to as the Lushai or Duhlian language.) These tribes were ruled by their 'Lals' or Chieftains who were bound by customary laws, which meant that it was their duty to protect the life and property of the villagers, to frame the general policy of making allotment of lands for cultivation, and to administer justice according to customary laws. Besides being a general supervisor of the village, the 'Lals' had to pay special attention to the maintenance of the village paths and water resources. The normal form of penalty he could inflict upon an offender was a fine, paid in cash or kind, ranging from rupees 5 to rupees 40 or its equivalent, in the form of pig or *Mithun*. Initially the British Lushai relationship was one of hostility, evident in the killings of Europeans and taking a small girl called Mary Winchester as captive. Hence more than promoting commercial interests, initially the British wanted to refrain from hostility so that the Mizos would not attack their territory. The Mizos, therefore, began to interpret this British attitude as one of love and respect for tribal traditions and values.

But in real fact the British, barring the missionaries, had no interest in the Lushai and left them where they were in 1947. There was yet another side to the Mizo movement at this stage, that being the idea of a "Crown colony of Eastern Agency" comprising of hill areas of Assam and Burma suggested by Prof. R. Copland, a constitutional expert. This idea of an independent state between Assam and Burma was also welcomed by A.R.M. Mc Donald, Superintendent of Lushai Hills during 1943-47.[47] Since this idea never took proper shape, the Mizos had to remain content with the status of "regional autonomy" under the state of Assam for some time. The colonial indirect rule in which the "Lal" or the Chief still retained his position deteriorated the relations between the Lals and the commoners. It led to social tensions among the emerging elite in the area; the Chief and the traditional elite class. The Lushai Hills as an "Excluded Area" meant that it was governed by the orders and regulations of the Governor of Assam, hence the provincial government and legislature were not responsible for its administration.[48] At the time up to the transfer of power by the British, the Lushais (Mizos), were not prepared to decide on their political future as regards joining either Burma or Pakistan. Some leaders of the Mizo Union wanted to stay within Indian territory but at the same time maintain "regional autonomy".

The anti-chief feeling among commoners grew even prior to the formation of a political Mizo party. On April 9, 1946, the Mizo commoners formed the first political party with the bare aim to abolish chieftainship. This mass based political movement demanding 'regional autonomy' put an end to chieftainship. The fact that the Mizos wanted to remain within India is also an interesting difference compared to the Naga movement which will be explained later. But certainly the different political leaders united together against Assam government took advantage of every social service scheme which was available to them. The call among the political parties was for a united Mizo struggle comprising of all ethnic groups and for the protection of their identity.

As Lalchungnunga points out, the abolition of chieftainship is the right step in the modernization of the Lushai Hills.[49] In July 5, 1947 the United Mizo Freedom Organization was formed, with the objective of joining Burma instead of India, as they felt that they would be able to enjoy greater autonomy. But the Mizo Union submitted a "Draft Constitution of Mizoram" to the Bordoloi Sub-Committee stating the following:

(a) *When India becomes independent, the present Lushai Hills District will be 'federated' with the province of Assam and be connected* therewith in certain subjects which shall be decided by negotiations between the provincial legislature and the Mizo National Council;
(b) There shall be a Legislative Council of 27 members... when those areas to Cachar District and Manipur State occupied by the Mizos are incorporated into Mizoram, the number of members will be increased;
(c) No Non-Mizo will be qualified to be a candidate for election;
(d) There shall be a National Court to be called "The Mizoram High Court";
(e) Any provincial legislation may be applied to the District only with the sanction of the National Council (of Mizoram) with any modifications;
(f) All the above items shall be subject to revision after ten years.

In August 1947, at a meeting at Aizawl under the Chairmanship of Mr. L.L. Peters, Superintendent of Lushai Hills, the Lushais said that if they were to enter the Indian Union then:

(i) the existing safeguards to their customary laws and land tenure should be maintained.

(ii) That the Chin Hills Regulation 1896 and the Bengal Eastern Frontier Regulation, 1873 should be retained until such time as the Lushais themselves through their District Council or other parallel District Authority declare that these can be abrogated;

(iii) That the Lushais will be allowed to opt out of the Indian Union when they wish to do so, subject to a minimum period of ten years.

The Bordoloi Sub-committee (1947) generally agreed to the demands made by the Mizo Union and leaders of other Mizo political parties, on matters of regional autonomy for all tribal customs etc., but nothing was known as to what the Committee felt regarding opting out of Indian Union. Thus, according to the Sixth Schedule the Mizo Hills were given District Autonomy.

After independence the Assam government continued to neglect the Mizo Hills which consequently led to an acute economic crisis. In 1959 the bamboo plants flowered all over, multiplying the rats, as a consequence there was a great famine or 'Mautam'. Upon the failure of the Assam Government to adopt insufficient relief measures, the Mizo Union MLAs, who had joined the Congress earlier, left the Congress Legislature, and came out openly for breaking with Assam. This demand of the Mizos showed in strength during the Village Councils education in 1960 in which the Mizo Union with the platform of separation from Assam was as many as 280 village councils out of 3000.[50]

This was also the beginning of Mizo National Front. At the beginning the MNF was a welfare organization calling itself the Mizo National Famine Front (MNFF), which once formed in 1960 was a collection of young workers who collected donations and rendered relief to the famine distressed people. Their work in the remote villages is praiseworthy, as the District Administration was unable to reach these areas. When famine was over, the MNFF dropped the word famine and became the MNF in 1961. The role of MNF in Mizo politics is remarkable. As a political party its objective was the creation of an independent and sovereign state of Mizoram. Their voice gradually became that of the entire people of the Mizo District. Their leader Laldenga, originally a clerk in the District Council and an ex-Havildar in the Army, quickly won the confidence of most Mizos across all political parties.

In fact, delays on the part of the Assam Government to send relief measures discredited the Mizo Union, and the Mizo National Front henceforth emerged as the saviour of the Mizo people. The Mizo Union had also parted company with the Congress Party on differences over the State language issue of 1960, and over the poor efforts made in giving famine relief. It was at this point, Prof. Roy Burman points out, that the MNF started double-talk and sought to exploit the differences between the Assam Government and the Mizo Union held District Councils.[51] However, the Mizo Union continued with their demand for a separate Hill State within India, while the MNF preached for a sovereign independent status and even sent its workers to East Pakistan for training.

During this time Nagaland was in trouble, and the then Prime Minister Nehru suggested the Scottish pattern of autonomy, protecting and preserving the identity and culture of the hill people, be implemented. After Nehru's death, Lal Bahadur Shastri appointed a Commission, which openly stated that the economic factors were the root cause of difference between the hill and the plain areas of Assam.

Though there were many common causes such as, neglect of hill areas by Assam, and Central Government, and a feeling of 'alienation' among the people, yet the Naga insurgency movement began on a different note. The Nagas, like the Mizos, had no written history in the pre-British days. However, Nagas were not unknown to the Kings of the Indo-Gangetic plain. They were often known or 'kiratas' in the Vedas and epics. The history of Kings of the Kamrup is silent on the Nagas (i.e., from fourth to twelfth centuries A.D.) Sukapha, the founder of the Ahom Kingdom, had entered Assam from Burma 1228 through the Tirag area of Arunachal Pradesh. The Ahoms first contact with the tribals Pradesh. The Ahoms first contact with the tribals were with the Aos and Lothas.[52] Despite clashes between the Ahom and the Naga tribes, in general, the Ahom maintained a cordial relationship and the Nagas paid tribute to the Ahom Kings in the form of Mithun and other commodities in return for revenue-free land and waters (beels). The British (from 1832-1850), undertook military attacks on the Nagas, later from 1850s, following a period of non-interference, they steadily tried to establish their authority over Naga hills from 1866 onwards.

In 1918, Naga club was founded in Kohima and Mokokchung, consisting of village chiefs and government officials to discuss the social and administrative contentious issues. The Naga Hills District Council, with the aim of uniting the Nagas, was established by Sir Charles Pawey in 1945. The Council met at Wokha and changed its name to Naga National Council, with the political objective to achieve autonomy for the hills, within the province of Assam and to train the people for self-government.[53] At first, there was no talk of separation from India, but its stand changed from June 1947, an ultimatum that the Naga Hills world cease to be a part of India, once Indian independence was attained, was issued. But the Naga leaders were divided in their opinions. While one group favoured immediate independence, some moderates favoured the continuance of governmental relations with India in some modified way, until they were trained in the running of a modern state. Yet a third group wanted to bring Nagaland into the position of a mandatory state under the British Government for a specified period of time. The idea of a 'Crown Colony', quite separate from India, was floated abroad and also that the United Kingdom with contributions from the Indian Government should meet the expenses of the Nagas.

While these events were taking place, in 1947, a delegation went to Delhi, carrying the view that Naga Hills, after their independence should be kept outside the Indian Union. As a result of prolonged talks between the Naga leaders and Sir Akbar Hydari, the Governor of Assam, a point memorandum was drawn up. Its preamble recognized the right of the Nagas to develop themselves according to their freely expressed wishes. It went on to establish that all cases, of civil or criminal nature, between the Naga's and Naga Hills tribes should be disposed of by duly constituted Naga Courts according to Naga customary laws. Gradually the extremists gained more control of the Naga National Council (NNC) voicing the opinion that Naga people ought to be treated as one with the rest of India and special efforts ought to be made to protect them from any danger of exploitation from outside, while at the same time they be given full opportunities for development, in their own particular way of life.

Nagas, however boycotted the General Elections of 1952, and a wide support of independence was taken by obtaining thumbprints of villagers. Civil disobedience movement became the nature of the political protest. In 1956, the insurgents founded the Naga Federal Government, but it was not supported by a wide range of people. Its constitution stated that 'Nagaland' was a people's sovereign republic. This had been from times immemorial. That there ought to be a Parliament with a strength of 100 M.P.s, the President be elected by the people and the cabinet consist of fifteen High Ministers. That Nagaland maintain a permanent military neutrality, and there be no standing army. It said that education was to be in the hands of the people.

In Nagaland the insurgency movement started in 1955. The Nagas were, perhaps, the earliest frontier tribes to come under British jurisdiction. Both the Ahoms and the British rule over the Nagas were bereft of any economic benefits. Their small states ruled by Chieftains were kept intact by the Ahom "Posa System", in which the plain people had to pay a small payment to the hill people and the latter never changed them. The Nagas instead gave them small territories (pieces of land), called the 'Naga Khats' for their cultivation.[54] Earlier in 1945, the Nagas had said that they were neither ready to join a democratic constitution nor compete with Indian politicians. That, they were dependent on the British, and considered themselves comfortable under the British Raj. It seemed as if an implicit trust had grown between the British and the Nagas.[55] It was far too costly for the British to administer the hill areas directly, and the Nagas interpreted this differently, feeling that the British had respected their independence and left them alone to govern their country. The Nagas looked across the Manipur border where some Naga tribes lived, felt that all these areas contain Nagas and would be theirs someday. In fact, most of the early Naga leaders as Christians, trained by the Baptist American Missions felt that their religion had something to do with their political aspiration. Nehru, himself, had realized that these Christian Nagas would not have anything in common with Indian culture. The idea of independence was already in the mind of the Nagas.[56] It sprang from the spread of education where there was a shift in the social, cultural, economic and ideological aspects of Naga life. Christianity brought them close to 'God' and by 1947 major Naga tribal languages like the Augami, Ao, Lotha, Sema had been translated into Roman scripts, for Bibles and the grammar books.[57]

Saroj Chakraborty rightly points out that 1947 had brought with it a new awakening among the elite of hill tribes. Money economy had perpetrated the hill area which few of the tribal leaders benefited from. They also had access to higher education and the articulate sections among them were restive and demanded 'self-determination'. Doses of self-government that was given to them, made the people of the hill districts demand autonomy. Ultimately they were allowed to hold elections and establish their statehood.[58] But the movement of the Nagas was based on personality cults and was different from the Mizos.

Refusing to join the North Eastern Council in 1971, the Nagas under their Angami leader Zapo Phizo had an underground Federal Government of Nagaland with him as their head. Phizo was supported by the British, and was given asylum in London, from where he maintained relationship with Kaito Sema whom he installed as leader of the insurgents. After the Chinese aggression, in 1962, Kaito contacted the Chinese Ambassador in London and made a secret agreement to train his rebels in collaboration with the British Agents and the CIA. Several Naga Youth escaped to Peking where they received training, money and hospitality, returning to India via Burma. In 1957, Nehru held a Peoples' Convention at Shillong and since then the successive

Indian governments have been trying to erode the mass base of the underground Nagas.

Unlike Mizoram, Nagaland's insurgency movement was more personalized and grew around the cults of political parties. Due to the frequent change of governments since 1963, the Nagas were not able to concentrate on developmental activities, of which education is a part.

Nagaland did not participate in the National Freedom Movement and therefore, Congress and other parties were not formed in the state prior to independence. Naga National Council, NNC, the first political party and a regional party formed in the area in 1946, prior to which in 1945 the Naga Hills District Tribal Council was formed in 1945 and which later became the NNC. Initially as a social and cultural organization it rapidly changed its colour and became a political mouthpiece of the Nagas, under the leadershp of A.Z. Phizo. It organized a plebiscite on the status of Naga Hills and boycotted the elections to the Assam Legislative Assembly. It spearheaded a non-violent movement and the underground violent struggle with the help of Federal Government of Nagaland (1956) and Naga Army for Naga independence.

The first All Tribes Naga People's convention was organized in Kohima on August 22-26, 1957 with 1750 delegates and 2000 visitors representing all tribes.[59] The second and third Naga People's Conventions were held in Ungma and Mokakchung in 1958 and 1959. The differences with Nehru were apparent and resulted into the 16-point agreement and the formation of Nagaland state. The Naga People's Convention was the forerunner of the Naga Nationalist Organization (NNO), which fought first Nagaland State Assembly Elections in 1964 and won against the D.P.N. (Democratic Party of Nagaland) and NFG, another party. Under the Chief Ministership of Shilu Ao, it sought to bring peace and initiated a programme for the general welfare of the Naga tribes. It wanted a Nagaland state as part of India by following constitutional methods.

In 1969 election manifesto, NNO promised modernization of agriculture, a communication network, free medical facilities, expansion of education, integration of contiguous Naga areas, and a stable and clean administration. Apart from promising implementation of the 16 point agreement, more emphasis on the development of Tuensang, separate university and high cost, protection of the rights of the minorities and reservation of non-gazetted and non-technical posts for the locals, it emphasized economic development programmes, such as agriculture, small scale industry, power to rural areas and youth welfare.

In 1969 it defeated the United Front of Nagaland (UFN) with the support of 7 independent MLAs and hence it once again came to power with Hoksie Sema as the Chief Minister. In 1972, the U.F.N. became the U.D.F. or United Democratic Front in 1974 elections with the help of independents and 4 N.N.O. The U.D.F. formed the Ministry with Vizol as the Chief Minister. Further defection took place, and hence after 10 days President Rule was imposed on the State for 32 months. The N.N.O. merged into Indian National Congress during this time.

The D.P.N. or the Democratic Party of Nagaland was formed in 1963 as the first opposition party with Kevichusa as its Chairman. The leader of the D.P.N. joined the U.F.N. from 1969 onwards. In 1972, Mr. S.C. Jamir of the U.D.F. jointed the U.F.N. along with N.N.O. Since the political manifesto of all these parties were the same, i.e., stressing the social, economic and educational development, they merged together and formed the N.N.D.P. or the Naga National Democratic Party, and they installed the NNDP ministry in June 1980 remaining in power till the next elections of 1982. During 1982 and 1987 elections Congress (I) ministries were formed and NNDP functioned as the recognized opposition the Nagaland Legislative Assembly. In matters of social policy and development the NNDP continued the policy of old UDF. Novel features were the formations of Village Development Boards and Village Development Funds.

Huska Sumi a former MLA was against the merger of UDF with NNP and hence the Nagaland People's Party or the NNP came into existence. It talked of a mass movement and of "Nagaism" and the establishment of a new social order based on the principles of justice, equality and liberty.

The Naga People's Council or NPC was formed due to defection of 13 Congress MLAs joining hands with the N.N.D.P. wanting to form a ministry, however in August 1988 Presidents Rule was once again imposed upon the state.

The picture of Mizoram is singularly different. The Mizos had gone forward to develop their hill territory all along. As explained earlier, urbanization and the expansion of the service sector had already created a demand for education after 1971. This phenomenon continued till late 1980s. And even now the educated Mizo are assets to the community. From 1952 to 1972 the only Mizo Party represented in the Assam Assembly elections was the Mizo Union as a part of the EITU with Lalmawia as Minister of State and A. Thanguma as the Chief Parliamentary Secretary. But in 1960 the latter refused to resign with other EITU members, instead he shifted his alliance to the Congress Party. This was the first time that the Mizo evinced interest in coalition parties. In fact as history records, unlike Nagaland where coalition parties was a feature, the Mizo have had only two coalition governments, that is, in 1972 in its first General Elections and in 1986, when the Mizo Peace Accord was signed. However, there were intra-party coalition between the Mizo Union (Mizo Union Council of Mizo Union of Pachhunga and R. Vanlawma) and the Mizo Union Rightwing of Lalsawia; the Congress factions of Dengthuama and Hrangchuema; People's Conference (A) of Chief Brigedier T. Sailo and People's Conference (B) Thargridema; and MNF (Laldenga) and MNF (Democratic of Chaungzuala. After the Mizo Union Ministry was formed in 1972, a merger took place on May 3, 1974 between the MU and the Congress, with Chhung, a senior Congress leader at the head. In the second General Elections in 1978, the Peoples Conference got the absolute majority and Brig. T. Sailo took over as the Chief Minister.

A mid-term election was held in April 1979 after Brig. Sailo's ministry lost its majority yet he was able to complete his five-year term. In 1984, a Congress (I) Ministry was sworn in, May 3, with Lalhanhawla as the Chief Minister.[60] But soon (by 1986) the Mizo Peace Accord was signed ending the twenty years' insurgency movement in Mizoram and an agreement was signed with Laldenga that a coalition Congress (I) and MNF government would be formed headed by Laldenga in 1987.

Thus, whether it was the party of Brig. Sailo, nor Lalthanhawla or Laldenga no differences were made regarding the educational policy by these parties. However, an interview with Mr. Zoramthanga[61] in 1993 has revealed that he disagreed with the formation of 'School Complex'.

The basic hypothesis of this study is that educational development is linked to the political, social and economic forces of the times especially in the North Eastern States. Its rationale is to find out how far these forces had a positive and/or negative effect on elementary education.

The specific objectives are to (i) trace the history of elementary education in the region; (ii) to understand the roles of the Christian missionaries and Colonial Government in the spread of literacy and elementary education; (iii) to study the expansion of educational facility; (iv) to link female literacy and the elementary education among girls in different tribal areas; (v) to review the process of decentralization of education and the role of local bodies by the aid of case studies on Lai Autonomous District Council of Mizoram and village education committee of Nagaland, in order to gauge the participation of local community in making primary education more responsive to local needs.

The methodology used in this study requires linking up educational development with political, social, and economic factors in an overall historical perspective, so as to ascertain how far the growth of elementary education is a product of these variables. It is largely based on empirical findings although some secondary sources of data have been made use of available in NCERT's First to Fifth All India Educational Surveys. Interviews with prominent leaders of Mizoram, Nagaland and educationalists from other North-Eastern States have been important inputs. Village level household surveys, conducted for obtaining primary data on causes of dropouts and non-enrolment of elementary school students in Meghalaya, (Barapari, East Khasi Hills district) Nagaland (Phesama, Kohima district), Manipur (Toubal district) have been sustentative source of information. The role of the community in enhancing the participation of primary school children has been gathered through visits to the Lai Autonomous District Council in Chhimtuipui district of Mizoram and the role of the Village Committee in Kohima district of Nagaland.

The present study maintains what in comparative education is generally known as the "problem approach" based upon George Z.F. Bereday's Comparative Method of Education. According to this approach it furnishes information to educational planners with a set of alternatives from which to select an appropriate policy. As no such study on educational development of the elementary stage has been conducted for the entire region, from the 1960s to 1980s, it was felt that this kind of study would be of both research value and contribute to policy formulation for the North East. Individual educational problems pertaining to each state and each level exists, but no such comparative analysis of different variables are available. As far as history is concerned the 1960s is a watershed in this region. It was at this time that the states developed their own identities, manifest even today. However, the rapid expansion of facilities educational and other, taking place in the two decades, is reflected in the picture of growth present today. Mizoram being one of the highest literate states in India only next to Kerala. On the other hand due to political instability, the Nagas have remained more backward.

Based on numerous field visits to all the seven states as a part of my official work I have taken the opportunity to visit villages and households to collect primary information. For secondary information I have used Delhi, Shillong, Aizawl, and NEHU Campus Libraries.

References

1. Syed Narulla and J.P. Naik, *Students History of Education in India (1800-1965)*, Revised Edition (Bombay: Macmillan, 1964), p.21.
2. *Ibid.*, p. 23.
3. *Ibid.*, p. 39.
4. *Ibid.*, pp. 120-21.
5. NCERT, *The Indian Year Books of Education 1961*, Part I (New Delhi: NCERT, 1965). pp. 220-228.
6. NCERT, *The Indian Year Book of Education 1961* Part II, p. 457.
7. Government of India, Ministry of Human Resource Development, Department of Education, *Programme of Action*, New Delhi, 1986.
8. Government of India, Ministry of Human Resource Development, Department of Education, *Programme of Action, 1992 (Draft)*, New Delhi, 1992.
9. Meena Sharma Barkataki, *British Administration in North East India 1826-1874. A Study of their Social Policy* (Delhi: Mittal Publications, 1985).
10. S.L. Baruah, *A Comprehensive History of Assam* (New Delhi: Munshiram Manohar Lal Publishers, 1985). p. 624.
11. Renu Debi, *Progress of Education in Assam* (Gauhati: Omsons Publications, 1987).
12. Bina Laskar, *Development of Women Education* (A Study of Assam) (Guwahati: Omsons Publications, 1987).
13. Cited in Prakash Singh, *Nagaland* (New Delhi: National Book Trust, 1972), pp. 18-19.
14. Government of India, *Census of India, 1961*, Vol. III, Assam Part IA, General Report, pp. 167-186.
15. R. Gopalakrishnan, *The North East India, Land, Economy and People* (Delhi: Vikas Publishing House, 1991), pp. 5-6.
16. R. Gopalakrishnan, *Insurgent North Eastern Region of India* (New Delhi: Vikas Publishing House, 1995).
17. *Ibid.*, p. 15-17.
18. B. Dutta Roy, Preface to *Insurgency in the Northeast India*, ed. B. Pakem (New Delhi: Omsons Publications, 1997), p. vi.
19. R. Borgohain, and B.J. Deb, "State, Ideology and Insurgency in Nagaland" in B. Pakem, ed., *op. cit.* p.328.
20. Sukhendu Mazumdar, "Insurgency in the Northeast: with special reference to Manipur and Nagaland" in B. Pakem, ed., *op. cit.*, pp. 308-311.
21. B.B. Kumar, *Tension and Conflict in North East India* (New Delhi: Cosmo Publications, 1995).

22. Deori Omen, "Northeast – A Perspective" in *Northeastern Region Problem and Prospects of Development*, ed. B.L. Abbi (Chandigarh: CRRID, 1984), p.183.
23. B.K. Roy Burman, "Issues in the North-East: An Appraisal" in B.L. Abbi, *op. cit.*
24. L.S. Gassah, ed., *Regional Political Parties in North Eastern India* (New Delhi: Omsons Publications, 1992), pp. vii–x.
25. M.M. Agarwal, ed., *Ethnicity, Culture and Nationalism in the North-East India* (New Delhi: Indus Publication, 1996).
26. B.L. Abbi, *Northeast Region Problems and Perspectives of Development* (Chandigarh: CRRID, 1984).
27. Hoksie Sema, *Emergence of Nagaland Socio-Economic and Political Transformulation and the Future* (New Delhi: Vikas Publishing House, 1986), p.184.
28. *Ibid.*, p. 135.
29. Animesh Ray, *Mizoram: Dynamics of Change* (Calcutta: Pearl Publishers, 1982), p.160.
30. *Ibid.*, pp.168-173.
31. *Ibid.*, p.176.
32. *Ibid.*, pp. 191-192.
33. Annual Reports of Deputy Inspector of Schools (1952-53) and Inspector of Schools (1967-71) [DEO (Aizawl West) Office] during my field visit.
34. S.N. Singh, *Mizoram: Historical, Geographical, Social, Political and Administrative* (New Delhi: Mittal Publications, 1999), p. 51.
35. V.S. Mahajan, "Mizoram at the beginning of next century: A case study" in *North East 2000 AD*, ed. R.B. Dutta Roy (New Delhi: Deep Publications, 1987), p. 231.
36. Interview with F. Lallura, Director School Education, Govt. of Mizoram, Aizawl, November 15th, 1999.
37. Interview with Mr. T.L. Thanga, then Commissioner and Secretary Education, Govt. of Manipur, Imphal, January, 1992.
38. Guha Roy, "Population Perspective of North East India in 2000 AD" in *North East 2000 A.D.* ed. R.B. Dutta Roy, *op. cit*, pp. 96-97.
39. Interviews with Mr.Tongpangshilu and Mr. Jack Secose Directorate of School Education, Government of Nagaland, Kohima, 1990 and with Ms. Mazo (SCERT), Ms. Sangpui Sailo (DIET) at Aizawl, 1995.
40. P. Roy Chowdhury, *The North East: Roots of Insurgency* (Calcutta: Firma KLM, 1986), pp.92-93.
41. M. Horam, "Problem of Understanding in Northeast India" in B.L. Abbi, ed., *op.cit*, pp.190-98.
42. V.I.K. Sarin, *Indias' North-East in Flames* (New Delhi: Vikas Publishing House, 1980), pp. 2-15.

43. H.K. Sareen, *Insurgency in North East India* (New Delhi: Sterling Publishers, 1980), p. 65.
44. Saroj Chakraborty, *The Upheaval Years in the North-East India* (Calcutta: Saroj Chakraborty and R. Chakraborty, 1982), pp. 206-207.
45. Bhupinder Singh, "Perspectives and Plans" in *Seminar*, 366, New Delhi, 1990. The North East – a symposium the problem of neglected region, p.21.
46. Interview with Mr. J.B. Raulhhinga. C.M. Lawngtlai, Lai Autonomous District Council, April 1995.
47. Lalchunmunga, *Mizoram: Politics of Regionalism and National Integration* (New Delhi, Reliance Publishing House, 1994), p.34.
48. *Ibid.*, p. 37.
49. *Ibid.*, p.40.
50. P. Roy Chowdhury, *The North East: Roots of Insurgency*, op. cit., p.103.
51. B.K. Roy Burman, *Demographic and Socio-Economic Pofiles of North East India. op. cit.*, p.33.
52. Verrier Elwin, *Nagaland*, Research Department, Advisors Secretariat, Shillong, 1961, p.12.
53. *Ibid.*, p. 51.
54. Lipi Ghosh, "Insurgency in Nagaland, The Historical Roots" in *Insurgency in the North East*, ed. B. Pakem, *op.cit.*, pp.338-345.
55. P.D. Stracey, *Nagaland Nightmare* (Bombay: Allied Publishers, 1968), p.12.
56. *Ibid.*, p.61.
57. V.K. Anand, *Conflict in Nagaland* (Delhi: Chanakaya Publications), p.53.
58. Saroj, Chakraborty, *The Upheaval Years in North-East India*, op.cit., p.93.
59. B.B. Kumar, "Regional Political Parties in Nagaland: An Appraisal" in *Regional Political Parties in North Eastern India*, ed. L.S. Gassch (New Delhi: Omsons Publications, 1992), pp. 106-210.
60. Interview with Lalthanhawla in 1993 at Aizawl where they did not spell out a different agenda for educational reform.
61. Interview with Mr. Zoramthanga, Aizawl, 1993.

1

A Background to the Development of Elementary Education in the North Eastern Region of India

1.1 The Region

Today, the North Eastern Region of India comprises of seven states of Arunachal Pradesh, Assam, Manipur, Meghalaya, Mizoram, Nagaland and Tripura. As a whole, the region accounts for 7.7 per cent of the total geographical area in the country with only 3.88 per cent of its total population, the majority of whom belong to one or other of the 209 Scheduled Tribes. It covers an area of 2.55 lakh kilometres of land, more than 80 per cent of which is mountainous. Twelve per cent of the area of this region comprises the Meghalaya-Karbi Plateau while the rest are Brahmaputra and Barak valley plains. The area also includes the Imphal valley and the Tripura plain.[1]

The relative isolation of the region from the mainstream Indian life had encouraged complex social sub-systems, rarely influenced by the outside world. Having lived for centuries in this isolated manner, the people have managed to retain their traditional life styles till the coming of the Ahoms 1228 and the British in 1826. Hinduism and Islam never disturbed their animistic beliefs, nor did the colonial economy affect their primitive form of 'slash and burn' method of cultivation, even in Assam. Economic policies which led to colonial economy and the creation of a new landed gentry, as a result of the Permanent

Settlement of 1793, and a 'comprador' class, involved in both agriculture and trading with East India Company, are particularly relevant to Bengal and parts of Bihar but not to the North East region. The region's geographical homogeneity[2] is the source of social, historical, cultural and political affinity between the states. Engrossed as they were in internecine tribal conflicts, they remained untouched by the rise and fall of Indian empires. However, this relative isolation was broken at the time of colonial rule in Assam, during which their strategic importance compelled the British to carve out a route through Manipur towards Burma. In the wake of imperialist aggression against the tribals also came missionary activities for conversion to Christianity. Thus, literacy and elementary education started growing at an unprecedented pace among the tribes of the region.

The educational significance of the region today lies in the high level of literacy and elementary education and the relatively lower-level of dropouts as compared with other regions of India. Table 1 gives comparative figures based on 1991 census.

Despite a great intra-regional variety in literacy (Arunachal Pradesh 41.22% and Mizoram 81.23%), the region as a whole fares comparatively well with the all-India average of 52.11%. Similarly, the dropout rates at the elementary level is also lower than the all-India average, in which the retention of the same 100 children enrolled in Class I in 1978-79 is as high as 89% in Meghalaya, 79% in Nagaland and 72% in Mizoram in Class VIII (1985-86). Even in Arunachal Pradesh the retention is as high as 79% as compared to the all-India average of 64%. This is notwithstanding the fact that Arunachal Pradesh has been classified as one of the most educationally backward states of India. Even Assam, another educationally backward state located in the same region, has a favourable literacy rate (53.42%) and retention (68%) rate at the elementary level. Thus, the success of the North-East in areas of literacy and elementary education is rooted in the nature of the historical development of education in this region as a whole, which deviated from the pattern of mainstream colonial education, as both the missionaries and the British rulers concentrated on literacy and elementary level education to the neglect of tertiary and professional education.

At first, inaccessible terrain and tribal hostility made the British withdraw from the hill regions in the North East, and concentrate mainly on the development of education in Assam plains. The hill areas were, therefore, left to the Welsh Methodist Mission, American Baptist

Table 1.1
North Eastern Region Basic Indicators for Education for All

States	*Literacy Rate 7 year +*						*Elementary*		*Stage*	*Class*
	M		*F*		*T*		*Class I*		*VIII*	
	1991	*2001*	*1991*	*2001*	*1991*	*2001*	*1978-79*	*1990-91*	*1985-86*	*1997-98*
Arunachal Pradesh	51.10	64.07	29.35	44.24	41.22	54.74	100	100	78	32
Assam	62.34	71.93	43.70	56.03	53.42	64.28	100	100	68	31
Manipur	72.98	77.87	48.64	59.70	60.96	68.57	100	100	75	29
Meghalaya	51.57	66.14	44.78	60.41	48.26	63.31	100	100	89	54
Mizoram	84.46	90.69	78.09	86.13	81.23	88.49	100	100	72	29
Nagaland	66.09	71.77	55.72	61.92	61.30	67.11	100	100	79	59
Tripura	70.08	81.47	50.01	65.41	60.39	73.66	100	100	66	32

Source: (1) Calculated on the basis of class-wise enrolment given in Education in India (1978-79 and 1985-86) New Delhi - Ministry of Education, Government of India.

(2) Census of India, 2001.

Mission, Lutheran Mission, Roman Catholic Mission and the German Education Mission as their field of operation. To the colonizers the missionary involvement in education was beneficial since it made the natives more 'peaceful and loyal'.[3] Moreover, the colonial government itself felt that education can be expanded more cheaply and efficiently through missionary activities.

1.2 Colonial Policy

Initially, the East India Company had a cautious attitude towards the missionaries because of its concern for the safety and stability of its Indian Empire and, therefore, did not encourage the missionaries from entering India. But despite this policy, some missionaries managed to come to India. At the private level, many of the Company's servants had tolerated and even encouraged missionary activity. Charles Grant, an Evangelist who had served in the Company's administration for forty years and had became Chairman of the East India Company, pleaded for the entry of the missionaries to India. He argued that Indians were sunk in darkness and ignorance, and only education could bring them light and convert them to Christianity.[4] Besides, educated Indians would become more loyal to British rule if they became Christians. Moreover, for commercial reasons, it was thought that the spread of Christianity would generate a greater demand for British manufactured goods in India. As J.C. Marshman had said "thus, commerce became the hand-maid of religion and under their combined influence, the gates of India were opened at once to the callous of England and the truths of the Bible".[5] The Company's attitude was that the missionary plan of education would, in the long run, create an "attachment" for the British nation among the Indians. For Duff, English education was likely to make Indians loyal to British rule, yet the over all policy of the government was not to interfere with the religious practice of the people. The missionaries, however, felt strongly about the need to convert Indians as a means of civilizing them. The Colonial state needed people to depend upon, as its apparatus was too small to run the country, independent of local people. Due to financial constraints, English education could only reach the upper classes of the people though it was hoped, that in due course, it would filter down to the masses.[6] The programme was a well-guarded excuse, in Treveleyan's reasoning, for bringing India securely under England's domination. The colonizers also justified their stand by saying that western education was for building up moral character. Yet right along colonial history, there persisted a fear in the minds of the colonizers that a religion-education nexus would lead to a backlash. The fact that such a backlash never took place in the North East is because of the peculiar way in which education developed in that region and also due to socio-political factors inherent in the tribal body politic itself. Except in the North East and some other tribal areas, the government was reluctant to allow the missionaries to preach Christianity in native schools. The period from 1807s to 1930s was characterized by a concerted attempt on the part of the Protestant Missions to bring about 'evangelization' in India, based upon a new perspective: "evangelization through the masses".[7] It would appear that till the first half of the 19th century, the Protestant Missions had near monopoly over English education. Wood's Despatch was the first plan of secular education from the primary to the tertiary level. In 1872, a major shift took place when the mission's previous policy of direct evangelism and conversion was replaced by a policy of diffusion of Christian ideas and principles. Moreover, since 1910, the change within the character of the missions due to Indian Christians gaining control over the region, led to giving a greater weightage to the policy of evangelization of the masses. Nationalist movements such as Home Rule were interpreted by the Indian Christian to mean Home Rule within the Indian Church. Unlike many nationalist leaders, the missionaries had faith that the British would make India a self-governing member of its Commonwealth; they also felt that the time was not yet ripe for complete Home Rule in illiterate India. Further, they were of the view that British rule, for the time being, was an indispensable factor. Therefore they did not support Gandhi's "Satyagraha" and "Non-Cooperation movement", for they did not feel it was justifiable to pull down a government which had given them protection and justice. It was only in 1944 that the missions identified themselves with the nationalist struggle.[8]

1.3 The Role of the Missions in Education

The missionaries, and to be more specific, the Protestant missionaries, often exalted the Bible as the ultimate source of authority and made it a condition that if an individual had to worship God aright, he must be able to read.[9] Thus, the involvement of the missionaries in educational programmes was viewed as supplementary to the primary task of communicating the 'spiritual' message to the people. The interest of the colonial officialdom in mission's educational programmes was not necessarily religious. It was both paternalistic and imperialistic. They understood that education imparted by the missionaries was effective in not only civilizing the natives but also in making them peaceful and loyal.[10] Closely intermingling with the main contents of colonial expansion, western education tended to make colonial occupation appear as beneficial in the eyes of the subject people. The authority of the government was thus compromised by the delegation of all educational and other philanthropic works to Christian missions because the latter could undertake such works more cheaply and efficiently than the government itself. In the process, the missionaries were placed in the position of official educationists. They submitted themselves to government inspections and to a measured control, as might be needed, to satisfy the government that its money was spent properly. Government on its part abstained from all interference in religious instructions. The strategy was to secure the cooperation of missionaries in implementing any measure which the government would wish to undertake. Thus, whereas the officials looked at the introduction of western education as a legitimizing process of colonial rule, the missionaries used it as a vehicle for communicating a Christian message to the subject people. The missionaries considered the three 'R's as the most effective means of winning converts by enabling pupils to learn the basic tenets of Christian faith. According to them educational institutions served a double purpose:[11] as a means of teaching Christian truth, and as a means of recruitment or training of future native workers. They, therefore, gave priority to the study of local vernaculars. these being according to them, the most effective means of preaching or educating. It would appear that the missions had almost a monopolistic control over education at the beginning of the 20th century. In the 1911 census, about 100 missions workers and students in the North East were engaged either as Supervisors or Enumerators. When the government decided to divide up the hill areas into subdivisions with direct official supervision at close quarters, the difficulty of manning their offices with clerks, their peon services with *Lambus*, their roads with *Mahorris* and supervisors, their hospitals with vaccinators, compounders, and dispensaries, were overcome by taking the help of the missions. The missions thus, supplied the manpower requirement of the colonial administration.[12] Moreover, they often acted as mediators between the colonial administration and the people.

The missionaries stressed on elementary education only. According to William Pettigrew, people's ignorance coupled with gross superstition and fatalistic beliefs in their animistic worship, an environment of remoteness and aloofness of the region from the outside world, were the compelling reasons for stressing the importance of elementary education.[13] Pettigrew was convinced that "it is necessary for such people as we have to deal with, not to have anything higher than a middle English school grade. The majority will, for many years to come, be content with an education that will enable them to read and write in their own vernacular". The missions tended to see in the "educated" groups a self-propagating, self-supporting and self-administering body of men and women in their evangelistic and elementary education work, freed from supervision and control of the missionaries. Education in the region was also closely related to the British policy in Assam, as prior to 1947 all other states barring Manipur and Tripura, formed parts of the erstwhile Assam Province. Prior to the Charter Act of 1833, education had not made any noticeable progress. David Scott, Agent to the Governor General for the whole eastern frontier favoured oriental learning. Scott feared that undue importance to western learning would hurt the native sentiments, thereby jeopardizing colonial interests. Thus, between 1815-1834 indigenous learning was encouraged and *Sashtras* were taught in Sanskrit. In order to attract people to education, those who passed out of indigenous schools, were initially absorbed into government service. But the new policy initiated by Lord Bentinck, that of employing English educated Indians in the subordinate revenue and judicial services, led them to abandon this policy in favour of the recruitment of Bengalees into lower administrative positions. Though schools in Assam grew in numbers between 1835 and 1901, Calcutta remained the centre of higher learning. During Ahom rule, patronage was given to the spread of Sanskrit literature, and religious teaching was imparted by Brahmins in the *Tols*; education being confined to only the priestly section of the official aristocracy or the *Kakotis*.[14] However, education was neglected by the royalty since the end of the 18th century, due to internal warfare and recurring Burmese invasions.

The British never helped the missionaries to spread the Gospel in Assam for fear of disturbing the religious sentiments, though at the personal level a lot of missionaries helped the government officials.[15] But whenever the company found it profitable to use the church as a means of disciplining and educating, they came forward as guardians of Christianity, donating land and giving generous contributions. The fear of jeopardizing the commercial interests of the company made the government take a cautious policy towards the expansion of missionary activities.

Lord Wellesley (1798-1806) tolerated missionary work privately. Even some of the missionaries themselves, such as the Serampore Baptist Mission, felt that their work was actually helping the government to stay in India; that every real convert was to become a friend of England and be attached to the British nation. Charles Grant felt that the Indians would become more loyal towards the British rule if they were converted to Christianity thereby enhancing the demand for British manufactured goods.

William Carey, of the British Baptist Mission of Serampore chose, Khasi Hills as the site for the publication of the New Testament in Khasi language in the Roman script in 1824 or 1827. The first missionary to work among the Khasis was Krishna Chandra Pal of Serampore mission. About the same time another Indian started a small school with 12 tribal children at Guwahati supported by the political agent Mr. Scott. The Serampore missionaries thus opened up modern education in Assam. In 1835, the American Baptist Mission Board decided to open a new mission among the Shan tribes of North Eastern part of Assam (now Arunachal Pradesh), at Sadiya in 1836 and Roman characters were introduced into the Shan tribal dialect. A Mrs. Brown started the first school for boys and a Mrs. Cutter for girls at Sadiya in July 1837.

In the meanwhile, due to shortage of funds, the Serampore Baptist Mission abandoned their mission in Assam in favour of the American Baptist Mission. Captain Hannay started the first mission station at Jaipur hoping to work among the Nagas who spoke Assamese, and with his help Bronson came into contact with the Nagas and prepared the first spelling book. Bronson soon moved to a Naga Hills village, Namsang, and got Christian literature translated into the Naga language.

By 1827, sixteen missions had started their work. In Khasi and Jaintia Hills the Presbyterians took over from the Baptists in 1841. At Cherrapunji, the house of Mr. Thomas Jones and his wife was besieged with the clamour "If we know English we could earn our living anywhere".[16] In 1842, Jones decided to start schools for the Khasis, in doing so, he reopened three schools started by Lish at Mawsmai, Mawluk and Cherrapunji. He accepted the Roman script as a means of spreading modern education, and henceforth education helped in the progress of evangelization in the Khasi and Jaintia Hills. By 1853, books had been published and several schools had been opened. At this juncture the missionaries were helped by the government of Lord Dalhousie who had become the Governor-General in 1853.

By 1880, there were 1659 converts in the seven main stations, and by 1895, five Presbyteries were established in Sohra-Shella, Shillong-Mawlai, Mawphlang-Moirang, Jowai-Shangpung and in Ridkhar. The Presbyterian church became the biggest organised church in the region.

Since the Brahmaputra valley, Mikir, Garo and Naga Hills, were dominated by the American Baptists' the Presbyterians moved to the Surma valley. A Mr. Pryse in 1850 started a school with 27 low caste Hindu boys. The following year they marched towards Manipur where he encountered native hostility towards Christianity. However, schools were opened in Lakshipur, Borkhola, Khatigara and Sunai. Teachers were sent to Hailakandi, Tatapore etc. Despite opposition, the missionaries managed to establish Sunday schools and other schools. In Cachar, 11 schools were opened consisting of more than 1,000 pupils.

In the Mizo Hills it was Rev. William Williams, the first missionary to be appointed by the Presbyterians, who entered the territory. But the actual work was done by Mr. J.H. Lorrain and Mr. F.W. Savidge from the Arthington Mission. They established their first centre at Aizawl in the North Lushai Hills from where they spread education throughout the Mizo Hills. Using the Roman script they translated the Bible and got the local dialect written in the Roman script. D.E. Jones was appointed to look after the Mizo Hills and the missionaries approached the tribal people through their chieftains. Darphaka was one of the first tribal chiefs to embrace Christianity.

By the second half of the nineteenth century, the Welsh Revival Movement had its effect on India and open air preaching was done in the area. They campaigned against drunkenness, feuds and restoration of property. Their appeal to the Mizo masses was made through social reform and the acceptance of an alien religion by the Mizo Chiefs or Lals (Tribal Chieftain).

The government soon entrusted education to the missionaries by giving them financial help, and elementary schools were opened in most part of the North Lushai Hills. Though, the average literacy became high among the Mizos due to their conversion to Christianity, they had to remain contented with elementary education only since government did not encourage higher learning. On the whole the Welsh mission had eight or nine missionaries including two hospital sisters in the North Lushai Hills while the Indian Baptist mission employed about the same number in the South Lushai Hills. The cost incurred by the government on education was minimum, i.e., expenditure never exceeded three and half pence, per head, of population per year. Thus, whatever progress was made was due to Christian Missions. More than in any other area the government and the missionaries worked in close concert in Mizoram.[17]

In view of the almost insurmountable communication problem, the missionaries were compelled to employ Lushais who worked in farflung areas. In the initial stages, school education was based upon teacher-pupil concept. The idea being that as soon as the pupil showed some aptitude, he was sent to teach the others.[18]

One significant development in the schools was the inclusion of some practical work such as basket-weaving and manual work in the curriculum. The problem was how to make education both practical and spiritual. The inclusion of practical subjects in Lushai Hill schools made education more appealing. Mr. E.L. Mendus virtually forced his students at Aizawl to work three periods a week at digging a playground out of a hill and also working in the school garden. The Governor of Assam gave money to Mendus to emphasize practical education for which he bought country tools. The basic concept of the missionaries was to fashion the youth in the "likeness of Jesus Christ" and that education instead of being a burden was useful and inspired work.

The practical side of education was emphasized more for the females, in order to break the prejudice against girl education. An educated girl thus came to be considered an asset to their community as they contributed to the family income.[19] The emphasis on the practical work orientation in female education also aimed at the principle of making some contribution towards the cost of education for girls. Therefore, the lady missionaries trained in such arts formulated a curriculum whereby the girls could give some of their time to work which would be both educational and profitable financially. The practical work which the girls were made to do was in addition to their normal subjects involved like cooking, basket making, weaving, etc.

The whole system of education was based upon the methods of the "project scheme".[20] During the first term, when the weather was fine, the children were taught weaving, farming and gardening. During second term, when the monsoons had begun; they were confined to schools and taught the three 'Rs' in classrooms. Even when vocational education was given, the religious purpose was never lost sight of. Along with elementary schools, modern medicine was introduced and by 1950s several Mizo girls had passed out of nursing schools. With the presence of the Presbyterians in the North Lushai Hills and Baptists in the South Lushai Hills, more than half of the population of the Mizo Hills became Christian. According to the 1961 census, 228,577 Mizos were Christians out of a total population of 263,877.

The principle and practice of missionary education laid down its religious character and purpose which was never hidden from the people. But operating within the limits of colonial structure, missionaries did nothing to subvert colonial interests. It was only with the Assam Bill of Education, 1946, that the missionary policy towards education underwent a change. This Bill sought to centralize all education and do away with the aided system which had monopolized education in the North East. According to it there was to be a Central Board at Shillong for the whole province and a District Board at Aizawl. To this, the missionary reaction was that the schools had a Christian foundation - with strong Christians in key positions and a Christian syllabus, and "Even if and when the time comes we shall have to give them up; we shall have the consolation of knowing that they have been impregnated with Christian spirit".[21]

In Manipur, the Princely State was divided into valleys in which the Vaishnav King and his Meiteis or Hindu subjects lived whereas the hills were dominated by Naga, Mizo, Kuki and Chin tribes, all of whom had embraced Christianity. The missionary influence was first felt in the work of Messrs. William Pettigrew of Kachar who wanted to use education for the spread of Christianity. Schools in Manipur were practically state sponsored and hence he evoked a strong reaction from the natives (mainly Vaishnavites). Though Pettigrew obtained the support of the Political Agent, Maxwell, yet the teaching of Christianity was banned in state schools. In Ukhrul, the land of the Thangkhul Nagas, however, Pettigrew was more successful, where he got the support of Kuki Christian volunteers to spread education. Threatened by the State Government's attitude of non-cooperation, Pettigrew preferred to ignore the dependence on state financial assistance.

The Naga Hills had practically no formal system of education prior to the arrival of the missionaries. Their traditional 'Morungs' or dormitories imparted education in hunting and wordly skills to youth prior to their entry to adult life. In 1838, Mr. Bronson from Jaipur established a station at Namsang village and in 1851, Mr. S.W. Whiting, a resident missionary at Sibsagar had baptized a Naga (Ao tribe) from Morangkong village. In 1869, Mr. E.P. Scott had visited the Naga Hills recruiting a few men to be trained at the Nowgong school. In 1854 when the Foreign Secretary of American Baptist Foreign Mission Society, visited Assam, 'the mission to Nagas' was much discussed.[22] Though they suggested full-time missionaries, yet no missionary was exclusively appointed for the Nagas. Since the Nagas would come down to Sibsagar for marketing, 'bazar-preaching' was practiced. Though the Naga Godhula was keen to preach Christianity to the Nagas, the latter looked upon him and all foreigners as British spies. They were thus extremely suspicious of missionary advances made upon them. The real change in missionary activities in Naga Hills came in 1857 when Mr. Clark abandoned the campaign in Assam Hills and advanced to the Naga Hills instead. The first mission was established at Molung in 1876. In 1878 C.D. King on reaching Assam wanted to open a station among the Angami Nagas, but denied government permission, he established himself at Samagoting, and following a Naga rebellion against the British, a station was opened in Kohima. Mr. King was joined by Mr. Goldsmith and a church was established.

The Molung Station was considered as a centre of Naga Christian activity and later in 1894 Impur also became a centre. The whole of Naga Hills was henceforth divided into two centres of work, namely Impur and Kohima.

The Ao Nagas embraced Christianity almost en masse. By 1892, there were 5 Ao Churches with 75 Christians. Like in Mizo Hills, the main concern of the church was to salvage Nagas from vices such as drinking, feuds etc. A fresh momentum to Christian activities came in 1886 and by 1905 there were 700 Christians in 20 villages around Impur alone.

The missionaries opened a third centre for the Lothas, and Wokha was selected for this purpose. In 1885, Mr. W.E. Witter moved to Wokha and prepared a small catechism and grammar book in Lotha language. He also planned to translate useful books. A small school with a boarding house was established, and small jobs were undertaken in the mission compound to meet the daily expenses of the school. Sunday schools were organised. As compared to the Aos, the Lothas were slow to take advantage of Christian education. Almost single handedly the American Baptists worked for the conversion of the Nagas and Mr. Clark even tried to introduce the English alphabet with Italian phonetics into the Naga dialects. Several books and Christian literature were published in Roman script; even modern medicine was introduced in Kohima by Mr. Rivenburg in order to impart the Gospel.

Among other missionary activities among the Nagas was the opening of a training school for Christian apostolic workers by Mr. S.A. Perrine, as leadership training was considered very important. Training was imparted in English so that the Nagas could act as interpreters. Besides the mission schools, a system of village schools, was also organized to eradicate illiteracy in which most of the school teachers were paid out of local church funds. Within twenty-five years, the Naga Mission grew to be financially self-sufficient.

Prior to the Second World War, the Christian missions controlled most of the primary schools in the Naga Hills district. Several new schools were established in the villages following the war, but due to financial difficulties, the government soon took over most of the so-called missionary or native schools in different places. Unlike the Mizo Hills, the spread of education was very slow in the Naga Hills where there were practically no middle schools, and students had to migrate to Assam or Manipur for education beyond the elementary level till the end of the last century. As Verrier Elwin observed in 1961 "Prior to the war, except in the case of the Aos, school going was still unpopular and looked upon as a necessary evil which had to be put up with somehow. Suddenly they found themselves clamouring for more and more schools in which they saw social progress and where the government could not build them, they went ahead and built their own. Existing schools were filled to overflowing".[23] After 1947, great stress was laid on the spread of education among the backward and hill tribes with special provision for their expansion.

In other parts of Assam as well, the American Baptist Missions and other denomination churches helped to spread elementary education. School literature was published by Mr. Brown as early as in 1841, and Mrs. Bronson opened a large mission and an Orphan institution in Nowgong. In 1854, there was a proposal from Mr. Solomon Peck, the then Foreign Secretary, to convert the institution to a central school for training native teachers and preachers. Several schools were organised at Guwahati under Mr. Baker with contribution from the local community. By 1855, there were six mission families in the three stations of Assam. Sibsagar – the Browns and Whitings, Nowgong – the Bronsons and Stoddards, and at Guwahati the Danfords and Wards. All these families concentrated on the plain areas of Assam. By 1870s it was found that the Mikirs and Kacharis had also been converted to Christianity and new missions arose in Goalpara and Kamrup. Though the first "mass movement" of conversion in the North East was mainly among the Garos, yet by the end of the 19th century, a large number of other hill tribes of Assam had also embraced Christianity and were being taught elementary education in schools with a Christian bias.

In the tea gardens, the government had invited the Salvatarian Mission of Italy to open schools for the Adivasis. Non-Catholics also attended these schools and got converted into Catholicism. The Catholic missions were resisted by the planters who feared that the missionaries would take their labourers away to Christian villages. Yet the first demand for educational institutions had come from the European and Anglo-

Indian communities in Shillong, constituting mainly of government officials who were able to pay for their children's education. The local Catholics, on the contrary, being poor, demanded free education. The Salesians of Don Bosco, another Catholic institution imparted more technical and job oriented education. In 1924, a handicraft-school was started in Shillong with the main purpose of helping young Catholics to earn their livelihood. Attractive courses such as carpentry, composing, printing, tailoring and shoe-making were introduced. Those who passed out of these schools received immediate employment from the government.

But on the whole, both the Baptist and the Catholic Missions were unable to spread elementary education in the plains in the same manner as they had done in the hill areas of the North East. The resistance to Christian and Western education by Brahmins dominating the plain areas stood in their way. The Christians found the simple tribal folk culture, with animism as their faith, an easy field for conversion. They were further helped by the attitude of the tribal chiefs who preferred the white man to the brown sahibs of the plain areas of Assam and Bengal. The importance of high levels of literacy and elementary education in Mizoram and Nagaland between 1960s and 1980s was not only due to missionary efforts but ethnic consciousness which grew among the tribes resulting in insurgency movements leading to their obtaining statehoods. However, despite these factors and other socio-economic commonalties that existed among the Mizos and Nagas, Mizoram's success can be attributed largely to the combination of the roles played by its politicians, church leaders, community members, the academic decentralization and voluntary associations such as the Young Mizo Christian Association. This combination, however, was found wanting in the history of Nagaland, between the 1960s and 1990s, to be discussed in detail in later section of the book.

References

1. R. Gopalkrishnan, *The North-East India-Land, Economy and People*, *op.cit.*, p. 5.
2. The region has international boundaries with Bhutan in the north, Burma in the east and Bangladesh in the south.
3. Laldena, *Christian Missions and Colonialism: A Study of Missionary Movement in North East India with Particular Reference to Manipur and Lushai Hills 1897-1947* (Shillong: Vendrame Institute, 1988), p. 90.
4. Charles Grant, *Observations on the State of Society among the Asiatic Subjects of Great Britain*, Parliamentary Papers, 1813, Vol. XI.

5. Quoted from John Clark Marshman, *The Life and Times of Carey* (London, 1859), Vol.2, pp. 45-46.
6. Krishna Kumar, *Political Agenda of Education* (New Delhi: Sage Publications, 1991), p. 31.
7. A. Mathew, *Christian Missions, Education and Nationalism* (Delhi: Anamika Prakashan, 1988), p. 2.
8. *Ibid.*, p. 197.
9. Quoted from M.A. Laird, *Missionaries and Education in Bengal 1793-1837* (Oxford, 1972) in Laldena, *op. cit.*, p. 90.
10. John Shakespeare to J.M. Lorrain as cited in P.N. Jones, *The Lushai Hills*, MSS, BNS, London (undated).
11. Laldena, *op. cit.*, p. 93.
12. *Ibid.*, p. 94.
13. Cited from William Pettigrew's Pamphlet, *Twenty five Years 1897-1922: Ukhrul Mission School*, 1922, in *Ibid.*, pp. 94-95.
14. Barkataki Meena Sharma, *British Administration in North-Eastern India (1826-1874) A Study of their Social Policy*, *op. cit.*, p.19.
15. Muttumama Mathew, *Christianity in Assam and Inter - 'Faith' Dialogue - A Study on the Modern Religion Movements in North Eastern India* (Indore: Satprakashan Sanchar Kendra, 1985), p. 9.
16. Cited from J.H. Morris, *History of the Western Calvinistic Methodist Foreign Mission*, in M. Mathew, *op. cit.* p. 30.
17. Quoted from A.G. McCall, *Lushai Chrysallis Aizawl*, 1977 (Reprinted) in Laldena, *op. cit.*, p. 95.
18. Quoted from David Kyles, *Lorrain of the Lushai Hills* (Edinburgh, 1944) in Laldena, *op. cit.*, p. 95.
19. Quoted from *An Educational Experiment 1920-1930*, Baptist Mission, South Lushai Girls' School, p. 2., in Laldena, *op. cit.*, p. 97.
20. Laldena, *op. cit*, p. 98.
21. Basil Ewart Jones, and Margaret Jones, *Letters and Reports 1940-1954* (Private Papers) in Laldena, *op. cit.*, p. 99.
22. M. Mathew, *op. cit.*, p. 62.
23. Verrier Elwin, *Nagaland*, *op. cit.*, p. 86.

2

Elementary Schooling Facilities in the Region

As we have seen, before the arrival of the British, hardly anyone could read or write English in Assam.[1] To economize on government expenditure, the employment of local people had become an administrative necessity for the colonists; Indians could be paid less. This required that Indians be given western education in English. Western education spread in the hill areas of Assam where Christian missionaries ran schools. However, the conversion of a large number of tribals to Christianity led to changes in the lives and beliefs of the people.[2] After 1947, the Government of India made special provision for the spread of education among the backward and hill tribes, and several government as well as private schools were established.

After Independence, the Constitution of India in its Article 45 (Part IV) under the Directive Principles of State Policy made provision for 'Free and Compulsory Education for Children'. It said that 'The State shall endeavour to provide, within a period of ten years from the commencement of this constitution, free and compulsory education for all children until they complete the age of fourteen years.' This emphasis on compulsory and free education was largely responsible for quantitative expansion of educational facilities between the 1950 and 1980. Further, under Articles 15 and 17 under Fundamental Rights: Prohibition of Discrimination on Grounds of Religion, Race, Caste, Sex or place of Birth, protection of the educational interests of the weaker sections of the Indian community, socially and educationally backward classes of citizens and scheduled castes and scheduled tribes was given special importance.

Education was also to be secular, but by Article 30 (1) all minorities, whether based on religion or language had the right to establish and administer educational institutions according to their choice. Hence, throughout the North East, three types of primary and upper primary schools grew, namely, government, aided and unaided private schools. In the Concurrent List Entry No. 25[43] education was made the joint responsibility of the State and Central Government and hence numerous centrally sponsored schemes were provided to the states for quality improvement of primary schools such as 'Operation Black Board', a scheme through which minimum of two rooms, one veranda, sitting arrangement, desks and teaching aids such as black-board etc. were made essential in every primary school. Often a second teacher was also introduced in single teacher school. A mid-day meals scheme, non-formal education package, Hindi teachers for the middle schools in non-Hindi speaking areas, were also introduced.

In the First Five Year Plan (1951-56) emphasis was given to the Gandhian model of Basic Education which incorporated a rural based craft into the curriculum of elementary education. However, the Kothari Commission, better known as the Indian Education Commission 1964-66, introduced 'Work Experience' to mean something wider than rural craft from the middle school onwards. It also stressed on the three-language formula, whereby the mother tongue or regional language, English as a link language and Hindi, or an Indian classical language or European language were to be taught in schools. The students of primary schools were to be taught either in the mother tongue or regional language, and two languages at the upper primary stage such as the mother tongue and the official or semi-official language. It is due to this language policy that English was given importance in the North Eastern States. The Commission by laying emphasis on health education also helped the Central Government to introduce measures like free medical check-ups for students and free vaccination.

In order to uplift the weaker sections of society the Central Government also started supplying the states with free textbooks and stipends from which some of the North Eastern Scheduled Castes and Scheduled Tribes and children benefited. Providing residential schools and staff quarters, in remote tribal areas, led to the increasing enrolment in elementary schools. In 1986, the Central Government came up with yet another package to give a boost to the elementary for Scheduled Castes and Scheduled Tribes in its Programme of Action by stating that not only all SC and ST students needed to be enrolled and retained in up to Class VIII, but they had to also perform satisfactorily. Several other incentive schemes were introduced such as pre-metric scholarships in addition to providing free uniforms, books, stationary etc. Moreover, constant micro-planning, which is planning at the grass-root level, was emphasized for ensuring enrolment, retention and successful completion of courses. The document also emphasized the need to employ teachers from Scheduled Castes and Scheduled Tribes. The preparation of primers for Classes I-II in tribal languages was considered a necessity. Infrastructure facilities in educational institutions was also its concern.[3]

In 1992, the Government of India announced that the drop out rates for the years 1987-88 for the Scheduled Castes and Scheduled Tribes in India being high for Classes I-VIII (68.81 for SC and 80.01 for ST), in addition to the post-metric scholarship, grant-in-aid to voluntary organizations would be given in order to encourage them to open schools in remote areas. Further, book banks, coaching and allied schemes were encouraged. Educational complexes were proposed to be set up for low literacy areas. For the tribal areas it was suggested that the 'educational plan would be implemented in an integrated manner through pre-school education (Balwadis), non-formal education, elementary education and adult education".[4] Decentralization and giving responsibility to local bodies to look after primary education was considered very important. Since 1992 onwards both the District Primary Education Programme in Assam and the Sarvya Shikshya Abhiyan in the North East States have each contributed to decentralization to education.

The First All India Educational Survey conducted by the NCERT in 1957 (data pertaining to 1951) when analyzed gives a clear picture of schooling facilities in the North Eastern States at the primary and middle stages, but no data is available for Nagaland. Even the Second Survey has no data on the Mizo Hills, hence it is only the Third NCERT survey (1979) that gives us the data on all the states of the region. Thus, for analysis of data prior to 1979, (the year of publication of the Third NCERT Survey), data on the region has to be gathered from the 1961 Census Report of Assam Vol. III Part 1A- under its general tables. Since the purpose of this chapter is to draw a comparative picture of the schooling facilities at the elementary level for the region as a whole, the data used is the Third NCERT Survey (1979) and the ones gathered thereafter have been used.

Primary Section

The NCERT data shows the criterion of schooling facilities at the primary level available within the habitation up to 1 km. (1978). Consequently, the all-India average shows that 76.12 per cent of its rural population were served with schooling facilities within walking distance of 1 km. of the place of residence. Moreover, as much as 90.34 per cent of the rural population were served by primary sections, located either within the habitation or at a distance of 1 km. As compared with these figures as much as 78.53 per cent of the population of Assam were served with primary sections, located either within the perimeters of residence or within a walking distance of 2 km. Manipur, one of the educationally advanced states of the region at that time, had as much as 96.57 per cent of its population served by primary schools within a distance of 2 km., and 95.78 per cent of its population were served by primary sections within a distance of 1 km. In Meghalaya, 87.55 per cent of the population were served by primary sections within a distance of 1 km. Meghalaya's relative backwardness in schooling facilities is largely due to small habitations where schools are difficult to provide. In Arunachal Pradesh, another backward state, the population was not provided with as many primary sections, due to both topographical reasons as well as their lack of interest in education at that time. It is worth mentioning here, that, unlike Meghalaya, Assam, Manipur, Nagaland and Mizoram; Arunachal Pradesh had neither any Christian missionary influence, nor a culture of Brahmanical education, which was prevalent in Tripura. Hence only 50.97 per cent of its population were served by a primary section within a walking distance of 2 km. Tripura's figures in the Third Survey are relatively better, that is, 94.76 per cent of the population were served by primary sections within a distance of 2 km. and 82.35 per cent within a distance of 1 km. Tripura also shares with Meghalaya the problem of providing educational facilities to smaller tribal groups. Tripura improved during the Third Survey period on account of the relative peacefulness of the state and a responsive administration.

By far the most impressive figures are those of Nagaland and Mizoram where the Baptist missions had been directly involved with the spread of elementary education. In Nagaland, as much as 98.98 per cent of its population was served by primary sections or schools within a distance of 2 km. Only 30 habitations were not served by schooling facilities within a distance of 2 km. of which 28 were in the population slab of below 500 persons.

The most impressive picture is that of Mizoram where 99.76 per cent of its population had schooling facilities within the perimeters of residence and there was only one habitation with a population of 0.24 per cent which did not have a schooling facility within 2 km. Mizoram may well be compared with Chandigarh, Lakshadweep and Pondicherry in which almost 100 per cent of their rural population were served by primary schools/sections within a distance of 2 km.

For the upper primary or middle stages which is Classes VI to VIII, the all-India average was 28.86 per cent of the rural population served by middle sections in the habitation of their residence; 71.97 per cent with facilities up to a distance of 3 km. and 86.91 per cent population within a distance of 5 km.

When compared with the all-India average, the North Eastern Region fares favourably. Even in Assam, which is considered as an educationally backward state, 86.89 per cent of its population was served with middle schools/ sections, in Manipur, 74.05 per cent and in Meghalaya 32.51 per cent. In Tripura, which has problems with small habitations, similar to Meghalaya, as much as 59.02 per cent of its population was served by middle schools/sections within their habitation. In Mizoram, however, almost all settlements had middle schools/sections within a distance of 5 km. and as much as 92.37 per cent of its rural population were served with middle schools within the village. An equally successful case is that of Nagaland where 56.67 per cent of the habitations were served with middle schools/ sections within their habitation and 64.97 per cent within a walking distance. The only exceptional case was Arunachal Pradesh where with 93.98 per cent of its population 'below' 500' population slab, had only 11.52 per cent of its population served by middle schools/sections within the habitation.

Thus, in terms of schooling facilities, as an indicator of educational development, the region as a whole had done well for itself even in the seventies. It is without doubt that the role played both by the missionaries and the colonial government earlier, if taken together, had put the North East on the map of educational achievement - both in literacy and elementary education.

According to the Fourth All India Education Survey of NCERT conducted in 1978, 98.35 per cent of Nagaland's total rural population had been provided with either primary schools or sections within their place of residence. This impressive figure is followed by similarly favourable account of Manipur (92.82%) and Assam (81.34%). The states which were below the all-India average (78.53%) were Tripura (54.42%), Arunachal Pradesh (55.90%); Mizoram (74.54%) and Meghalaya (76.12%) (see Appendix VI for details). Barring Arunachal Pradesh

(60.69%), Mizoram (74.63%) and Meghalaya (88.53%) all other states of this region have schools within a distance of 1 km. from the place of residence of the children (all-India average being 92.82%).

For the middle school level, (64.32%) of Mizoram's rural population was provided with such facilities within the habitation, followed by Nagaland (50.72%) and Manipur (38.62%). The all-India average was, that, only 33.47 per cent of rural population had such facilities within their habitation. The states of this region which were below this figure were Assam (20.91%), Tripura (19.79%), Arunachal Pradesh (18.14%); and Meghalaya (15.72%). However, barring Arunachal Pradesh (28.15%) and Meghalaya (53.03%) all other states of the region had over seventy per cent of its rural population provided with such facilities within a distance of 3 kilometres, which was close to the all-India average of 78.83 per cent.

In 1986, Mizoram had provided 80.37 per cent of its rural population with primary schools within the habitations, while in most other states the rural population was given the same facilities, within a distance of 3 kilometres. As far as middle schools were concerned all of these states had provided their rural population with schooling facilities, the range being 73.35 per cent in Arunachal Pradesh to 99.45 per cent in Nagaland, the all-India average being 94.60 per cent.

In 1993, most of the villages of Mizoram (586 out of 667), were provided with primary schooling facilities in the vicinity, though the state was lacking in these facilities at the middle school level. Appendix XI gives details as per the Sixth All India Educational Survey's Provisional Statistics (1995). According to the state level report on Meghalaya for the same year there are indications that 70 per cent of all habitations in Meghalaya have schooling facilities within a distance of 1 kilometer. Even if the state norms are relaxed to provide 200+ population with a schooling facility in the vicinity of the dwellings, they would still be left with 1288 habitations bereft of such facilities (that is 20 per cent of the total habitations involving 30,000 children). This would affect the districts of West and South Garo Hills, with more than 250 each of school-less villages with a population below 200.[5]

In relation to the national norm of 300+ population having access to upper primary/middle schools, within a distance of 3 kilometres, in Meghalaya in 1993, only 59 per cent of its total habitations and 70 per cent of its rural population had these facilities. In fact as much as 419 of their habitations are in need of these facilities. The state government has, therefore, suggested that apart from non-formal centres, formal schools be established in all 'viable villages/habitations' and the upgrading of existing primary schools to 'upper primary schools'. Moreover, hostel facilities would have to be extended to select upper primary schools to be utilized by both primary and upper primary students.

Growth of Primary and Upper Primary Schools

The pattern of the growth of primary and upper primary schooling facilities in this region has not been uniform or rational. For example, at the primary level, Arunachal Pradesh which had the lowest participation of girl students for the elementary level has had, however, the fastest growth rate of primary schools, that is, 52.17 per cent increase in the years 1973-78, and again 22.48 per cent increase between the years 1986 and 1993. Yet Mizoram, whose performance is the best in the area of enrolment, retention rate and girls' participation, and has witnessed the lowest growth of primary schools, that is, 8.40 per cent, from the years 1973 to 1978, and -2.69 per cent from the years 1986 to 1993. Similarly, Nagaland has seen -1.02 per cent decrease from the years 1973 to 1978, but 15.38 per cent increase from 1986 to 1993. This is because in Mizoram the schooling facilities were sufficient and what from 1973 the Mizos concentrated on was the employment of teachers and the introduction of centrally sponsored schemes rather than an expansion of educational facilities.

Table 2.1
Growth Rate in Primary Schools

States	*% age of increase from 1957-1965*	*% age of increase from 1965-1973*	*% age of increase from 1973-1978*	*% age of increase from 1978-1986*	*% age of increase from 1986-1993*
Arunachal Pradesh	N.A	N.A.	52.17	29.52	20.38
Assam	44.39	7.94	9.68	19.76	11.66
Meghayala	N.A.	N.A.	17.44	3.27	11.02
Mizoram	N.A.	N.A.	8.40	94.77	-6.17
Manipur	165.50	59.76	8.76	19.78	9.94
Nagaland	N.A.	N.A.	-1.02	16.72	8.31
Tripura	42.78	13.95	5.78	22.50	4.93

Source: Calculated from All India Educational Surveys, New Delhi, NCERT

The percentage increase in middle schools/middle sections was the highest during the years 1973 to 1978 in Tripura 981.48%), followed by Nagaland (177.31%). Table 2.3 gives the total number of recognized primary and middle schools which existed between 1993-94.

Table 2.2
Growth Rate on Middle Schools

States	*% age of increase from 1957-1965*	*% age of increase from 1965-1973*	*% age of increase from 1973-1978*	*% age of increase from 1978-1986*	*% age of increase from 1986-1993*
Arunachal Pradesh	N.A.	N.A.	77.97	73.33	52.20
Assam	3.27	50.98	53.42	36.63	39.11
Meghalaya	N A.	N.A.	28.08	77.81	23.11
Mizoram	N.A.	N.A.	16.11	88.98	31.22
Manipur	272.62	-32.90	80.00	15.34	61.01
Nagaland	N.A.	N.A.	177.31	-11.82	32.30
Tripura	-37.21	-5.00	981.48	43.49	3.58

Source: Calculated from All India Educational Surveys, NCERT, New Delhi.

Table 2.3
Total Number of Recognised Primary and Middle Schools in North-East

States	*Primary*		*Middle*	
	1993-94	*2001-02*	*1993-94*	*2001-02*
Arunachal Pradesh	1205	1315	277	347
Assam	28876	33236	6729	8019
Manipur	3076	2573	633	796
Meghalaya	4175	5646	725	1041
Mizoram	1082	1377	609	851
Nagaland	1409	1499	418	479
Tripura	2063	2095	431	432

Source: (1) Ministry of Human Resource Development, Department of Education, Annual Report 1993-94, New Delhi.
(2) Selected Education Statistics, MHRD, New Delhi.

One may also summarize the poorest percentage increase in the number of primary school between the years 1981-82 and 1992-93 was in Meghalaya (12.86), in Nagaland (10.22%) and Manipur (11.19%). The upper primary sections/schools in Nagaland have one of the poorest percentage increase of (15.16%) followed by Assam (29.91%).

School Buildings

Majority of the primary schools of this region consist of semi-pucca buildings of Assam type with tin or straw roofing and bamboo partitions. Most of the states held primary classes in open space or in tents after 1978 except in Tripura. In fact, in 1986, only sixty-eight primary schools were held in the open space in Tripura. In the same year, nine of these schools were held in tents in Meghalaya. Mizoram had no pucca building and even in Assam there existed only 1962 pucca buildings out of a total of 25873 schools. Pucca buildings were rare, especially in Manipur (61), Tripura (69) and Nagaland (79). Thatched huts predominate in Assam and Meghalaya. Table 2.4 gives details on the types of buildings existing for primary schools. Once again the situation is equally dismal in the upper primary or middle schools. Two of such schools were being held in open space in Tripura in the same year (see Table 2.5). Playgrounds are equally uncommon in this region, and only 8.20 per cent of Assamese primary schools have any use for playgrounds.

Table 2.4
Statewise Primary School According to Type of Buildings 1986

States	*Pucca Building*	*Partly Pucca Building*	*Kachha Building*	*Thatched Huts*	*Tents*	*Open Space*	*Total*
Arunachal Pradesh	142	51	144	615	0	0	952
Assam	1962	7578	10503	5830	0	0	25873
Manipur	61	479	1371	846	0	0	2757
Meghalaya	288	698	1215	1482	9	0	3692
Mizoram	0	578	355	72	0	0	1005
Nagaland	79	401	506	145	0	0	1131
Tripura	69	43	1553	194	0	68	1927

Source: Fifth All India Educational Survey 1986, New Delhi, NCERT.

Table 2.4.1
Statewise Primary School According to Type of Buildings 1993

States	*Pucca Building*	*Partly Pucca Building*	*Kachha Building*	*Thatched Huts*	*Tents*	*Open Space*	*Total*
Arunachal	306	241	369	230	0	0	1146
Assam	4102	10464	8568	4695	352	709	28890
Manipur	292	807	1279	63	8	14	3031
Meghalaya	884	1647	889	674	3	2	4099
Mizoram	23	433	433	54	0	0	943
Nagaland	49	500	606	70	0	0	1225
Tripura	349	252	1131	260	3	34	2029

Source: Sixth All India Educational Survey (1993), New Delhi, NCERT.

Table 2.5

Middle School According to Types of Buildings 1986

States	*Pucca Building*	*Partly Pucca Building*	*Kachha Building*	*Thatched Huts*	*Tents*	*Open Space*	*Total*
Arunachal Pradesh	75	23	19	65	0	0	182
Assam	415	2086	1830	660	0	0	4991
Manipur	14	117	262	43	0	0	436
Meghalaya	150	224	186	105	0	0	665
Mizoram	0	295	154	14	0	0	463
Nagaland	89	82	113	7	0	0	291
Tripura	11	30	360	16	0	2	419

Source: Fifth All India Educational Survey (1986), New Delhi, NCERT.

Table 2.5.1

Middle School According to Types of Buildings 1993

States	*Pucca Building*	*Partly Pucca Building*	*Kachha Building*	*Thatched Huts*	*Tents*	*Open Space*	*Total*
Arunachal Pradesh	115	73	56	31	0	2	277
Assam	726	3001	2276	904	19	17	6943
Manipur	63	210	376	52	1	0	702
Meghalaya	203	393	160	63	1	0	820
Mizoram	23	310	253	22	0	0	608
Nagaland	92	114	165	14	0	0	385
Tripura	29	71	306	26	0	2	434

Source: Sixth All India Educational Survey (1993), New Delhi, NCERT

Ancillary Facilities

The NCERT Fifth All India Educational Survey data gives details about facilities in primary schools, such as, drinking water, urinals, and separate urinal for girls, lavatory, separate lavatory for girls, medical-checkups and vaccinations. In 1986, drinking water was in short supply both in Mizoram and Nagaland. Even in 1995, the schools in the districts of Lunglei and Chhimtuipui, in Mizoram, had hardly any drinking water during the dry seasons. The case study on Lai Autonomous District Council of Mizoram revealed that even district headquarters lacked these facilities in primary schools.[6] Similarly, the urinal facilities were hardly existed in Assam, with practically no separate urinal for girls. The whole region suffered from lack of these facilities. There was also hardly any separate lavatory for girls in Assam, Meghalaya, and Nagaland. Assam conducted no medical checkups for primary school students. The medical facilities such as vaccination, in addition to checkups being poorest in Assam followed by Tripura. Though in Manipur medical checkups had taken place for primary school students, yet there were no vaccination schemes (See Table 2.6 for details). The Sixth All India Educational Survey, however, gives no data on medical check-ups and vaccination.

Table 2.6

Statewise Primary Schools Having Ancillary Facilities in North East 1986

State	*Total No. of Schools*	*Primary Schools Having Facilities for*						
		Drinking Water	*Urinal*	*Separate Urinal for girls*	*Lavatory*	*Separate Lavatory for girls*	*Medical check-up*	*Vaccination*
Arunachal Pradesh	952	468	218	80	88	23	185	305
Assam	25873	3978	1866	0	1735	0	0	0
Manipur	2757	711	465	118	155	29	152	0
Meghalaya	3692	437	440	67	68	13	279	501
Mizoram	1005	317	502	109	201	40	55	127
Nagaland	1131	283	424	125	21	11	46	130
Tripura	1927	718	259	70	103	29	5	88

Source: Fifth All India Educational Survey (1986), New Delhi, NCERT.

Table 2.6.1

Statewise Primary Schools Having Ancillary Facilities in North East 1993

State	*Total No. of Schools*	*Primary Schools Having Facilities for*				
		Drinking Water	*Urinal*	*Separate Urinal for girls*	*Lavatory*	*Separate Lavatory for girls*
Arunachal Pradesh	1146	466	154	41	87	29
Assam	28890	5711	3475	470	558	112
Manipur	3031	481	511	118	241	58
Meghalaya	4099	421	392	76	102	26
Mizoram	943	301	684	158	310	63
Nagaland	1225	160	273	139	66	50
Tripura	2029	376	222	33	63	11

Source: Sixth All India Educational Survey (1993), New Delhi, NCERT.

The ancillary facilities in the upper primary schools were also poor in most of the North Eastern states. Both Mizoram and Nagaland lack drinking water facilities. Assam had the poorest medical facilities; followed by Tripura. Table 2.7 gives details on each facility for this level.

Table 2.7
Statewise Upper Primary Schools Having Ancillary Facilities in North East 1986

State	*Total No. of Schools*	*Upper Primary Schools Having Facilities for*						
		Drinking Water	*Urinal*	*Separate Urinal for girls*	*Lavatory*	*Separate Lavatory for girls*	*Medical check-up*	*Vaccination*
Arunachal Pradesh	182	116	71	37	43	18	65	84
Assam	4991	2306	2758	659	1040	86	1	0
Manipur	436	210	218	88	85	35	42	0
Meghalaya	665	254	279	132	125	42	90	153
Mizoram	463	130	222	66	152	50	27	63
Nagaland	291	128	139	112	52	39	29	44
Tripura	419	219	189	86	50	11	1	18

Source: Fifth All India Educational Survey (1986) New Delhi, NCERT.

Table 2.7.1
Statewise Upper Primary Schools Having Ancillary Facilities in North East 1993

State	*Total No. of Schools*	*Upper Primary Schools Having Facilities for*				
		Drinking Water	*Urinal*	*Separate Urinal for girls*	*Lavatory*	*Separate Lavatory for girls*
Arunachal Pradesh	277	150	86	38	56	25
Assam	6943	2958	2434	1013	475	148
Manipur	702	259	350	182	254	118
Meghalaya	820	217	305	169	126	59
Mizoram	608	266	553	201	330	66
Nagaland	385	140	212	152	95	65
Tripura	434	180	156	38	53	8

Source: Sixth All India Educational Survey (1993) New Delhi, NCERT.

Furniture and Mats for Students

In Arunachal Pradesh, as early as in 1978, almost fifty per cent of its primary schools had adequate mats and furniture for their students (i.e., 393 out of a total of 735 schools). The situation improved even further in 1986. This is quite contrary to the situation in Assam, where as many as 3948 out of 21603 of its schools had no such facility in 1978, and 40705 schools still lacked these facilities in 1986. In Manipur, 498 schools had adequate furniture and this figure rose substantially to become 5717 in 1986. Though in Meghalaya these facilities were not available to a majority of the schools in 1978 (460 schools had adequate mats and furniture out of 3575 total primary schools), the situation improved in 1986 (3402 schools had adequate facilities). In Mizoram out of 516 primary schools, as many as 254 had adequate furniture and mats for their students in 1978 and the situation went on improving in 1986. In Nagaland too these facilities were adequate both in 1978 and in 1986. Whereas there were 205 schools with these facilities in 1978, almost 50 per cent of the primary schools had added these facilities in 1986. Tripura needs to add more of these facilities in their primary schools. For example, in 1978, out of 1573 schools only 333 had these facilities but the situation did not improve substantially in the next decade.[7]

At the middle school stage very few schools had these facilities in this region in 1978 barring Mizoram. For example, out of 105 middle schools in Arunachal Pradesh only 41 schools provided these facilities to their students. In Assam, 1520 out of 3653 schools had such facilities. In Manipur, only 89 out of 378 middle schools had these facilities. In Mizoram, over 55 per cent of their schools were provided with such facilities (135 out of 245 middle schools). In Nagaland also the situation was not too bad as 33.94 per cent of the schools had these facilities (112 out of 330 in middle schools). In Tripura, only 20 per cent of their schools had these facilities (59 out of 292 schools). There is no national published data available on these facilities before or after 1978.

Furniture for Teachers

Data on furniture for teachers in primary schools is available only for the years 1978 and 1986. It shows that while all schools in Arunachal Pradesh in 1978 provided teachers with chairs, the situation deteriorates in 1986 with only 321 primary schools, out of 952, providing their teachers with such equipment.[8] This is because the furniture had broken and there was to money in plan and non-planned expenditure to replace or repair them.

All the primary schools of Assam had similar resources in 1978 (21603 schools with equal number of chairs for teachers). It is possible that each school was provided with at least a chair for the Head Teacher. However, with the growth of the number of teachers per school; chairs were added for the teaching staff in 1986 (40218 chairs out of a total of 25873 schools). In Manipur, 1978 data also reveals the same pattern. All the 3437 schools had chairs for at least the Head Teacher. In Meghalaya too there were similar amenities for primary school Head Teacher. However, there seems to be a decline in these facilities with the growth of teachers in primary schools in both these states in 1986. Even an educationally advanced state like Mizoram had failed to provide all its primary schools with adequate chairs for their teachers in the year 1986. (Mizoram had provided all of its 516 primary schools with chairs for their teachers in 1978). In Nagaland too, as compared with all its 962 primary schools with adequate number of chairs for their teachers in 1978, in 1986 only 498 schools were left with these facilities. In Tripura, there is a definite improvement in the availability of such facilities between 1978 and 1986. While all of its 1573 primary schools had these facilities, 1752 out of 1927 schools continued with these facilities in 1986. Tripura has thus faired substantially well in providing their teachers with necessary equipment.

Arunachal Pradesh had provided all of its 105 middle schools with adequate chairs for their teachers in 1978. Similarly, Assam (3653); Manipur (378); Meghalaya (374); Mizoram (245); Nagaland and Tripura. There is no data available for the provision of these facilities for middle schools before and after 1978.

Black Boards

Since the implementation of the scheme of Operation Black Board, to improve minimum facilities available in primary schools the situation in primary schools has improved; and classrooms have been provided with education and aids. Data analyzed for the years 1978, and 1986 indicates an increase in the use of blackboards. In Arunachal Pradesh, 412 primary schools/sections out of 735 had blackboards in 1978. There was an increase in number to 2457 in 1986 but the percentage usable was as low as 8.60. In Assam only 4639 primary schools/sections, out of a total of 21603 had blackboards in 1978, but this situation had improved and there were 44849 blackboards for 25873 schools/sections in 1986. Despite the increase in the number of blackboards in 1986, the percentage of those that were used decreased, indicating a lack of their maintenance, along with buildings and furniture (about 12.54 per cent were in use).

In Manipur, 1704 primary schools/sections were provided with blackboards in 1978, out of a total 3437, which was far from satisfactory. However, the situation improved in 1986 with 6432 out of 3757 primary schools/sections being provided with these facilities, out of which only 7.89 per cent were not fit for use.

In Meghalaya, 1148 primary schools had blackboards in 1978; the figures grew to 10665 in 1986, and according to the Fifth All India

Educational Survey as little as 3.52 per cent of these were still fit to be used. Figures of 1978 as compared with 1986 indicate the same trend, i.e., there were only 402 blackboards out of 516 schools in 1978, as compared with their increase to 4257 in 1986, only 3.68 per cent of the equipment could not be made use of, according to the Fifth Survey. In Nagaland, despite the increase in the number of blackboards from 662 in 1978 to 4057 in 1986, the percentage non-functional was as high as 9.35. Thus, making Nagaland second to Assam in the lack of adequate blackboard facilities in primary schools/sections in this region. In Tripura, however, the blackboards seem to have been better maintained, as only 5.88 per cent appeared non-functional in 1986. The increase in the number of blackboards being 551 in 1978 to 4705 in 1986.

As far as middle schools/sections are concerned data is available only for 1978. In Arunachal Pradesh there were only fifty-eight blackboards for 105 middle schools. However, in Assam the situation is better; 63.67 per cent of their schools had this facility (2326 blackboards out of 3653 schools). Even in Manipur, most schools were likely to have them (i.e., 302 schools out of at total 378 schools had blackboards). In Meghalaya, 77 per cent schools/sections had blackboards (i.e., 288 out of 374 schools). In Mizoram, as high as 87.75 per cent of their schools had this facility (i.e., 215 out of 245 schools). In Nagaland, as well, 80.91 per cent of schools were provided with this facility (267 out of 330 schools). In Tripura, only 41.78 per cent of schools had these facilities. Thus, apart from Arunachal Pradesh, Tripura also lacked blackboards at the middle stage of schooling.

One may conclude that in addition to the lack of pucca buildings, there is also a shortage of classrooms, drinking water, toilets, blackboards and teaching aids in most middle schools. Provision of playgrounds is equally unsatisfactory at both the primary and middle school level. What needs to be emphasized is that there is a crying need to share such resources wherever available, through a network of school complexes, as has been attempted in Mizoram from 1987.

Teachers

The growth rate in the number of teachers from 1957 to 1995 indicates that the years 1978 to 1986 witnessed a greater percentage increase of teachers in the primary schools/sections. The percentage increase was as high as 69.46 in Mizoram, followed by Arunachal Pradesh with 70.41 per cent. Though the tendency (between the years 1973-1978 and 1978 to 1986), had been to give primary importance to providing adequate teaching staff this emphasis declined from 1986. In fact, in

Arunachal Pradesh with (-7) and Tripura with (-10.00) showed a decrease in growth rates. Further, even in educationally forward states like Mizoram, there is only 0.08 percentage increase in primary school teachers between 1993 and 1995. Nagaland with an increase in (1.88 per cent), Arunachal Pradesh (4.74 per cent) and Manipur (5.56 per cent), the overall picture is one of low percentage increase. In 1986, as many as 55.25 percent of primary schools in Arunachal Pradesh had only one teacher in position. Even in Meghalaya the situation was similar in as many as 53.33 schools at the primary level.

Table 2.8

Percentage Increase in Number of Primary School Teacher

States	*1957-1965*	*1965-1973*	*1973-1978*	*1978-1986*	*1986-1993*
Arunachal Pradesh	N.A.	N.A.	79.29	70.41	32.82
Assam	78.37	10.15	30.97	27.66	25.06
Meghalaya	N.A.	N.A.	28.64	11.98	26.52
Mizoram	N.A.	N.A.	17.95	69.46	4.95
Manipur	244.08	65.93	17.35	N.A	23.17
Nagaland	N.A.	N.A.	13.95	20.51	10.23
Tripura	97.13	33.58	28.17	58.31	18.60

Source: Calculated from All India Educational Surveys, New Delhi, NCERT.

For most of the North Eastern states the tendency was an increase in the number of teachers during the late seventies through the mid-eighties. Though none of the states had a consistent pattern of growth, nevertheless, states like Arunachal Pradesh, Meghalaya, did not, but Mizoram, Nagaland and Tripura showed consistent pattern in increasing their staff strength. From 1993, however, this trend decreased, and barring Nagaland which showed a 28.81 per cent increase, all the other states evinced a trend in minus figures.

The percentage of female teachers is low in the area for both the lower and upper primary stages; often lower than the all India average. The growth from 1978 to 1993 was slow. Only Arunachal Pradesh and Manipur seem to have taken pains to add to the number of female teachers. On the contrary, in Tripura the percentage of female teachers has declined, from 28.16 per cent in 1978 to 22.39 per cent in 1993. There was, however, a steady growth of female teachers in Assam, Meghalaya, Mizoram and Nagaland (see Table 2.10 for their growing numerical strength between 1978 and 1993) for the primary stage.

Table 2.9

Percentage Increase in Number of Middle School Teachers

States	*1957-1965*	*1965-1973*	*1973-1978*	*1978-1986*	*1986-1993*
Arunachal Pradesh	N.A.	N.A.	90.57	95.63	51.29
Assam	129.29	1.26	69.20	36.28	61.82
Meghalaya	N.A.	N.A.	45.26	58.09	33.04
Mizoram	N.A.	N.A.	44.22	91.63	55.05
Manipur	390.38	4.88	4.22	76.08	96.03
Nagaland	N.A.	N.A.	26.14	17.63	27.43
Tripura	335.98	42.63	28.84	36.63	45.66

Source: Calculated from All India Educational Surveys, New Delhi, NCERT.

Table 2.10

Percentage of Female Teachers in Primary Schools

States	*1978*	*1986*	*1993*
Arunachal Pradesh	12.66	17.34	23.01
Assam	20.71	25.59	28.84
Manipur	12.88	21.43	30.49
Meghalaya	36.16	39.96	46.18
Mizoram	30.60	44.11	46.16
Nagaland	25.49	29.90	34.00
Tripura	28.16	21.86	22.39

Source: 1. Fourth All India Educational Survey (1978), New Delhi, NCERT.
2. Fifth All India Educational Survey (1986), New Delhi, NCERT. (Unpublished Data).
3. Sixth All India Educational Survey, Provisional Statistics (1993), New Delhi, NCERT.

Table 2.11

Percentage of Female Teachers in Upper Primary Schools

States	*1978*	*1986*	*1993*
Arunachal Pradesh	12.36	17.88	20.92
Assam	12.61	19.14	17.88
Manipur	15.90	21.95	33.14
Meghalaya	33.16	37.02	37.78
Mizoram	17.96	21.16	22.27
Nagaland	20.56	21.56	27.43
Tripura	23.27	22.56	22.68

Source: 1. Fourth All India Educational Survey (1978), New Delhi, NCERT.
2. Fifth All India Educational Survey (1986), New Delhi, NCERT (Unpublished Data).
3. Sixth All India Educational Survey, Provisional Statistics (1993), New Delhi, NCERT.

Upper primary school figures show a steady increase in female teachers between 1978 and 1993 in Arunachal Pradesh, Manipur, Mizoram and Nagaland. Both Assam and Tripura's performances are unsatisfactory. Yet measured by the All India figures, this region lacks adequate female teachers, All India being 35.8 per cent of female teachers in 1993.

Data shows low number of female teachers in Arunachal Pradesh in 1993-94 where there were only 670 female teachers in a total of 2713 primary school teachers. In Manipur too, at the upper primary level there were only 2186 female teachers out of 6932 total teachers strength. The lack of female teachers at the upper primary level is more alarming, in the states of Mizoram (3738 total and 806 females) and in Nagaland (4180 out of a total of 904 were females). Even Tripura faces the same shortage of female teachers with only 1016 out of a total of 4780 teachers being women at the same school level. The reason being that female teachers prefer to serve at the primary level since schools are located near homes.[9]

Teacher-Pupil Ratios

The teacher-pupil ratio was favourable in these states. As table II.12 reveals Manipur had the best teacher-pupil ratio in 1986, both for its rural and urban primary schools (16 rural and 18 urban). In Naga schools too, the teacher-pupil ratio was favourable to the student (19 rural and 30 urban). Arunachal had also a favourable teacher pupil ratio for both its rural (16) and urban (27) upper primary schools. In fact all other states barring Assam and Tripura, had a favourable teacher-pupil ratio in 1986, for the upper primary stage, Mizoram being the best (12 rural and 17 urban). Mizoram's teacher-pupil ratio was better than the all India average of 29 (rural) and 35 (urban) see Table II.12 for details.[10] According to the data furnished by the Department of Education, Government of India for the 1992-93, by Ministry of Human Resource Development in its Itanagar Conference on the North Eastern states, held in October 24-25, 1994, the teacher-pupil ratio in lakhs was 3 (Arunachal Pradesh), 39 (Assam); 18 (Manipur); 36 (Meghalaya); 30 (Mizoram); 19 (Nagaland) and 23 (Tripura) as against the all India figures of 45 at the primary level. For the upper primary or middle level, the figures given were 23 (Arunachal Pradesh); 31 (Assam); 11 (Manipur); 19 (Meghalaya); 12 (Mizoram); 21 (Nagaland); and 25 (Tripura) against the all India figure of 43.

Table 2.12
Statewise Pupil-Teacher Ratio at Primary and Upper Primary Stages in North East 1986

States	*Primary Stage*			*Upper Primary Stage*		
	Rural	*Urban*	*Total*	*Rural*	*Urban*	*Total*
Arunachal Pradesh	34	31	34	16	27	17
Assam	37	30	36	29	35	30
Manipur	16	18	17	14	21	16
Meghalaya	35	51	37	20	25	21
Mizoram	29	24	27	12	17	13
Nagaland	19	30	20	13	21	15
Tripura	36	42	36	27	45	29

Source: Fifth All india Educational Survey (1986), New Delhi, NCERT.

Table 2.12.1
Statewise Pupil-Teacher Ratio at Primary and Upper Primary Stages in North East 1993

States	*Primary Stage*			*Upper Primary Stage*		
	Rural	*Urban*	*Total*	*Rural*	*Urban*	*Total*
Arunachal Pradesh	27.65	19.93	26.57	23.80	29.63	24.49
Assam	35.25	30.92	34.80	19.67	20.89	19.77
Manipur	14.25	13.26	14.03	14.36	17.40	15.17
Meghalaya	23.42	25.36	23.60	18.56	20.73	18.85
Mizoram	24.60	21.18	23.03	11.83	16.65	13.63
Nagaland	11.63	11.39	11.61	12.40	17.97	13.63
Tripura	22.79	24.47	22.95	21.43	19.49	21.18

Source: Sixth All India Educational Survey (1993), New Delhi, NCERT.

Staff Strength

As far as staff strength is concerned the majority of the primary schools of the region had one or two teachers in position in 1986. In Meghalaya (15), Arunachal Pradesh (4) and Tripura (1); the primary schools had no pre-teachers in position during the Fifth All India Educational Survey.[11] In Tripura (26.41%), Mizoram (23.18%) and Manipur (20.75%) had three teachers in position. In Nagaland 22.19 percent of these schools had five teachers in position, and as many as 28.67 of schools had more than six. Nagaland's performance as far as both primary teachers in position as well as their growth and qualifications have been the best in the past three decades in this region (see Table 2.13).[12]

Table 2.13
Percentage of Teachers in Position in Primary Schools in 1986

States	*1.*	*2.*	*3.*	*4.*	*5.*	*6 & above*
Arunachal Pradesh	55.25	26.89	8.51	2	1.78	5.15
Assam	34.41	41.14	12.24	6	3.22	2.98
Manipur	18.50	29.74	20.75	11.93	7.18	11.90
Meghalaya	53.33	28.33	9.61	3.87	1.22	2.60
Mizoram	11.84	27.16	23.18	17.61	8.36	11.84
Nagaland	3.71	11.67	14.85	19.10	22.19	28.47
Tripura	7.52	26.57	26.41	15.83	9.18	14.43

Source: Fifth All India Educational Survey (1986), New Delhi, NCERT.

Table 2.13.1
Percentage of Teachers in Position in Primary Schools in 1993

States	*1.*	*2.*	*3.*	*4.*	*5.*	*6 & above*
Arunachal Pradesh	45	35	7	3	2	7
Assam	21	49	16	7	3	4
Manipur	19	21	23	13	7	17
Meghalaya	37	38	14	5	2	3
Mizoram	15	20	18	15	13	19
Nagaland	7	14	13	15	18	32
Tripura	8	25	19	13	9	25

Source: Sixth All India Educational Survey (1993), New Delhi, NCERT.

Teacher Qualification

Though there were more trained primary teachers in 1978 than in 1965 in Assam, Manipur and Tripura, Arunachal Pradesh, Meghalaya, (Mizoram and Nagaland not having attained statehood during the conduct of the Third All India Educational Survey), in 1986 only Manipur (56.05%) and Nagaland (44.47%) showed an increase in the percentage of trained teachers from 1978. In all the other states of this region, the percentage of trained primary teachers declined between 1978 and 1986, perhaps because the emphasis was to provide better infrastructural facilities such as school class-rooms and toilets rather than on improving the qualification of teachers. Data on the middle schools/sections also indicates the same trend. However, Meghalaya like Manipur and Nagaland has added more trained teachers in 1986 in its middle schools (see Tables 2.14 & 2.15 for details).

In 1995, the districts of Assam which lacked trained primary (22%) and middle school teachers (13%) were Sibsagar, North Cachar Hills (10.67%) Assam was also lacking in trained teachers.[13]

Table 2.14
Percentage of Trained Primary School Teachers

States	*1965*	*1978*	*1986*	*1993*
Arunachal Pradesh	-	55.97	42.86	34.80
Assam	61.49	64.93	62.87	65.55
Manipur	26.41	49.24	56.05	44.48
Meghalaya	-	38.56	49.99	51.16
Mizoram	-	60.67	57.58	83.91
Nagaland	-	38.33	44.47	36.02
Tripura	40.87	67.75	40.36	54.04

Source: Second All India Educational Survey (1965), New Delhi, NCERT.
Fourth All India Educational Survey (1978), New Delhi, NCERT.
Fifth All India Educational Survey (1986), New Delhi, NCERT.
Sixth All India Educational Survey (1993), New Delhi, NCERT.

Table 2.15
Percentage of Trained Middle School Teachers

States	*1965*	*1978*	*1986*	*1993*
Arunachal Pradesh	-	56.34	37.32	42.35
Assam	27.75	30.48	29.37	23.82
Manipur	16.79	20.74	36.26	34 63
Meghalaya	-	18.20	30.41	22.65
Mizoram	-	36.22	48.87	74.46
Nagaland	-	30.28	36.22	26.79
Tripura	43.91	67.12	42.33	51.33

Source: Second All India Educational Survey (1965), New Delhi, NCERT.
Fourth All India Educational Survey (1978), New Delhi, NCERT.
Fifth All India Educational Survey (1986), New Delhi, NCERT.
Sixth All India Educational Survey (1993), New Delhi, NCERT.

Data as furnished by the Department of Education, Ministry of Human Resource Development, Government of India for the years 1992-93 indicate that Mizoram (84%) and other states of this region had inadequate number of trained teachers for the primary schools (Arunachal Pradesh 40%; Assam 66%; Manipur 54%; Meghalaya 42%; Nagaland 48% and Tripura 33%). At the upper primary or middle school level too, Mizoram had as much as 80 per cent of trained teachers. Percentage of trained teachers of the other states being Arunachal Pradesh (40%);

Assam (28%); Manipur (29%), Meghalaya (35%); Nagaland (29%); and Tripura (34%).

There were a substantial number of teachers who had passed the matriculation examination in rural primary schools of this region both in 1978 and in 1986; though there is no nationally compiled data available which gives details on their educational qualifications prior to 1965. There were a number of teachers not trained to teach below the middle class level, between the years 1965 and 1986; especially in remote areas within each state, even in an educationally advanced state like Mizoram;[14] such teachers were employed way back in the sixties.

In Assam out of 34117 primary teachers in 1965 as many as 27405 were qualified below the middle class pass level. Only 5858 were matriculates and 175 had an intermediate pass. There were no graduate or post-graduate degree holders, teaching at primary level in urban primary schools. In Tripura, however, only 349 out of 3704 primary school teachers had middle level pass certificates. There were 2837 matriculates and 413 intermediate degree holders. Like Assam none of the primary schools had graduates or postgraduate teachers.

As Table 2.16 indicates that most of the primary school teachers both in 1978 and in 1986 were matriculates except for in Arunachal Pradesh which had a large percentage of "outsiders" employed in the school teaching profession. Thus, if compared with the other states of this region there were more graduate primary teachers in that state both in 1978 (36.74%) and 1986 (42.36%). Arunachal Pradesh's educational backwardness was not due to under-qualified teachers, but the multiplicity of tribal languages, hostile climatic condition in the far-flung areas, and the reluctance on the part of teachers to serve in remote and inaccessible parts of the region. On the other hand Mizoram with as little as 0.39 per cent graduate teachers even in 1986, has performed a miracle at the elementary level. For that several socio-economic and political factors are responsible, but the most important one was the direct advantage derived from education in Mizoram, which created a condition for making education attractive. The rapid expansion of the service sector in the state coupled with 'anti *vai*' (anti outsiders) agitation, made education a promising phenomenon to the newly growing middle class. Education gave this bourgeois class a direct access to state government jobs.

Table 2.16

Qualifications of Primary School Teachers in Percentage

	Matriculate		Intermediate		Graduate		Post-Graduate	
	1978 %	1986 %	1978 %	1986 %	1978 %	1986 %	1978 %	1986 %
Arunachal Pradesh	35.50	25.14	10.17	19.71	36.74	42.36	4.66	5.58
Assam	46.67	54.74	4.07	0.11	1.38	2.11	0.01	N.A
Manipur	29.11	33.80	7.58	14.39	5.97	10.14	0.20	0.04
Meghalaya	14.15	21.57	2.69	3.90	1.37	1.29	0.08	0.16
Mizoram	12.49	34.77	2.11	14.29	0.67	0.39	0.10	N.A.
Nagaland	11.98	32.74	1.39	7.88	0.79	2.81	0.02	0.07
Tripura	36.52	35.83	45.44	55.19	12.71	8.33	0.01	0.12

Source: Fourth (1978) & Fifth (1986) All India Educational Survey, New Delhi, NCERT.

Table 2.16.1

Qualifications of Primary School Teachers in Percentage (1993)

States	*Up to Secondary*	*Higher Secondary*	*Graduate and above*	*Any other*
Arunachal Pradesh	17.19	32.61	50.20	0
Assam	74.54	15.86	9.56	0.04
Manipur	53.36	23.19	23.45	0
Meghalaya	81 42	14.19	4.35	0.04
Mizoram	87.60	8.88	3.52	0
Nagaland	73.58	16.19	10.08	0.15
Tripura	57.95	33.74	8.82	0.09

Source: Sixth All India Educational Survey (1993), New Delhi, NCERT.

The qualifications of the middle school teachers had not increase in this region as would have been normally expected. As explained earlier, the case of Arunachal Pradesh is quite unique in this region (53.42 graduates in 1978 and 63.07 in 1986). Both Manipur and Tripura, which had a history of having tertiary level education earlier than the other states, also had a favourable percentage of graduate teachers both in 1978 and 1986. (See Table 2.17). On the other hand, Assam, (33.18%) Meghalaya (53.85%), Mizoram (36.82%) and Nagaland (27.96%) had matriculates teaching at the middle school level. Either the middle school teachers were promoted or they under qualified in remote areas. It may be mentioned here that lack of housing facilities in rural areas makes the educated persons seek jobs other than the teaching profession.

Table 2.17

Qualifications of Middle School Teachers in Percentage

	Matriculate		*Intermediate*		*Graduate*		*Post-Graduate*	
	1978 %	*1986* %	*1978* %	*1986* %	*1978* %	*1986* %	*1978* %	*1986* %
Arunachal Pradesh	4.18	0.87	1.90	3.21	53.42	63.07	37.07	21.48
Assam	42.99	33.18	23.24	42.22	20.60	19.20	0.19	0.07
Manipur	9.26	17.63	20.83	22.42	64.52	54.61	1.58	1.02
Meghalaya	22.21	53.85	45.86	20.52	14.09	11.12	0.20	0.55
Mizoram	42.86	36.82	19.84	38.44	14.86	16.23	0.36	0.71
Nagaland	28.15	27.96	11.44	16.08	19.44	23.63	1.04	1.74
Tripura	4.01	8.30	0.10	12.23	71.50	74.91	4.23	1.64

Source: Fourth (1978) & Fifth (1986) All India Educational Survey, New Delhi, NCERT.

Table 2.17.1

Qualifications of Primary Middle School Teachers in Percentage (1993)

States	*Up to Secondary*	*Higher Secondary*	*Graduate and above*	*Any other*
Arunachal Pradesh	3.49	8.65	87.75	0.11
Assam	22.73	37.97	38.87	0.43
Manipur	12.07	20.16	67.65	0.12
Meghalaya	47.08	34.84	17.86	0.22
Mizoram	33.43	36.16	30.28	0.13
Nagaland	40.66	20.18	38.78	0.38
Tripura	14.22	12.19	73.15	0.24

Source: Sixth All India Educational Survey (1993), New Delhi, NCERT.

Non-formal Education

Non-formal Schooling Education was introduced as an alternative to the formal by the Central Government in 1976. Data on most North Eastern States (barring Tripura) is available for 1978.[15] This compared with 1986 data indicates their rise at the primary level in Assam (709 to 6859) and Meghalaya (188 to 380). But at the upper primary stage there is no growth from 1978 to 1986. In fact, both for the primary and upper primary stage states had reduced the number of non-formal education centres in 1986, with Nagaland and Tripura abandoning the scheme, totally. In Mizoram, there was only one additional centre at the primary level in 1986 and none for the upper primary level. (There existed 7 centres for the age group of 14-35 years in 1978).

Table 2.18

State-wise Village with Non-Formal Education Centres and Enrolment, 1978

States	*No. of Villages with Non-formal education centres for the age group*			*Enrolment in non-formal education centres for the age groups*		
	6 to14 yrs	14 to 35 yrs	Above 35 yrs	6 to14 yrs	14 to 35 yrs	above 35 yrs
Arunachal Pradesh	79	228	71	849	5964	549
Assam	709	141	4	21148	3407	89
Manipur	50	100	-	1809	3393	-
Meghalaya	188	233	170	4822	5078	2535
Mizoram	3	7	4	52	269	64
Nagaland	80	239	157	138	7139	3175
Tripura	-	398	33	-	7820	54

Source: Fourth All India Educational Surveys (1978), New Delhi, NCERT.

Table 2.18.1

Number of Villages with Centre at

	Only Primary		*Only Upper Primary*		*Both Upper Primary and Primary*	
States	*1986*	*1993*	*1986*	*1993*	*1986*	*1993*
Arunachal Pradesh	31	39	0	4	0	1
Assam	6170	6251	0	119	0	277
Manipur	154	491	0	40	0	93
Meghalaya	345	533	181	0	34	0
Mizoram	4	72	0	11	0	8
Nagaland	0	0	0	0	0	0
Tripura	0	0	0	0	0	0

Source: Fifth and Sixth All India Educational Surveys, New Delhi, NCERT.

Table 2.19
Non-Formal Education Centres and Enrolment 1986

States	*Rural*					*Urban*				
	No. of Centres		*Enrolment*			*No. of Centres*		*Enrolment*		
	Pri.	*U. Pri.*	*Boys*	*Girls*	*Total*	*Pri.*	*U.Pri.*	*Boys*	*Girls*	*Total*
1	*2*	*3*	*4*	*5*	*6*	*7*	*8*	*9*	*10*	*11*
Aruna-chal Pradesh	31	-	407	274	681	1	-	8	6	14
Assam	6859	-	108160	86795	194955	39	-	746	577	1323
Manipur	160	-	1865	1712	3577	9	-	106	112	218
Meghalaya	380	215	8920	7293	16213	2	1	32	30	62
Mizoram	4	-	79	57	136	-	-	-	-	-
Nagaland	-	-	-	-	-	-	-	-	-	-
Tripura	-	-	-	-	-	-	-	-	-	-

Source: Fifth All India Educational Surveys (1986), New Delhi, NCERT.

Table 2.19.1
Non-Formal Education Centres and Enrolment, 1993

States	*Rural*					*Urban*				
	No. of Centres		*Enrolment*			*No. of Centres*		*Enrolment*		
	Pri.	*U. Pri.*	*Boys*	*Girls*	*Total*	*Pri.*	*U.Pri.*	*Boys*	*Girls*	*Total*
Arunachal Pradesh	41	4	572	459	1031	0	0	0	0	0
Assam	7849	138	150571	133085	283656	86	0	1541	1257	2798
Manipur	635	47	10163	10195	20358	38	10	488	716	1204
Meghalaya	555	0	5868	5421	11289	11	0	119	147	266
Mizoram	80	12	745	655	1400	8	0	98	93	191
Nagaland	0	0	0	0	0	0	0	0	0	0
Tripura	0	0	0	0	0	0	0	0	0	0

Source: Sixth All India Educational Surveys (1993), New Delhi, NCERT.

'Out of school' children are as much a phenomenon in the villages as in the urban areas. The 1986 data also indicates that both rural and urban centres enrolled more boys than girls. Hence the theory that the girl child, preoccupied with domestic and agricultural work during school hours, would be more interested in the non-formal centre does not hold true. What was required was to initiate a campaign for enrolling girls into these centres. Further, the 1978 data reveals that in Tripura (7820), Nagaland (7139), Arunachal Pradesh (5964) and Meghalaya (5078), the majority of non-formal centres enrolled the age group of 14-35 years, thereby attracting the adult learner.

In 1986, barring Arunachal Pradesh (34.43%) and Assam (45.00%) all other states of the region had a higher percentage of students in the age group of 11-14 years, enrolled in the non-formal centres, as compared with the all India percentage. The fact that in 1978 and in 1986 non-formal centres tended to attract higher age groups of students indicates that these were not regarded as substitutes to primary education. At best they were being used for middle school dropouts, but more so, for high school dropouts and adult learners.

2.9 Finance of Elementary Education 1975-76-1993-94

As far as allocation of resources is concerned the plan revenue expenditure in Mizoram, which was only 117.33 lakhs in 1975-76 was as much as 529.75 and non-plan from 120.31 to 2581.78, for the same years – less than that of Nagaland or other states of the North East (see Tables 2.19 to 2.25). However, as far as utilization of the funds are concerned Mizoram had utilized all the funds allotted to it under the Central Assistant Schemes for Operation Black Board (8.87). Non-Formal Education (2.06), Integrated Education for Disabled Children (24.79), Teacher Programme including training (31.85), Vocational Education (16.68), Science education (84.42) in the year 1990-91, as against Nagaland for Operation Black Board; (9.36) for Integrated Education for Disabled Children (28.00) Teacher education and only 14.84 for Vocational education. The fact that despite the inability of Naga poor children to attend formal schools, Nagaland did not use any opportunity to avail non-formal education. Two, though the total plan and non-plan expenditure may have been small for Mizoram, as compared to other states in the region, Mizoram has taken every opportunity to improve the standard of its elementary schools from Central Assistance schemes which was gathered in my field visit to rural areas in Aizawl's Aibawk circle in 1995; we found not only did all these schemes existed but that the elementary teachers were nearly all trained. Their staff strength being 6-8 in each school. Classroom had all the necessary equipments. Science equipments were used and 'work education' was introduced in the making of small teaching aids, furniture repair, school garden etc., as a kind of vocational training.

Table 2.20

Arunachal Pradesh : Data on Finance on Elementary Education 1975-76 – 1993-94

(Rs. in Lakhs)

1 *Expenditure (Revenue Account)*	*1975-76*	*1980-81*	*1985-86*	*1990-91*	*1991-92*	*1992-93*	*1993-94*
a. Plan	25.78	55.08	123.31	472.62	1299.98	1365.69	1670 78
b. Non-Plan	68.31	261.39	593.31	1823.09	1646.57	1852.99	2059.15
c. Total	94.09	316.47	716.62	2295.71	2946.57	3218.68	3729.93
2 Percentage Expenditure to Total (Revenue Account)	54.70	55.23	42.89	62.26	66.11	63.52	64.33
3 Central Assistance for							
a. Operation Blackboard				82.16	0.00	106.57	33.21
b. Non-formal Education Scheme				-		-	-
c. Integrated Education for Disabled Children				-		-	-
d. Teacher Programme*				-	-	0.00	0.00
e. Vocationalisation Scheme				-	6 36	-	-
f. Science Education Scheme				-	-	-	-
g. Education Technology Scheme				-	-	4.8	-
h. Enrolment Education Scheme				-	-	1.00	-

Source: 1. DPEP Studies

2. Budgetary Resources for Education 1951-52 to 1993-94, Department of Education, Ministry of Human Resources, New Delhi, 1995
3. Annual Reports, various years, Ministry of Human Resources, Department of Education.

Table 2.21

Assam : Data on Finance on Elementary Education
1975-76 – 1993-94

(Rs. in Lakhs)

1 Expenditure (Revenue Account)	*1975-76*	*1980-81*	*1985-86*	*1990-91*	*1991-92*	*1992-93*	*1993-94*
a. Plan	229.67	307.33	1296.01	3724.55	5489	8009.00	11022.00
b. Non-Plan	1740.95	3490.69	11094.40	21216.35	2543.60	27429.45	29164.14
c. Total	1970.62	3798.02	12390.41	24940.93	30923.08	35438.45	40186.14
2 Percentage Expenditure to Total (Revenue Account)	44.80	45.97	58.21	56.63	58.15	52.11	58.86
3 Central Assistance for							
a. Operation Blackboard				0.0	420.48	1628.46	512.04
b. Non-formal Education Scheme				159.40	192.09	350.16	488.46
c. Integrated Education for Disabled Children				-	-	-	-
d. Teacher Programme*				35.00	98.95	319.41	316.55
e. Vocationalisation Scheme				42.62	140.28	100.24	291.54
f. Science Education Scheme				141.66	146.27	-	-
g. Education Technology Scheme				73.53	-	127.24	-
h. Enrolment Education Scheme				-	12.85	10.89	-

Source: 1. DPEP Studies
2. Budgetary Resources for Education 1951-52 to 1993-94, Department of Education, Ministry of Human Resources, New Delhi, 1995
3. Annual Reports, various years, Ministry of Human Resources, Department of Education.

Table 2.22

Manipur : Data on Finance on Elementary Education 1975-76 – 1993-94

(Rs. in Lakhs)

1 *Expenditure (Revenue Account)*	*1975-76*	*1980-81*	*1985-86*	*1990-91*	*1991-92*	*1992-93*	*1993-94*
a. Plan	8.97	30.76	92.05	428.73	423.13	599.55	424.84
b. Non-Plan	1389.74	819.13	1454.31	2483.75	3053.75	3507.72	3643.46
c. Total	398.71	849.89	1546.36	2912.48	3476.88	4107.27	4068.30
2 Percentage Expenditure to Total (Revenue Account)	58.04	47.01	43.34	43.12	40.79	42.95	43.51
3 Central Assistance for							
a. Operation Blackboard				47.88	57.30	0.00	32.30
b. Non-formal Education Scheme				24.59	62.40	43.78	92.28
c. Integrated Education for Disabled Children				3.97	3.98	5.00	22.40
d. Teacher Programme*				1.00	110.30	12.11	7.64
e. Vocationalisation Scheme				-	44.00	7.18	7.40
f. Science Education Scheme				87.05	-	-	-
g. Education Technology Scheme				10.08	16.19	-	-
h. Enrolment Education Scheme				-	-	-	-

Source: 1. DPEP Studies

2. Budgetary Resources for Education 1951-52 to 1993-94, Department of Education, Ministry of Human Resources, New Delhi, 1995

3. Annual Reports, various years, Ministry of Human Resources, Department of Education.

Table 2.23

Meghalaya : Data on Finance on Elementary Education 1975-76 – 1993-94

(Rs. in Lakhs)

1 *Expenditure (Revenue Account)*	*1975-76*	*1980-81*	*1985-86*	*1990-91*	*1991-92*	*1992-93*	*1993-94*
a. Plan	11.07	32.66	41.02	649.39	1185.28	1392.60	1890.00
b. Non-Plan	107.93	288.47	725.58	2452.43	2809.22	3219.02	3643.81
c. Total	119.00	321.13	766.68	3101.82	3994.50	4611.62	5533.81
2 Percentage Expenditure to Total (Revenue Account)	33.43	35.48	37.03	55.47	59.19	59.76	60.76
3 Central Assistance for							
a. Operation Blackboard				100.49	90.04	0.00	399.53
b. Non-formal Education Scheme				-	-	-	-
c. Integrated Education for Disabled Children				-	-	-	-
d. Teacher Programme*					77.60	0.00	208.10
e. Vocationalisation Scheme				20.75	-	-	-
f. Science Education Scheme				35.20	-	0.80	-
g. Education Technology Scheme				5.00	5.08	14.50	-
h. Enrolment Education Scheme				-	-	-	-

Source: 1. DPEP Studies

2. Budgetary Resources for Education 1951-52 to 1993-94, Department of Education, Ministry of Human Resources, New Delhi, 1995

3. Annual Reports, various years, Ministry of Human Resources, Department of Education.

Table 2.24
Mizoram : Data on Finance on Elementary Education
1975-76 – 1993-94

(Rs. in Lakhs)

1 *Expenditure (Revenue Account)*	*1975-76*	*1980-81*	*1985-86*	*1990-91*	*1991-92*	*1992-93*	*1993-94*
a. Plan	17.33	75.61	123.43	346.60	495.61	491.85	529.75
b. Non-Plan	120.31	373.30	933.74	1961.57	2290.35	2634.33	2581.78
c. Total	137.64	448.91	1057.17	2308.17	2785.96	3126.18	3111.53
2 Percentage Expenditure to Total (Revenue Account)	37.30	59.22	54.05	54.30	57.02	56.13	56 39
3 Central Assistance for							
a. Operation Blackboard				8.87	68.80	13.42	3.98
b. Non-formal Education Scheme				2.06	3.16	2.96	8.58
c. Integrated Education for Disabled Children				24.79	31.72	45.36	1.92
d. Teacher Programme*				31.85	23.50	17.72	0.00
e. Vocationalisation Scheme				16.68	-	24.88	21.92
f. Science Education Scheme				84.42	31.76	-	-
g. Education Technology Scheme				-	0.11	-	-
h. Enrolment Education Scheme				-	2.80	2.50	-

Source: 1. DPEP Studies
2. Budgetary Resources for Education 1951-52 to 1993-94, Department of Education, Ministry of Human Resources, New Delhi, 1995
3. Annual Reports, various years, Ministry of Human Resources, Department of Education.

Table 2.25

Nagaland : Data on Finance on Elementary Education 1975-76 – 1993-94

(Rs. in Lakhs)

1 *Expenditure (Revenue Account)*	*1975-76*	*1980-81*	*1985-86*	*1990-91*	*1991-92*	*1992-93*	*1993-94*
a. Plan	22.48	99.19	62.30	329.80	280.10	262.00	304.56
b. Non-Plan	365.69	649.79	1645.18	2414.17	2690.84	3190.06	3474.37
c. Total	388.77	748.98	1707.48	2743.97	2970.94	3452.06	3778.93
2 Percentage Expenditure to Total (Revenue Account)	63.12	63.26	60.53	58.35	60.06	61.33	62.99
3 Central Assistance for							
a. Operation Blackboard				5.85	0.00	7.84	-
b. Non-formal Education Scheme				-	-	-	-
c. Integrated Education for Disabled Children				9.36	10.79	12.61	5.74
d. Teacher Programme*				28.00	-	10.30	27.94
e. Vocationalisation Scheme				14.84	-	-	-
f. Science Education Scheme				-	-	-	-
g. Education Technology Scheme				-	-	-	-
h. Enrolment Education Scheme				-	-	-	-

Source: 1. DPEP Studies

2. Budgetary Resources for Education 1951-52 to 1993-94, Department of Education, Ministry of Human Resources, New Delhi, 1995
3. Annual Reports, various years, Ministry of Human Resources, Department of Education.

Table 2.26
Tripura : Data on Finance on Elementary Education
1975-76 – 1993-94

(Rs. in Lakhs)

	Expenditure (Revenue Account)	*1975-76*	*1980-81*	*1985-86*	*1990-91*	*1991-92*	*1992-93*	*1993-94*
1	a. Plan	23.48	59.73	268.52	860.34	826.14	814.36	888.08
	b. Non-Plan	326.66	504.13	1191.06	3199.51	4175.22	4626.64	4613.12
	c. Total	350.14	563.86	1459.58	4059.85	5001.36	5441.00	5501.20
2	Percentage Expenditure to Total (Revenue Account)	39.25	37.97	36.34	39.27	43.29	41.35	41.15
3	Central Assistance for							
	a. Operation Blackboard				7.70	64.41	4.23	56 13
	b. Non-formal Education Scheme				-	-	-	-
	c. Integrated Education for Disabled Children				-	-	-	-
	d. Teacher Programme*				-	-	20.00	0.00
	e. Vocationalisation Scheme				-	-	-	4.12
	f. Science Education Scheme				0.74	-	-	-
	g. Education Technology Scheme				0.06	-	0.41	-
	h. Enrolment Education Scheme				9.12	-	2.00	1.88

Source: 1. DPEP Studies
2. Budgetary Resources for Education 1951-52 to 1993-94, Department of Education, Ministry of Human Resources, New Delhi, 1995
3. Annual Reports, various years, Ministry of Human Resources, Department of Education.

Table 2.27 State-wise Data on Finance on Elementary Education 1994-95 – 2001-02 BE

(Rs. in Crores)

	1994-95	*1995-96*	*1996-97*	*1997-98*	*1998-99*	*1999-00*	*2000-01RE*	*2001-02BE*
Arunachal Pradesh: Data on Finance on Elementary Education								
Budget Expenditure on Education (Revenue Account)								
Plan	35.33	34.09	48.45	60.08	67.23	67.23	77.44	75.93
Non-Plan	37.29	44.38	47.76	48.85	54.75	54.75	59.04	64.73
Total	72.62	78.47	96.21	108.93	121.98	121.98	136.48	140.66
Percentage to total Budget Expenditure (Revenue Account)	14.6	13.96	14.39	15.14	15.13	13.76	12.44	
Assam: Data on Finance on Elementary Education								
Budget Expenditure on Education (Revenue Account)								
Plan	336.89	358.41	364.43	471.34	451.38	546.77	563.50	587.91
Non-Plan	595.16	669.56	722.67	876.23	958.48	1257.52	1938.13	2107.16
Total	932.05	1027.97	1087.10	1347.57	1409.86	1804.29	2501.63	2695.07
Percentage to total Budget Expenditure (Revenue Account)	25.95	25.90	28.26	28.23	30.42	27.86	29.55	29.28
Manipur: Data on Finance on Elementary Education								
Budget Expenditure on Education (Revenue Account)								
Plan	29.79	32.41	57.57	56.79	42.69	58.30	62.30	49.12
Non-Plan	111.90	133.17	77.71	169.48	155.81	296.58	278.64	251.87
Total	141.69	165.58	135.28	226.27	198.50	354.88	340.94	300.99
Percentage to total Budget Expenditure (Revenue Account)	24.51	23.30	16.44	23.66	22.88	22.73	24.16	22.41

Contd.

	1994-95	1995-96	1996-97	1997-98	1998-99	1999-00	2000-01RE	2001-02BE
Meghalaya: Data on Finance on Elementary Education								
Budget Expenditure on Education (Revenue Account)								
Plan	24.65	44.05	28.31	48.38	50.49	47.49	54.81	64.99
Non-Plan	70.27	75.38	151.27	95.41	124.01	158.83	161.98	177.78
Total	94.62	119.43	179.58	143.79	174.50	206.32	216.79	242.77
Percentage to total Budget Expenditure (Revenue Account)	18.77	18.86	26.97	19.34	19.72	20.53	16.48	16.21
Mizoram: Data on Finance on Elementary Education								
Budget Expenditure on Education (Revenue Account)								
Plan	18.61	23.74	34.65	30.49	31.98	46.30	56.07	67.33
Non-Plan	65.48	67.37	92.77	87.64	90.17	112.95	126.11	129.03
Total	84.09	91.11	127.42	118.13	122.15	159.25	182.18	196.36
Percentage to total Budget Expenditure (Revenue Account)	14.14	13.74	16.34	15.46	15.91	15.78	15.19	18.59
Nagaland: Data on Finance on Elementary Education								
Budget Expenditure on Education (Revenue Account)								
Plan	26.53	19.39	26.09	23.26	23.10	24.16	32.08	51.22
Non-Plan	86.24	97.14	101.68	113.04	119.09	138.60	179.76	187.64
Total	112.77	116.53	127.77	136.30	142.19	162.76	211.84	238.86
Percentage to total Budget Expenditure (Revenue Account)	12.24	11.63	12.05	11.36	12.19	12.58	13.04	13.83
Tripura: Data on Finance on Elementary Education								
Budget Expenditure on Education (Revenue Account)								
Plan	50.41	58.38	82.40	76.49	79.27	79.27	109.83	131.38
Non-Plan	118.04	131.24	163.43	182.88	196.25	196.25	289.88	325.29
Total	168.45	189.62	245.83	259.37	275.52	275.52	399.71	456.97
Percentage to total Budget Expenditure (Revenue Account)	21.20	21.64	24.01	21.06	20.80	20.80	23.51	21.53

Source: Analysis of Budget Expenditure on Education, MHRD, Various years, New Delhi, Government of India.

References

1. Meena Sharma Barkataki, *British Administration in North Eastern India 1826-1874, A study of their social policy*, op.cit.
2. S.L. Baruah, *A Comprehensive History of Assam* (New Delhi: Munshiram Manoharlal Publishers, 1985), p. 264.
3. Government of India Ministry of Human Resource Development. Department of Education, *Programme of Action*, New Delhi, 1986.
4. Government of India, Ministry of Human Resource Development, Department of Education, *Programme of Action*, 1992 (Draft), New Delhi, 1992.
5. Tourist Mark. "Status of Elementary Education in Meghalaya", Shillong, September 1997. Mimeo.
6. Jayashree Roy Jalali, N. Somorendro Singh, *Decentralizing Primary Education - The Role of Lai Autonomous District-Council of Mizoram*, NIEPA, September 1996.
7. NCERT, *Fourth (1978) and Fifth All India Educational Surveys* (1986), New Delhi.
8. *Ibid.*
9. Interview with Ms. Lynden, Inspector of Schools, Shillong, 1996.
10. Interviews with Mr. Laltwanga and Mr. Hrangthanga, 1995, Ex-members of Mizo Board of Secondary Education, Aizawl.
11. Note that according to Operation Black Board there was to be at least 2/3rd teachers in position at the primary stage.
12. Nagaland always employed many teachers from other states due to its language problem of having English as the medium of instruction.
13. Directorate of Elementary Education, Government of Assam, *Sixth All India Educational Survey*, 1996.
14. The necessity of employing 2/3 teachers at least in primary schools in rural areas meant that many of the older teachers were not qualified.
15. Tripura had 17 Gram Vidhyapiths and 129 centres classified on as other in 1973.

3

Female Literacy and Elementary Education for Girls

Literacy and the Tribal Dimension

Several research studies have indicated the close relationship between low female literacy and its adverse effect on girls' education for the elementary sector.[1] However, the dropout rate for girls is not necessarily based on any gender bias in this region. The matriarchical tribes such as the Khasis, Garos and Jaintias attached great importance to female education. But even in the so-called patrilineal tribes such as the Lushais of Mizoram, female education was given utmost importance, as it was believed that an educated mother or daughter would be of an economic and social asset to the family. Both in Manipur and in Mizoram, females always participated in the workforce, at all levels, and the expansion of the service sector in Mizoram at present has enhanced the demand for female education. Only among some patriarchal and patrilineal tribes there was gender bias against girls education.

In 1991, in all the North Eastern states the percentage of female population to the total population was above 46 per cent, though literacy varied from 29.69 per cent (Arunachal Pradesh) to 78.60 per cent (Mizoram). The literacy performance of Nagaland (54.75%) was also better than the all-India average. Barring Assam and Tripura, most of the women work as cultivators in this region. This is despite the high literacy percentages in Mizoram and Nagaland. The reasons being that there is practically no industry in these states and hence cultivation

Table 3.1. Economic Classification of Population 1991

Name of the States	*Literacy*	*Population*	*Main workers*	*Cultivator*	*Agricultural Labourers*	*Household Ind. Manuf. Proc. Serv. repairs*	*Other than household Ind.*	*Marginal Workers*
Arunachal	T-41.59%	864558	390976	235987	20054	742	9725	8806
	F- 29.69%	46.21%	36.34%	50.45%	36.27%	28.44%	9.50%	87.31%
Assam	T- 52.89%	22414322	6992056	3559117	844964	61455	217661	1096879
	F- 43.03%	47.99%	19.33%	19.34%	19.22%	47.71%	6.35%	88.67%
Manipur	T- 59.89%	1837149	708283	437499	47350	41089	16344	66621
	F- 47.60%	48.92%	41.43%	44.39%	59.55%	85.34%	31.05%	85.05%
Meghalaya	T- 49.10%	1774778	715587	395804	89492	2885	12509	41735
	F- 44.85%	48.86%	37.16%	42.35%	41.69%	43.36%	10.04%	88.39%
Mizoram	T- 82.27%	689756	290317	178101	9527	2958	4605	47028
	F- 78.60%	47.95%	38.68%	46.73%	35.12%	32.49%	16.55%	67.32%
Nagaland	T- 61.65%	1209546	511497	371597	7233	1991	6767	4740
	F- 54.75%	46.98%	41.46%	51.84%	29.36%	54.99%	9.37%	77.26%
Tripura	T- 60.44%	2757205	802063	305523	187538	11384	28243	56454
	F- 49.65%	48.57%	16.93%	16.68%	22.10%	30.31%	9.16%	86.01%

Source : Census of India 1991, New Delhi T = Total F = Female

Table 3.1.1. Total Workers (main+marginal) and their categories-India, North Eastern States: 2001

Name of the States	*Sex*	*Literacy Rate*	*Population*	*Total workers*	*Cultivators*	*Agricultural Labourers*	*Household Industry workers*	*Other workers*
Arunachal	Total	54.74	1091117	482206	281822	18569	4130	177685
Pradesh	Female	44.24	47.4	39.1	51.3	45.6	48	18.9
Assam	Total	67.11	1988636	849982	544433	33852	18072	253625
	Female	61.92	47.6	42.6	50.1	46.4	63.9	24.5
Manipur	Total	68.87	2388634	1069578	492996	120991	97955	357936
	Female	59.7	49.5	44.4	43.7	56	80	31.8
Meghalaya	Total	88.49	891058	469597	253161	27494	6572	182370
	Female	86.13	48.4	43.7	49.1	52.7	51.9	34.7
Mizoram	Total	73.66	3191168	1158190	311378	278334	33535	534943
	Female	65.41	48.7	28.2	29	41.1	59.5	19.1
Nagaland	Total	63.31	2306069	956425	457195	172975	17956	308299
	Female	60.41	49.4	41.7	45.2	47.6	55.5	32.3
Tripura	Total	62.78	26638407	9557064	3741912	1289902	328541	4196709
	Female	56.03	48.2	28	28.9	34.1	64.2	22.4

Source: Census of India 2001, New Delhi.

and agriculture are the main occupations of the women. Women also partake in high percentages as marginal workers, doing part-time jobs. In Manipur, women are largely employed in household and other industries (see Table 3.1).

Economic classification of the population as available in 1991 census indicates that where the female literacy is high such as in Mizoram (78.60%) the completion rates for girls for the first five years of schooling is also as high as 64.22 per cent (See Tables 3.1 and 3.2 for details).

As Table 3.2 indicates, the higher the female literacy the greater the tendency of the females to participate in types of workforce other than cultivation; provided that there is an opportunity. We see that female literacy has had a positive effect on both enrolment and retention of girls.

Female literacy has grown at a faster rate in the last decade (1981-91) in Arunachal Pradesh (169.41%) than in any other state in this region, followed by Assam (130.97%) between the years 1971-91.[2] The reasons being the numerous literacy campaigns that have been conducted in the area by both government and voluntary organizations. As both these states had been declared as educationally backward, special centrally sponsored schemes had been in operation in them. The female growth rate in literacy in Tripura has however declined from 1961-71 to 1981-91[3] (that is from 107.94 per cent to 56.96 per cent). Table 3.3 gives details on the growth rate from 1961 to 1991 for each state.

Table 3.2
Elementary Education

Sl. No.	*State*	*Completion Rates of Five Years of Schooling (in %)*	
		1991-92	
		Boys	*Girls*
1.	Arunachal Pradesh	48.90	33.55
2.	Assam	-	-
3.	Manipur	62.42	55.11
4.	Meghalaya	29.23	19.27
5	Mizoram	67.13	64.22
6.	Nagaland	-	-
7.	Tripura	44.41	44.88

Source: A.K. Sinha, Indicators of School Education Unpublished Draft Report. New Delhi, NIEPA, 1994

Table 3.3
Growth Rate on Literacy in Percentage

S.No.	States		(1961-1971)	(1971-1981)	(1981-1991)	(1991-2001)
1	Arunachal Pradesh	Total	58.34	77.94	107.01	31 62
		Female	161.27	197.03	169.41	49.01
2	Assam	Total	3.56	no census in 1981	87.88 (1971-1991)	21.54
		Female	8.88		130.97	30.21
3	Manipur	Total	8.18	27.59	42.63	14.49
		Female	22.59	57.14	55.09	25.42
4	Meghalaya	Total	59.66	12.65	47.80	28.94
		Female	59.89	19.22	53.17	34.69
5	Mizoram	Total	N.A	10 61	38 27	7.56
		Female		12.54	49.51	9.58
6	Nagaland	Total	52.99	53.25	46.82	8 86
		Female	64.46	80.80	62.36	13 10
7	Tripura	Total	53.06	34.21	45.36	21.87
		Female	107.94	49.13	56.96	31.74
	All India	Total	22.55	22.82	44.07	-
		Female	44.32	33.12	58.44	-

Source: Census of India 1961, 1971, 1981, 1991, 2001.

Inter-district disparity - a reflection of tribal groupings

Inter-district disparities reveal pockets of backwardness, which are common to states like Arunachal Pradesh and Nagaland. This is because the same tribal population lives in both these states. For example, both Tirap district of Arunachal Pradesh and Tuensang district of Nagaland have remained backward, as both of these are inhabited by the same tribal groups, such as the Mishmi, Monpa, Nocte, Singhpo, Tangsa, Wancho and Yobin of Arunachal Pradesh, cutting across state boundaries. Both in 1981 and in 1991, the female literacy percentage of Mon district of Nagaland remained low, that is, 12.35 (1981) and 29.10 (1991). Mon being inhabited by the Konyak tribe. These districts had difficulty in producing literacy primers.

In Arunachal Pradesh, apart from Tirap valley, East Kameng had the lowest in female literacy during this decade (2.88 in 1981 and 14.02 in 1991). The district was inhabited by the educationally backward tribes such as Kooa, Khamba, Miji, Monpa Sherdukpen, Sulung[4], Tangsa and Aka; none of them had developed literacy primers.

In Assam, the Darrang district, though not occupying the lowest position in female literacy (32.53 in 1991), had over 10 per cent tribal population consisting of the Boro, Kacheri, Deori, Hojai, Kacheri including Sonwal, Lalung, Mech, Miri and Rabha, out of which only Boro and Kacheri had made attempts to develop literacy primars and impart teaching in the mother tongue at the lower primary stage.

Meghalaya, though an educationally advanced state in the sixties, had one of the lowest female literacy percentages in the decade 1981-91 in West Garo Hills. This was despite the development of Garo language almost a century ago. The low participation of women may be explained by factors such as irrelevant curriculum, unattractive school building - which will be discussed in the section on dropouts. West Garo Hills had as poor a female literacy percentage as 31.32 in 1991, doing somewhat better than 19.50 per cent in 1981. In the West Garo Hills district, the sub-tribes such as the Kuki, Mon, Mikir, Mizo and Naga had problems of integrating with the Garo population, and this could have been the reason for their remaining aloof from the formal education system.[5]

Though the states, mentioned above, need special attention, yet the position of female literacy is not much better in other states, like Manipur, Tripura and across the eastern and western borders of Mizoram state. In Manipur female literacy was low in districts such as Manipur North (20.20 per cent), Manipur West (26.06) and Tengnoupal (25.16) in 1981. The low level of literacy in these districts may be attributed to the lack of textbook, for imparting literacy in the mother tongue to the tribal sub- groups inhabiting Aimol, Anal, Chothe and Chiru (Manipur North); Gangte, Hmar, Kabui, Kacha Naga (Manipur West); and Simte, Thadou, Vaipei and Zou in Tengnoupal. Other tribes like the Angami and Thangkuls had their own primars. Even in 1991, Manipur was left with five low female literacy districts inhabited by tribes as mentioned above (see Table 3.5 for details on literacy percentage for 1991).

In 1991, South Tripura inhabited mostly by Riang, Santal, Tripuri and Uchai tribes had as low as 39.75 per cent female literacy. It may be mentioned here that Mizoram's pockets of low literacy is in the areas where the Brus, Riangs and Chakmas inhabit areas right across the western and eastern borders of Aizawl, Lunglei and Chhimtuipui districts (See Maps I).

Inter-District Disparities in Literacy 1981 and 1991

The criteria used for ascertaining levels of educational development in the area of literacy between the years 1981 and 1991 is somewhat different for this region than what may be applied to other regions of

Table 3.4
Districtwise Levels of Educational Development 1981

Criteria used :-

A. Above 53.72 - Very High
C. 27.76-40-74 - Moderate
B. 40.79-53.72 - High
D. Below 27.26 - Low

A.	*Very High*	*B.*	*High*	*C.*	*Moderate*	*D.*	*Low*
1.	Nagaland	1.	Nagaland	1.	Nagaland	1.	Nagaland
i.	Mokokchung	i.	Kohima	i.	Phek	i.	Mon
	T-61.78		T-48.94		T-37.99		T-19.89
	F-57.18		F-38.69		F-25.27		F-12.35
		ii.	Wokha	ii	Tuensang	2.	Arunachal Pradesh
						i.	West Kameng
			T-45.60		T-30 49		T-20.97
	Manipur Imphal		F-34.82		F23.32		F-12.48
	T-64.53						
	F-54.03						
		iii.	Zunheboto	2.	Manipur		
				i	Manipur North	ii.	East Kameng
3.	Mizoram		T-45.59		T-31.03		T-7.73
i.	Aizawl		F-38.10		F-20.20		F-2.88
	T-65.09						
	F-61.00	2.	Manipur	ii.	Manipur West	iii.	Lower Subansiri
		i.	Manipur South		T-36.38		T-19.51
ii.	Lunglei		T-44 85		F-26.06		F-10.01
	T-56.89		F-36.09				

Contd.

Contd.

Criteria used :-

A. Above 53.72 - Very High
B. 40.79-53.72 - High
C. 27.76-40-74 - Moderate
D. Below 27 26 - Low

A. Very High	*B. High*	*C. Moderate*	*D. Low*
F-50.46	ii. Manipur Central T-43.28 F-29.77	iii. Tengnoupal T-34.23 F-25.16	iv. Upper Subansiri T-12.89 F- 5.29
	iii. Manipur East T-41.99 F-30.99	3. Mizoram i. Chhimtuipui T-37.07 F-28.73	v. West Siang T-22.44 F-13.39
	3. Tripura i. W. Tripura T-46.21 F-35.80	4. Tripura i. Tripura South T-34.83 F-24.50	vi. East Siang T-26.04 F-15.57 vii. Dibang Valley T-26.28 F-13.49
	ii. N. Tripura T-41.96 F-32.53	5. Arunachal Pradesh I. Lohit T-28.26 F-17.54	viii. Tirap T-19.33

Contd.

Contd.

Criteria used :-

A. Above 53.72 - Very High B. 40.79-53.72 - High
C. 27.76-40-74 - Moderate D. Below 27.26 - Low

A. Very High	*B. High*	*C. Moderate*	*D. Low*
			F-9.68
	4. Meghalaya I. E. Khasi Hills T-43.73 F-40.30	6. Meghalaya I. W. Khasi Hills T-31.97 F-29.40	3. Meghalaya I. Jaintia Hills T-24.51 F-24.70
		ii. Garo Hills T-33.51 F-27.70	ii. W. Garo Hills T-25.91 F-19.50

Sources: 1. Statistical Handbook of Nagaland 1989.
2. " " Manipur 1983.
3. " " Meghalaya 1989.
4. Statistical abstract of Arunachal Pradesh 1989
5. Mizoram at a glance 1983, Government of Mizoram. Directorate of Economics and Statistics
6. Some Basic Statistics of Tripura 1985. Directorate of Statistics Govt. of Tripura.
7. Assam had no census in 1981.

Note: The above data excludes Assam where 1981 Census could not be held.

Table 3.5
District-wise Levels of Educational Development 1991

Crieria used:-

A. Above 65 - Very High (9 districts) B. 55-65 - High (14 districts)
C. 45-55 - Moderate (23 districts) D. Below 45 - Low (14 districts)

A.	*Very High*	*B.*	*High*	*C.*	*Moderate*	*D.*	*Low*
A	ASSAM	A.	ASSAM	A.	ARUNACHAL PRADESH	A.	ARUNACHAL PRADESH
i.	Kamrup	i.	Nalbari	i.	W. Kameng	i.	Tawang
	T-65.04		T-55.99		T-46.31		T-29.80
	F-55.01		F-44.19		F-35.22		F-16.83
ii.	Jorhat	ii.	Lakhimpur	ii.	W. Siang	ii.	E. Kameng
	T-65.51		T-58.96		T-45.64		T-26.20
	F-56.88		F-48.85		F-35.85		F-14.02
B.	MANIPUR	iii.	Golaghat	iii.	Dibang Valley	iii.	Lower Subansiri
			T-58.54		T-46.88		T-41.57
			F-49.75		F-33.27		F-30.70
i.	Imphal	iv.	Sibsagar	iv.	Lohit	iv.	Upper Subansiri
	T-70.74		T-64.46		T-49.21		T-38.31
	F-58.32		F-56.14		F-36.21		F-27.24
C.	MIZORAM						
i.	Aizawl	v.	Dibrugarh	B.	ASSAM	v.	East Siang
	T-88.06		T-58.32	i.	Bongaigaon		T-44.30
	F-85.51		F-48.89		T-49.06		F-34.43
ii.	Lunglei	vi.	N. Cachar Hills		F-38.72	vi.	Changlang

Contd.

Contd.

A. Above 65 - Very High (9 districts)
C. 45-55 - Moderate (23 districts)
B. 55-65 - High (14 districts)
D. Below 45 - Low (14 districts)

A.	*Very High*	*B.*	*High*	*C.*	*Moderate*	*D.*	*Low*
	T-77.73 F-72.58		T-51.76 F-47.30	ii.	Goalpara T-46.81 F-37.58		T-43.20 F-29.64
D.	NAGALAND	vii.	Cachar T-59.19 F-48.76			vii.	Tirap T-32.06 F-18.52
i.	Kohima T-69.16 F-61.41			iii.	Sonitpur T-48.14 F-38.60		
ii.	Wokha T-73.92 F-65.99	B. i.	MANIPUR Churachandpur T-58.17 F-49.30	iv.	Dhemaji T-53.84 F-41.12	B. i.	ASSAM Dhubri T-38.31 F-28.75
iii.	Mokokchung T-77.85 F-74.88	ii.	Ukhrul T-62.54 F-51.57	v.	Marigaon T-47.99 F-39.19	ii.	Kokrajhar T-40.57 F-30.92
E.	TRIPURA	C.	MEGHALAYA	vi.	Tinsukia T-50.28 F-39.99	iii.	Barpeta T-43.24 F-33.20
i.	W. Tripura T-65.83 F-55.15	i.	E. Khasi Hills T-60.04 F-57.04	vii	Karbi Anglong T-45.57 F-34.35	iv.	Darrang T-42.00 F-32.53

Contd.

Contd.

A. Above 65 - Very High (9 districts) B. 55-65 - High (14 districts)
C. 45-55 - Moderate (23 districts) D. Below 45 - Low (14 districts)

A. Very High	*B. High*	*C. Moderate*	*D. Low*
	D. MIZORAM I. Chhimtuipui T-59.11	viii. Nagaon T-54.74 F-46.30	C. MEGHALAYA i. Jaintia Hills T-35.32 F-36.31
	E. NAGALAND i. Phek T-62.59 F-51.34	ix. Karimganj T-54.76 F-44.74 x. Hailakandi T-53.07 F-41.04	ii. W. Garo Hills T-39.32 F-31.32
	ii. Zunheboto T-64.36 F-57.63	C. MANIPUR	D. NAGALAND i. Mon T-36.02 F-29.10
	F. TRIPURA i. N. Tripura T-60.37 F-50.31	i Senapati T-46.04 F-36.13 ii Tamenglong T-50.16 F-39.68	

Contd.

Contd.

A. Above 65 - Very High (9 districts) B. 55-65 - High (14 districts)
C. 45-55 - Moderate (23 districts) D. Below 45 - Low (14 districts)

A. Very High	*B. High*	*C. Moderate*	*D. Low*
		iii. Chandel T-46.68 F-34.80	
		iv. Thoubal T-52.47 F-36.31	
		v. Bishnupur T-54.94 F-41.13	
		D. MEGHALAYA	
		i. W. Khasi Hills T-50.52 F-47.94	
		ii. E. Garo Hills T-48.38 F-41.70	

Contd.

Contd.

A. Above 65 - Very High (9 districts) B. 55-65 - High (14 districts)
C. 45-55 - Moderate (23 districts) D. Below 45 - Low (14 districts)

A. Very High	*B. High*	*C. Moderate*	*D. Low*
		E. NAGALAND i. Tuensang T-48.39 F-41.98 F. TRIPURA i. S. Tripura T-51.35 F-39.75	

Source: Statistical Database for Literacy. National Institute of Adult Education 1993.
Note: The above criteria used is exclusively for the North Eastern States.

India. The rationale behind this is, that barring Arunachal Pradesh and Meghalaya, the levels of both male and female literacy in the region are somewhat higher than other parts of the country for sociological and religious reasons[6]. Thus in 1981 the low literacy districts were Mon (Nagaland); West and East Kameng; Lower and Upper Subansiri, West and East Siang; Dibang valley and Tirap (Arunachal Pradesh); and Jaintia and West Garo Hills (Meghalaya), that is, the rates below 27.76 per cent. Most other states fell into the categories of moderate, which was between 27.76 and 40.74. Only Mokokchung (Nagaland); Imphal (Manipur); and Aizawl and Lunglei (Mizoram) fell into a very high category that is above 53.72. See Table 3.4 for details.

The districts with low female literacy in 1981 were Kohima (38.69); Wokha (34.82); Zunheboto (38.10), Manipur South (36.09); Manipur Central (29.77); Manipur East (30.99); West Tripura (35.80); North Tripura (32.53); and East Khasi Hills (40.30). It was as low as 2.88 in East Kameng and 5.29 in Upper Subansiri.[7]

According to 1991 census data the low literacy districts are confined to Assam, Arunachal Pradesh, Meghalaya and Nagaland which is below 45 per cent. In Arunachal Pradesh we have Tawang (Total 29.80, female 16.83); East Kameng (total 26.20, female 14.02); Lower Subansiri (total 41.57, female 30.70); Upper Subansiri (total 38.31, female 27.24); East Siang (total 44.30, female 34.43); Changlang (total 43.20, female 29.64); and Tirap (total 32.06, female 18.52) (See Table 3.5).

Table 3.6

List of State-wise Distribution of Backward Districts with low age specific (6-11 years) enrolment ratio for Girls in Rural areas, 1986

States - Categories of Districts by Enrolment ratio for rural girls in age group 6-11 years in the range 26-50.

1.	Arunachal Pradesh	-	A. East Kameng
			B. Tirap
			C. Lower Subansiri
			D. West Kameng
			E. Tawang
2.	Nagaland	-	A. Mon
			B. Tuensang
			C. Wokha
			D. Zunheboto
			E. Kohima
			F. Mokokchung
3	Assam	-	A. Karbi Anglong
4.	Meghalaya	-	A. East Garo Hills
			B. East Khasi Hills
			C. Jaintia Hills.

Source: Usha Nayar, Universal Primary Education of Rural Girls in India - NCERT, 1991, New Delhi.

Table 3.6.1
Classification of Districts according to Total Literacy Levels

Very High (above 70)	*High (60-70)*	*Moderate (50-60)*	*Low (below 50)*
Arunachal Pradesh	Changlang	West Siang	Dibang Valley
	Papum Pare	East Siang	West Kameng
			Lohit
			Upper Subansiri
			Upper Siang
			Lower Subansiri
			Tawang
			Tirap
			East Kameng
Assam			
Jorhat	Sibsagar	Cachar	Karbi Anglong
	Kamrup	North Cachar Hills	Barpeta
	Dibrugarh	Nalbari	Darrang
	Golaghat	Dhemaji	Kokrajhar
	Lahimpur	Nagaon	Dhubri
	Karimganj	Tinsukia	
		Sonitpur	
		Morigaon	
		Goalpara	
		Bongaigaon	
		Hailakandi	
Manipur			
Imphal West	Imphal East	Thoubal	Tamenglong
	Churchandpur		Chandel
	Ukhrul		Senapati
	Bishnupur		
Meghalaya			
East Khasi Hills	West Khasi Hills	East Garo Hills	South Garo Hills
	Ri Bhoi	Jaintia Hills	West Garo Hills
Mizoram			
Aizwal			Lawngtlai
Serchhip			
Champhai			
Kolasib			
Lunglei			
Saiha			
Mamit			
Nagaland			
Mokokchung	Kohima		
Wokha	Zunheboto		Tuensang
Dimapur	Phek		Mon
Tripura			
West Tripura	North Tripura	Dhalai	
	South Tripura		

Source: Census of India 2001, New Delhi.

Table 3.6.2
Classification of Districts according to Female Literacy Levels

Very High (above 70)	*High (60-70)*	*Moderate (50-60)*	*Low (below 50)*
Arunachal	West Kameng	Dibang Valley	Upper Siang
Pradesh	East Siang	Lohit	Lower Subansiri
Papum Pare	West Siang	Changlang	Tirap
		Upper Subansiri	Tawang
			East Kameng
Assam			
Jorhat	Lakhimpur	Hailakandi	Dhubri
Sibsagar	North Cacher Hills	Morigaon	
Kamrup	Cacher	Karbi Anglong	
Dibrugarh	Nalbari	Goalpara	
Golaghat	Karimganj	Barpeta	
	Dhemaji	Darrang	
	Tinsukia	Kokrajhar	
	Nagaon		
	Sonitpur		
	Bongaigaon		
Manipur			
Imphal West	Ukhrul	Tamenglong	
Imphal East	Thoubal	Chandel	
Churchandpur		Senapati	
Bishnupur			
Meghalaya			
East Khasi Hills	Ri Bhoi West	South Garo Hills	
	Khasi Hills	Jaintia Hills	
	East Garo Hills	West Garo Hills	
Mizoram			
Aizwal		Lawngtlai	
Serchhip			
Champhai			
Kolasib			
Lunglei			
Saiha			
Mamit			
Nagaland			
Mokokchung	Zunheboto	Tuensang	Mon
Wokha			
Dimapur			
Kohima			
Phek			
Tripura			
West Tripura	Dhalai		
North Tripura			
South Tripura			

Source: Census of India 2001, New Delhi.

In Assam, the low literacy districts are Dhubri (total 38.31, female 28.75); Kokrajhar (total 40.57, female 30.92); Barpeta (total 43.24, female 33.20); and Darrang (total 42.00, female 32.53). In Meghalaya the low literacy districts are Jaintia Hills (total 35.32, female 36.31); and West Garo Hills (total 39.32, female 31.32). For Nagaland, only Mon falls into this category (total 36.02, female 29.10).

The moderate category of 23 districts, with literacy below 55 per cent, have substantial inequalities between male and female percentages. Arunachal Pradesh, Assam, Manipur, Meghalaya, Nagaland and Tripura. (See Table 3.5 for details). Among the literate districts the females of Nalbari, Lakhimpur, Golaghat, Sibsagar, Dibrugarh, North Cachar and Cachar (Assam) need special assistance. Similarly, Churachandpur and Ukrul (Manipur); East Khasi Hills (Meghalaya); Chhimtuipui (Mizoram); Phek and Zunheboto (Nagaland) and North Tripura (Tripura) districts need to pay special attention to female literacy. Even the high literacy districts of Imphal (Manipur), Aizawl and Lunglei (Mizoram), Kamrup and Jorhat (Assam), and West Tripura (Tripura) have about a ten per cent gap between male and female literacy percentages.

State and District-wise Position of Female Literacy and Enrolment of Girls

There are many discrepancies between the ranking of female literacy and girls' enrolment in Arunachal Pradesh. Though in 1986, East Kameng district had a female literacy rate of only 2.88 (the lowest in the state) yet the ratio of girls enrolled in the age group of 6-11 years was 27.00 and for 11-14 years 10.13.[8] This is despite 55.04 of the population being served by primary schools/sections within a distance of 1 km. and 23.03 by upper primary schools/sections within the distance of 3 kms. Lower Subansiri with only 10.01 female literacy rates had a more positive picture of the participation of girls at the elementary level (48.00 ratio for 6-11 years and 32.23 ratio for 11-14 years).

No census was conducted for Assam in 1981; however, there was low enrolment of girls for the elementary stage in the districts of Karbi Anglong (36.31 for 6-11 years and 38.27 for 11-14 years) in 1986.[9] This was despite the fact that 97.15 percentage of primary schools available within 1 km. and 86.58 of upper primary schools within 3 km.

In Manipur, the enrolment ratio for girls of both age groups was as low as 56.29 for ages 6-11 years and 30.31 for ages 11-14 years for Senapati district which had 94.5 of its population served by a primary section within the habitation, and 66.35 of upper primary within 3 kms. of habitation.

In Meghalaya, West Garo Hills district which had only 19.55 female literacy rate in 1981 had an enrolment ratio as high as 51.06 for girls belonging to 6-11 years and 72.39 for the age group of 11-14 years. The provision of schooling facilities for both primary and upper primary level are not satisfactory; for example, only 82.39 per cent habitations have schooling facilities within 1 km., for the primary level, and 67.06 with in an area of 3 km. for the upper primary level in West Garo Hills district.

The overall picture of both female literacy and the participation of girls at the elementary level is more satisfactory in the case of Mizoram when compared with any other North Eastern States. However, Chhimtuipui is in more need of administrative attention, as only 19.42 of its population are served by primary schools within their reach, and 69.42 per cent of population are provided upper primary schools, within a circumference of 3 km.

In Nagaland, besides Mon, Tuensang and Phek with low female literacy rates; the girl enrolment in Kohima was especially low, (35.13 for years 6-11 and 31.37 for 11-14 years). Female literacy in Tripura was hardly any criteria for girl enrolment, which is the highest among all North Eastern States (100.28 for 6-11 years and 42.63 for 11-14 years), even in the low female literacy district such as South Tripura.

District-wise Percentage of Girls to Total Enrolment in Class I-V in 1986-87 in SC/ST Categories

In Arunachal Pradesh, Tirap district's performance in literacy was the second worst; out of a total of 34.50 percentage girls enrolled only 0.27 per cent were SC and 20.47 per cent ST - all belonging to the rural areas. East Kameng as has been earlier mentioned had the worst picture-out of a total of 28.05 girls enrolled (female literacy rate being 2.88 for 1981) only .04 were SC and 21.10 STs.[10]

In the case of Assam two districts which have a greater SC/ST population (such as in Dhubri and Kachar) also had low girl enrolment. In Dhubri, the total was 41.20 – (43.78 SC and 43.65 ST). In Cachar the total was 41.72, (43.73 SC and 41.89 ST). In Manipur, Chandel districts, the two which had the lowest total enrolment of 41.77, there were 47.37 SCs and 41.52 STs. In Meghalaya, the West Garo Hills performance is the lowest; (in the total of 46.60) there were 48.62 SCs and 46.80 STs. In Mizoram, Chhimtuipui performance was the worst in 1986-87, out of 42.39 total and a ST population of 42.39. It may be mentioned here that no SC population is registered in Mizoram. In Nagaland too, no SC population is registered. Kohima district's performance was the worst with 32.87 per cent of girls enrolled, all belonging to the ST category. In Tripura, South

Tripura district does not present an encouraging picture. Out of a 42.96 total of girls, there are 44.31 SCs and 37.02 STs.

Table 3.7
Literacy by SC, ST in North-Eastern States

State	*Population (1000)*		*% of SC Literate Population*	*% of ST Literate Population*	*% of Total Literates*	
	1991	*2001*	*1991*	*1991*	*1991*	*2001*
Arunachal P.	865	1091	0.47	63.66	41.59	54.74
Assam	22414	26638	7.40	12.82	52.89	64.28
Manipur	1837	2388	2.02	34.41	59.89	68.87
Meghalaya	1775	2319	0.51	85.53	49.10	62.6
Mizoram	690	891	0.10	94.75	82.27	88.49
Nagaland	1210	1989	NA	87.70	61.65	67.11
Tripura	2757	3199	16.36	30.95	60.44	73.2

Source : Census of India, 1991, 2001.

While comparing the literacy rate between the years 1981 and 1991, and especially the female literacy rates, one realizes their certain peculiar characteristics. As for example, whereas Mizoram is consistent in its literacy growth and is performing the best as far as literacy is concerned, the case of Arunachal Pradesh is quite the contrary. The great difference in these states may be explained not only historically, but also by the freedom given in Mizoram to their three Autonomous District Councils namely; Mara, Lai, and Chakma to impart literacy and primary education and now the upper primary education (from 1995) in their mother tongue. This has helped the state to grow substantially in its literacy rate and explains the phenomena of its female literacy. However, there are pockets of backwardness running right across the North Eastern and North Western sides, of the state, even in the educationally forward districts such as Aizawl and Lunglei, which have nomadic mobile tribes like the Brus, Riangs and Chakmas.

The progress in female literacy made by Nagaland, Tripura and Meghalaya may also be attributed to the development of certain tribal languages in these states which have had a positive effect on girls education at the elementary level. However, even in Nagaland, the Mon and Tuensang districts need more attention, as do many parts of Kohima district, where the literacy rate has fallen substantially between the years 1971 to 1991, Mon and Tuensang are inhabited largely by the same tribes being a part of the NEFA and hence administered centrally. In Kohima, the population is no longer confined to Angamis and Aos, but have had a substantial increase of SC labourers involved in construction work. In Meghalaya, the low female literacy needs further investigation to discover the reasons behind it. In Tripura, the floating plantation workers from Bihar coupled with a constant tension prevailing between what is originally the Tripuris, and the migrant population from Assam and Bangladesh, has adversely affected female literacy. In Manipur, the development of the Meitei language and the promotion of the original script has helped to develop literacy in some districts in the last decade.

Girl Enrolment and Dropouts from the Elementary Level

In general, the percentage of girls enrolled into the primary classes has increased from 1957 to 1993. The highest percentage increase of girls enrolled between the years 1957-1965 was in Manipur (255.80), Tripura (152.42) and Assam (127.66). However, there is no substantial increase in girl enrolment except in Tripura (77.32) between the years 1965 and 1973. In the period 1973-1978, Arunachal Pradesh witnessed the highest percentage of increase in girl enrollment, that is, 97.25. Manipur showed a similar decrease in girl enrollment in the same period (-7.95). Arunachal Pradesh also continued with an increase in the percentage of girls enrolled between 1978-86 (123.94), followed by Tripura (86.14). The gap between girls and boys enrollment decreases between 1986-1993 in all the North Eastern States, except for Arunachal Pradesh.

Table 3.8

Growth Rate on Enrolment at Primary Level Total and Girls in Percentage

States	*% age of increase from 1957-1965*	*% age of increase from 1965-1973*	*% age of increase from 1973-1978*	*% age of increase from 1978-1986*	*% age of increase from 1957-1965*
1	*2*	*3*	*4*	*5*	*6*
Arunachal P.	N.A.	N.A.	63.90	78.16	42.52
" Girls	N.A.	N.A.	97.25	123.94	53.29
Assam	68.97	17.79	20.84	29.09	11.56
" Girls	127.66	25.44	25.14	44.24	16.47
Manipur	144.82	59.60	-14.21	-10.21	50.40
" Girls	255.80	59.60	- 7.95	- 6.43	53.25
Meghalaya	N.A. .	N.A.	15.25	35.44	10.58
" Girls	N.A.	N.A.	16.46	36.57	10.92

Contd.

1	2	3	4	5	6
Mizoram	N.A.	N.A.	1.21	53.16	12.15
" Girls	N.A.	N.A.	1.69	51.63	11.61
Nagaland	N.A.	N.A.	14.61	16.03	4.20
" Girls	N.A.	N.A.	18.50	23.92	5.64
Tripura	130.65	63.70	6.71	73.84	13.96
" Girls	152.42	77.32	9.95	86.14	16.97

Source: All India Educational Surveys 1957-1993, New Delhi, NCERT.

At the middle school level, 1957-1965 a phenomenal increase of girl enrollment was in Tripura (503.03%), Manipur (498.55%) and Assam (275.96%). Though Assam (82.38%) and Tripura (118.67%) maintain an increase in girl enrollment for the years 1965-1973, in Manipur there is no substantial increase - (30.04% girls out of total 34.91% increase in enrolment).

The years 1973-78 witnessed a substantial increase in the enrollment of girls in Arunachal Pradesh (268.43), although in the other states of the region there was no sharp difference between this decade and the previous two. Arunachal maintained the highest rate of increase even in 1978-1986 and 1986-1993. There is a trend towards the increase in the growth rate of girls enrolled between 1973 and 1993 in all North Eastern States, barring Arunachal Pradesh, hence the gender gap tended to decrease between 1986 and 1993.

Table 3.9 : Growth Rate in Middle School Enrolment Total and Girls in Percentage

States	*% age of increase from 1957-1965*	*% age of increase from 1965-1973*	*% age of increase from 1973-1978*	*% age of increase from 1978-1986*	*% age of increase from 1957-1965*
Arunachal Pradesh	N.A.	N.A.	161.54	157.24	85.80
" Girls	N.A.	N.A	268.43	238 84	97.25
Assam	127.47	51.90	19.53	48.75	27.14
" Girls	275.96	82.38	24.64	56.21	37.85
Manipur	177.36	34.91	17.23	36.40	53.18
" Girls	498.55	30.04	40.27	51.00	65.58
Meghalaya	N.A.	N.A.	25.83	90.98	14 13
" Girls	N.A.	N.A.	33.14	100.00	13.00
Mizoram	N.A.	N.A.	10.89	36.48	40.80
" Girls	N.A.	N.A.	13.74	45.27	39.50
Nagaland	N.A.	N.A.	30.05	11.75	52.32
" Girls	N.A.	N.A.	39.61	15.93	67.84
Tripura	292.34	71.11	18.30	12.04	11.16
" Girls	503 03	111.67	19.89	122.06	17.90

Source. All India Educational Surveys 1957-1993, New Delhi, NCERT.

The dropout rates of girls in 1986 were nearly the same as that of total dropouts of middle schools in states such as Arunachal Pradesh, Meghalaya, Mizoram and Tripura (data on dropout rates for primary schools are not available for the region for that year). Data pertaining to 1988-89 as supplied by the Ministry of HRD, Government of India for the elementary stage, indicate the same trend in the primary schools. Thus there is no substantial difference between the percentages of total dropouts to girl dropout between Classes I-V. 1993 data however shows a marginal gap between the sexes, with girl dropout rates being higher in all the states especially in Tripura (See Table 3.10 for details).

Although girl enrolment had increased substantially in Arunachal Pradesh and Manipur between 1986-1993, yet data on dropout of girls shows that the participation of the girl child in education was far from satisfactory especially at the primary stage. The situation gets worse at the middle-school stage where more than 70 per cent of the girl students drop out of formal schools.

Table 3.10

North Eastern States : Enrolment and Dropout Rates at Primary Schools 1986, 1993

States	*Year*	*Enrolment*		*Dropout Rates*	
		Total	*Girls*	*Total*	*Girls*
Arunachal Pra.	1986	88029	-	-	-
	1993	125462	54420	60 05	61.09
Assam	1986	2627634	-	-	-
	1993	2931511	1331949	39.05	39.55
Manipur	1986	179834	-	-	-
	1993	270476	127133	68.26	68.53
Meghalaya	1986	251502	-	-	-
	1993	278119	138761	32 06	34.43
Mizoram	1986	104044	-	-	-
	1993	116686	55319	57.58	58.58
Nagaland	1986	126812	-	-	-
	1993	132142	63448	37.65	24.13
Tripura	1986	364769	-	-	-
	1993	415690	190077	63.49	66.95

Source : Fifth and Sixth All India Educational Survey, New Delhi, NCERT, 1986, 1993.

In Manipur, in spite of the incentives and programmes initiated for development of girls education, there exists a high gap between the education of boys and girls in all stages. The most serious problems are the low enrolment, wastage and stagnation. This may be due to poverty

Table 3.11
North Eastern States: Enrolment and Dropout Rates at Middle Schools 1986, 1993

States	*Year*	*Enrolment*		*Dropout Rates*	
		Total	*Girls*	*Total*	*Girls*
Arunachal Pra.	1986	17284	-	79.19	79.15
	1993	32114	13027	68.72	67.62
Assam	1986	761848	-	68.09	70.96
	1993	968639	429752	67.55	71.80
Manipur	1986	68467	-	75.40	77.89
	1993	104878	48566	72.34	72.26
Meghalaya	1986	64435	-	69.90	69.45
	1993	73546	34841	57.65	57.11
Mizoram	1986	28659	-	40.54	40.82
	1993	40354	19558	52.44	50.60
Nagaland	1986	28769	-	60.10	56.82
	1993	43882	21158	38.13	39.58
Tripura	1986	109029	-	66.17	65.50
	1993	121197	54209	68.39	70.92

Source : Fifth and Sixth All India Educational Surveys. New Delhi, NCERT, 1986, 1993.

and ignorance on the part of the parents. Girls are engaged in domestic and occupational work at home by their parents. Apart from this, there still remains a prejudice against girls' education, even if the parents are not poor. The parents lack knowledge about the practical value of education. Even in 1996 the rural folk did not favour education of girls. Social factors such as early marriage and parental apathy for girl's education also are the causes of wastage and stagnation.[11]

In most Muslim and even Meitei (Vaishnav) dominated areas there is a demand for separate schools for girls after the primary stage.[12] In Thoubal district though there existed a government co-educational school for the middle level, within walking distance, both Muslim men and women expressed their concern about co-education, as it was against their cultural norms. The other factors affecting girl participation in elementary education were lack of female teachers in rural areas; insurgency movement and hence lack of security and poor hostel and transport facilities in villages situated at a distance from Imphal, the state capital.

In Meghalaya, the dropout rate is the highest in Classes I and II.[13] The physical facilities are poor in rural primary schools. Most schools have only one room, insufficient drinking water, and no separate toilet for girls. This is true even for Barapani whic belongs to Khasi Hills, a district with high literacy and higher enrolment of girls. During a household survey, conducted in the region parents explained at length the socio-economic constraints faced by them in sending their children to these schools. One major factor was the school hours which clashed with the harvesting time, and for which the parents required children participation. Secondly, there hardly existed any non-formal education centres, and even if they did they were often without Instructors. There was also practically no early childhood education centre or any alternative centre for the parents to leave their young children; hence the daughters remained at home looking after their siblings. They suggested the opening of more non-formal centres especially for girls.[14]

In Tripura, in spite of the provision of schooling facilities and incentives; 19.4 per cent of ST girls were outside the formal schooling system especially in Jirania block of West Tripura District.[15]

The case study revealed that both poverty and illiterate parents, especially the mothers, were causes of low enrolment. Interviews held with parents, Panchayat members, and field workers revealed that formal school timetable clashed with harvesting season. The school curriculum was also irrelevant. Meghalaya and Tripura case studies revealed that the local-specific curriculum, which is being tried out today, in the Lai Autonomous District Council of Mizoram State (Jalali, NIEPA, 1995), might help to solve some of the problems. The details have been discussed in the case study of Mizoram.

Quite in contrast to studies already mentioned, a study conducted on Arunachal Pradesh (K. Sujatha, NIEPA; 1988) revealed formal schools were more in demand there. But the unqualified tribal primary teachers adversely affected the performance of these students, especially in the remote areas. The lack of training to impart NCERT textbooks at the middle school is a common constraint faced by most North Eastern States and hence more teacher training courses need to be conducted there. In Phesema, Kohima District in Nagaland (Jalali, NIEPA; 1990) it has been pointed out that there was a need to impart teacher training. The lack of physical facilities within the government schools made the parents send their children to both primary and middle privately-managed schools often situated three kilometres away from home and took as long as one hour to walk each way.[16] This was despite the active community participation by the Angami parents to construct playgrounds and school equipment in the government schools.

However, several case studies conducted both at Ukhrul, Churachadpur districts of (Manipur), Nagaland and Mizoram reveal that where Christians constituted the ST population the drop out rates of girls was less. Yet, after all, a district is not always a true indicator of the actual situation as is the example of Mizoram. In Mizoram, 67.13 per cent boys and 64.22% girls completed five years of schooling in 1991-92. Not only this, but there is also a lack of housing facilities for women teachers, and an acute shortage of female teachers in both primary and middle school in all these states. Studies conducted (by Shilo Ao[17] and Sangtam[18]) revealed that since teachers had to travel for several hours to their block headquarters, to collect their salaries, after three months, they usually preferred to be posted out and refused to join school in the remote areas of each district. Moreover, even the Inspector of schools rarely has a vehicle to travel for inspection of schools. Thus, even the policy of posting a married couple together in schools, as has been tried out in Arunachal Pradesh and Nagaland, has not provided the required incentive.

References

1. Usha Nayar, *Universal Primary Education of Rural Girls in India*, (New Delhi, NCERT, 1991).
2. In Arunachal Pradesh the Rama Krishna Mission and Done Polo are voluntary agencies that have helped to spread female literacy in Assam. The literacy campaigns like Total Literacy Mission and National Literacy Mission have also done some work.
3. Tripura has had political problems and often the literacy missions were looked upon as the methods through which the centre is infiltrating into the society of opposition states. Moreover, there has been no follow-up activity in the way of post-literacy movement and rural libraries for neo-literates, which is behind the success of Midnapore and Burdwan districts of West Bengal. Further, the Tripuri tribals were seldom brought into the literacy classes. language being a constraint as the question whether literacy would be in Kak Borah or Bengali has been the bone of contention.
4. Sulungs are bonded labourers even in 2001, Interview with N. Dutta, Joint Director, School Education, Itanagar 2001.
5. Interview with Dr. Wolflang, Director SCERT, Shillong, 1996, who also explained the Bangladeshi immigrants were reluctant to study Garo or Khasi and hence were not counted in the census as Literates.
6. There is no taboo to educating a girl child and besides Christian Mission always encouraged girl's education since the 19th century. The inter-district disparities reveal that where the same background tribes live, no primers are available in their mother tongue, and the tribes are not able to learn either English or any other tribal language other than their own. It may be mentioned here that both in Arunachal Pradesh and Nagaland there does not exist a state language – hence either English, Nagamese or Hindi is the common

medium of inter-tribal communication. Therefore, other advanced tribal language primers are of no use to those tribes that live in districts where Adi, Mishmi (Arunachal Pradesh) and Ao, Angami, Lotha (Nagaland) are not in existence.

7. The low female literacy could have the same reason as given in footnote 6, except for Kohima district where the immigrant Bihar, Nepali, Oriya and U.P. female labour, engaged in roadways and construction work, has brought down the literacy percentage in the district.
8. Due to enrolment drive in the State.
9. Karbi Anglong, Autonomous District Council for Karbi tribes is backward. Unlike Mizoram's Lai Autonomous District Council, this Council has not been paying attention to education on account of inner politics of the Council.
10. East Kameng is a hilly area where the villages are sparsely populated and often the school is difficult to reach since one has to travel across hills for many hours to reach the place. This district like Dhubri is very rural in character with little transport facilities.
11. Interview with N.B. Debnath, Department Education, Government of Tripura, New Delhi, 1993.
12. Jayashree Roy Jalali, "Village Educational Survey", Thoubal district, Manipur, NIEPA, 1992.
13. Tourist Mark, "Issues Confronting the State in Universalization of Elementary Education", Directorate of School Education Government of Meghalaya, Shillong, 1996.
14. Josephine Yazali, and Jayshree Roy Jalali, "Village Education Survey", Barapani, Meghalaya, NIEPA, 1991.
15. N. Debnath, "A study on the causes of low Enrolment and high drop-out of ST. girls in Five Primary Schools in Jirania Block, West Tripura District, DEPA Dissertation, NIEPA, 1991. The parents said that the school curriculum was irrelevant and had nothing to do with the agricultural activities of the child.
16. Phesama, June-July, 1990.
17. Shilo Ao, "Role of the Village Education Committee on Primary Education - A Case Study of Kohima District of Nagaland", DEPA, NIEPA, 1995.
18. A. Santam, "Inspection and Supervision Elementary Schools in Tuensang District of Nagaland", DEPA, NIEPA, 1996.

4

Decentralization of Education

Decentralization in the Indian context refers to "reversing the concentration of administration at a single centre and conferring powers to local government".[1] It involves the delegation of responsibilities to lower levels in a territorial hierarchy, whether the hierarchy is one of the government within a state, or offices within a large-scale organization. It is different from delegation of powers to a subordinate authority. The subdivision of India's vast territory into smaller areas, including the education system, and the creation of political and administrative institutions in those areas have been a continuing process since the fifties. The philosophy of decentralization derives from the very concept of democracy which India has been practising. The decentralization process takes cognizance of the ethics and norms of a democratic society. In this "all decisions which are to effect the lives of the people of a particular area or region, whether in economic, social or administrative areas, are to be based on the collective decision of all the people of that area or region".[2] Democratic decentralization, hence, has its roots in the desire to associate more and more people with the work of the government in all intermediary levels in general and at the local level in particular. It acknowledges "people's right to initiate their own projects for local well being and the authority to execute and operate them in an autonomous manner".[3] It aims at widening the area of people's participation, authority and autonomy through dispersal of powers, from top to bottom levels, in political decision-making, financial control and management and administrative operation to be exercised by people's representatives. It is a necessary condition for development as it takes note of local circumstances in development plans and their implementation.

The Indian Constitution provides for the formal division of powers between the Centre and the State Governments and lower levels of administration. The Balwant Rai Mehta Committee (1957) had recommended the constitution of statutory elected local bodies with the necessary resources, power and authority which became the basis of a decentralized administrative system, known as Panchayati Raj system. In India, local governments which fall within the jurisdiction of the state have some notable variations in nomenclature.[4] The Report of the Working Group on District Planning in its Seventh Five Year Plan Document had accepted that "decentralization enables a better perception of the needs of the local areas".[5] It has been, therefore, accepted that "decentralized planning has become both necessary and possible".[6] The unique system of decentralization in North East India has been the District and Autonomous District Councils in that region provided by the Constitution of 1950.

During British colonial rule, the present North East India consisted of the Province of Assam and the two Princely States of Manipur and Tripura. Under the Government of India Act, 1935, the Hill Areas of Assam were divided into Excluded and Partially Excluded Areas. In the Excluded Areas the Provincial Ministry had no jurisdiction. The Governor of Assam, as an agent of the Governor-General in Council, was invested with authority over the excluded areas.

After independence, the recommendations of the Bardoloi Committee (which formed the basis of Sixth Schedule in the Constitution), advocated the creation of District Councils in the Hill Areas of Assam. The basic consideration for providing District Councils was, that, "The areas are on the frontier and if the frontier is to be well protected the political aspirations of the people of this area should be satisfied. The only way by which this could be satisfied was by the creation of district councils".[7]

The idea behind the scheme contained in the Sixth Schedule was to "provide the tribal people with simple and inexpensive administration of their own, which would safeguard their tribal customs and ways of life, and assure them maximum autonomy in the management of their characteristically tribal affairs",[8] at the same time in no way affecting the unity and integrity of the state. Autonomy was to be exercised in matters pertaining to the peculiar customs and institutions of the tribal people, without hindering the unity of administration or lessening the general responsibility of the State and Union Government to "secure to them the benefits of a progressive and liberal administration".[9]

In 1952, the District Councils were constituted in all the districts excepting the Naga Hills, where the demand was for complete independence. Apart from the District Councils, Regional Councils were established for the Pawi-Lakhars, in the Mizo Hills. In 1972, by an amendment to the Constitution, District Councils were established for the Pawis and Chakmas in Mizoram, and for the tribals in Manipur Hills. Thus, in all the tribal areas in North East India there were District Councils except for Tripura.[10]

Powers and Functions of the District Council

Broadly speaking, the powers and functions of the District Council are four: legislative, executive, financial and judicial. The legislative power includes the power to make laws on the allotment, occupation or use or setting apart of land, other than the reserved forests. The district councils also has the power to make laws, regulate the practice of *Jhum* or other forms of shifting cultivation, establish town or village councils with special functions; others, relating to village or town administration including town or village police, public health and sanitation, the appointment or succession of chief or headman, the inheritance of property, marriage and divorce, social customs, money-lending and trading by persons other than schedule tribes.[11] As regards the executive powers, the District Council has the power to establish, construct or manage primary schools, dispensaries, markets, cattle-pounds, ferries, fisheries, roads and waterways. It has also the power to determine the language and the manner in which primary education ought to be imparted in the primary schools within its jurisdiction.[12]

The District Council has also powers of taxation such as assessing and collecting land revenue, levying taxes on lands and buildings, professions, trades, and employment, for the maintenance of schools, dispensaries and roads, licences or leases for the purpose of prospecting or for extracting minerals.

The judicial powers include constitution of village courts for tribal suits or cases in which both the parties are tribals. It makes for the appointment of suitable persons as members of the village courts, and such officers, as may be necessary, for the execution of laws made by the District Council.[13]

The Development Departments, transferred to the control of the District Councils, are agriculture, public works, flood control and irrigation, soil conservation, animal husbandry, veterinary services, fisheries, forests, Panchayati Raj and community development, cottage industries, roads and buildings, education - primary to middle schools, health and family planning and development. The district level officers are responsible to the state government for implementing schemes which had been transferred to the control of the District Council.[14]

District Council and State Government

The only relationship existing between the Government of Assam and the various District Councils was the approval of their legislation by the Governor, in sanctioning of loans and grants to meet the normal cost of their administration or the expenditure for certain development works. Thus, the District Councils have been functioning, more or less independently of the State Government and the Union Government, and were extremely jealous of the powers given to them by the Sixth Schedule, and at the same time suspicious of even the best intentions of the State Government.[15]

The Governor has sledge hammer type of powers. He may, at any time annul or suspend any act or resolution of the District Council which is likely to endanger the safety of the country or is prejudicial to public order and take even such steps as the suspension of the Council if necessary. He may assume to himself all or some of the powers of the Council during the period of suspension for a period of six months at a time. But he has no power to dissolve the Council without the recommendation of the Commission to be appointed, under para 14 of the Sixth Schedule and hold fresh elections.[16]

Nevertheless the State Government "did not exercise effective control over the District Councils. It allowed the District Councils to function as independent political units, and the administrative machinery brought into existence for the implementation of the decisions of the District Councils was adequate".[17]

District Councils and Their Functioning

The District Council is a corporate body, having perpetual succession. The Council consists of representatives elected by adult franchise to administer the functions and exercise the powers entrusted to it. The District Council also consists of certain number of persons nominated by the Governor to represent the minorities and the unrepresented communities".[18] The term of a Council is five years, with provision for extension for a period of one year at a time.

A member of a Council must be a citizen of India, be not less than 25 years of age and have the right to vote at the election to District Council.

No person can become a member of two District Councils. If a member is absent continuously for a period of 30 days, he forfeits his seat in the Council. Government servants, State or Central, employees of the District Council, lunatics, persons not citizen of India etc., are excluded from membership of the District Council.[19]

The rights and obligations of the members of the District Councils are more or less the same as those of the members of any legislature. They should pay the dues to the District Council or the government or corporative societies in due time, and evince interest in any contract made with the District Council. There is no provision for the recall of members. Any question relating to disqualification is referred to the Governor and his decision is final. A member may resign at any time from the Council without assigning any reason.[20]

A voter must be a resident in a constituency for not less than 180 days and must belong to a Scheduled Tribe. A non-tribal is required to have resided permanently for not less than 12 years. The decision of Governor is final in any dispute relating to election.[21]

The first meeting of the newly elected District Council is fixed by the Governor and is presided over by the Deputy Commissioner (D.C.). Regular meetings after every 3 months and special meetings can also be called for. The forum to constitute a meeting of the District Council has six members or one third of the total strength of the Council, whichever is greater.

Evolution of the Role of Local Authorities in Primary Education in India

The association of Indian local bodies with the administration of education in general and that of primary education in particular was the result of several factors.[22] They were initially a fall out of the attempts of the East India Company's officials to establish modern educational institutions and maintain them partly from voluntary grants-in-aid sanctioned by the government. In this respect the Despatch of 1859 becomes significant. "Obviously, the establishment of local bodies and their association with the administration of primary schools follow as a corollary from this order although the Despatch makes no specific reference to them".[23]

The second factor which helped the development was the ever present desire of British Officials to introduce English precedents, through the implementation of the Elementary Education Act of 1870. This act provided for elementary education of the masses by entrusting to local bodies the power to levy rates and to enforce compulsory attendance.[24] The third factor was an attempt to check the evils of a wasteful system of centralized financial administration and thus Lord Mayo passed the Decentralization Order of 1870. "The decentralization, that thus began on financial grounds, soon came to stay as a measure of general administrative reform and the levy of local rates to meet a specific situation of financial stringency ultimately resulted in giving local bodies a share in the administration of education in general and of primary education in particular".[25] Lord Ripon's contribution in 1880s is already mentioned in the introduction to this thesis.

In the 1880s under Ripon's Local Self Government Act, the Government of the Presidencies concerned set up local committees at the district and the 'taluka' levels. The Mughals devised a policy of delegating more and more powers to the provinces. They also associated people in local administration. District and 'taluka' boards were established by the British replacing existing local committees. The most significant step in this direction was taken by Lord Ripon in 1882. He sought to change the basic approach to local self-government. Ripon advocated the extension of local self-government, primarily as an institution of political and popular education. He, therefore, urged for an early establishment of local boards not only in cities and towns but also in rural areas. These boards were to be predominantly elected bodies with non-officials as chairman.

Though the local bodies failed to function democratically, yet they played a significant role in the administration of rural areas during the next eighty years. Lord Ripon's injunction had made one significant omission, namely the establishment of village 'Panchayats' which had existed in Ancient India. Local self-government under him was limited to the district and 'taluka' levels. The idea of the village panchayats was introduced by the Montagu-Chelmsford Reforms in 1919. The fourth and probably the most important factor behind the establishment of local bodies was political. As Indian nationalism began to develop, the British decided to utilize local bodies as a "half-way house", by "Indianizing" them on the one hand, and granting them larger powers and responsibilities on the other. The centre of the administration of primary education was transferred to local bodies soon after the Government of India Act, 1919. In other words, the local bodies represented "Self Government" for the people, and these were entrusted with important tasks for social service, which, among others, included primary education as well.[26]

During the colonial days the association of local bodies, in the administration of primary education, gave wrong priority to certain objectives. The primary aim ought to have been the decentralization of authority or the harnessing of local leadership to the cause of mass education. But neither of these was properly implemented. Decentralization started late and was carried on slowly in a half-hearted manner. Moreover, real decentralization hardly materialized and the wheels turned back to centralized authority. Above all, the British administration maintained a bureaucratic character right to the end – a feature which made it difficult, if not impossible, to build up a non-official or local leadership in primary education.

Incidentally, it may be said that the two other minor aims of associating local bodies with the administration of primary education had "succeeded" fairly well. On the one hand, local bodies had made a large financial contribution to the spread of primary education. The second objective partly fulfilled was political, viz., the transfer of central authority was a method of diverting the public mind from direct political struggle; but this objective has naturally ceased to have any bearing on the problem in independent India.[27]

Further, since during British rule the comparatively small scale and the half-hearted manner in which the experiment of associating local bodies with the administration of primary education seems to have been tried, "taking a bird's eye view of the role of local bodies in the administration of primary education in India, as a whole, during the last hundred years, therefore, one cannot help feeling that the experiment has not had a fair trial".[28]

The problem of creating local bodies for administering primary education in rural areas was hardly taken into account. Attempts to revive village panchayats date back to 1921, but the potential for independent administration of primary education had not been fully exploited anywhere. In other words, the ideal method of harnessing local leadership in the cause of primary education in rural areas is yet to be discovered.

Throughout the last 100 years of British rule, local bodies remained financially poor. The transfer of such a costly responsibility, as that of primary education, ought to have been followed by simultaneously providing sufficiently large resources to enable local bodies to discharge that responsibility; but no such steps were taken. At least liberal grants-in-aid ought to have been given, but even this was not done and government grants have been neither liberal nor given on right principles. Moreover, proper training and guidance that the British officials were expected to give to Indians in the management of local bodies, was not generally available. Therefore, it may be said, without fear of contradiction, that the conditions laid down by Lord Ripon for the successful working of the experiment of local self-government were never fully satisfied in practice, at least in so far as the administration of primary education is concerned.

Finally, history has disproved the view, commonly held in certain quarters, that the cause of primary education has suffered by its association with local bodies and that the one panacea to ensure satisfactory progress is to "centralize" its control in the State Department of Education. It is not our claim that local bodies did not commit any mistakes or that they always rose to the occasion and did their duty efficiently. It is only suggested that to blame local bodies alone or even mainly for the slow progress of primary education is an over-simplification of a very complex problem and that it is not justified by history. The Kher Committee suggested some reforms with a view to improving the efficiency of administration and making the introduction and enforcement of universal, free, compulsory primary education, easier and more fruitful.[29]

Several reasons are advanced in favour of associating local bodies with the administration of primary education. Such association, it is argued, "brings the schools closer to the communities they serve; it harnesses local knowledge, local enthusiasm and local resources to the cause of mass education and furthers it materially; it brings in additional finances to support primary education which is neither possible nor desirable for the state governments to forego and the loss of which would result in giving a great setback to the spread of primary education; it creates a multiple-source-system of finance which works much better in practice than a single-source-system. It leads to decentralization of authority which results in securing greater effectiveness and economy, especially when allied services like public health are decentralized and delegated to local bodies. It is democratic in principle and trains leadership for public administration of local and even higher levels.

Moreover a comparative study of the administration of primary education in the progressive countries of the world shows that the educational legislation of most nations leaves some room for initiative and activity on the part of local bodies. Hence the task of local bodies in the field of education is very important.

In view of these cognate reasons which we generally accept and the widely prevalent practice of progressive nations we feel, that in India also, it would be an advantage to associate local bodies with the administration of primary education in some form or other. Therefore, the Kher Committee felt strongly that the interests of mass education should be the "only criteria" to decide whether authority over primary education should be delegated to local bodies, and if so, to what extent. Emphasizing its importance the committee stipulated, "We are recommending here that local bodies should be associated with the administration of primary education because we believe that such association would further the cause of mass education and bring the goal of universal education nearer.

The Kothari Commission's recommendation was in agreement with the Kher Committee that local authority should be given the right to administer education as a privilege, subject to two conditions - promotion of the cause of education and good administration. This privilege would be withdrawn if either of these conditions is violated.

Education under Local Bodies in the North East

Seventy-eight per cent of the area of the North East region is managed by indigenous, self-governing institutions of the tribals. These traditional village and community based institutions have been retained and legitimized as local institutions for all purposes by most of the state governments.[30]

The valleys and plains of Assam, Manipur and Tripura, however, share the political history and traditions of the mainland. These areas were either princely states or under the direct administration of the British during the pre-independence period. In North-East there is a clear cut division between hills and plains, with the hills having traditional tribal councils and the plains adapting modern panchayat bodies as self-governing institutions with the exception of Arunachal Pradesh. Arunachal Pradesh opted solely for the panchayat system, despite the existence of tribal councils among the 100 odd tribes of the state.

Each group was organized under chiefs who for centuries enjoyed more or less sovereign powers over their territorial jurisdiction. The chief, by virtue of his sheer physical and intellectual powers, was the guardian and defender of his people. Each village had its well-defined territory which was the common property of the whole group. All members of the group had the right to practice shifting cultivation and carry out other livelihood related activities like hunting and fishing within the village territory. That right was socially sanctioned and behind that lay the force of custom.[31]

This mode of living gave rise to strong regulatory systems at the village and community levels in the forms of (i) autocratic chieftainship, and (ii) republican type of village councils.[32] Both had objectives of defending the village and the community against external aggression and managing the common property resources of land and forests, maintaining peace and order in the village.

Chieftainship prevalent among most tribes such as Semas and Konyaks of Nagaland, Kukis of Manipur, Mizos, Lais and Maras of Mizoram, Khasis and to some extent Garos of Meghalaya. The chiefs were at the same time the chief administrators, chief justices, the protectors and the guardians of their communities. However, in running the village administration, the chiefs were assisted and advised by a council of village elders representing different groups, but mainly men of the chiefs' choice, nominated or selected without much consideration for the opinion of the people they represented.

The village council comprised of honest leaders, other important village functionaries like the priests and interpreters presided over by a village chief or traditional village headman. The relationship of the Ahom kings of Assam and Maharajas of Imphal and Barak Valley with the village councils remained cordial.

During British rule (1873), 'inner line' regulation was introduced to regulate the entry of outsiders, partly as a measure to insulate the primitive tribes from the influence of the outside world, and partly to ensure the safety and security of the visitors to the hills. The Government of India Act 1919 classified these areas as 'backward tract' which were wholly or partially excluded from the application of the Acts passed by Central and Provincial legislatures. The Government of India Act, 1935, while retaining the special status of these areas, further sub-classified the hills into two categories :

(i) Wholly excluded areas and;
(ii) Partially excluded areas.

The wholly excluded areas included the North-East frontier districts or present Arunachal Pradesh, Naga hill district or present Nagaland, Lushai hills district or present Mizoram and North Cachar hills district of Assam. The partially excluded areas included the Garo Hills district, Khasi - Jaintiya hills district (present Meghalaya) and Mikir hills district (Karbi Anglong district of Assam). The Governor of the province was entrusted with absolute power to administer these areas. The wholly excluded areas were kept outside the purview of the provincial legislature. In the case of the partially excluded areas, the Central or Provincial Acts could be extended there only with the concurrence of the Provincial Governor. The advice of the Council of Ministers were not binding on the Governor, as he had the power to reject or modify the laws passed by the legislatures with prior approval of the Governor General of India.

In Manipur, after the Treaty of Yanbadu in 1826, the administration of the hill areas was separated from the administration of the valley. In 1891, the administration of the hills was brought directly under the control of the British. Further, in 1916 the British appointed their Resident to oversee the affairs of the Manipur Kingdom. This made the Meitei Maharaja only an ornamental supervisor and the hill areas came directly under the British Resident, assisted by the Assistant Commissioners. In Tripura, however, the Maharaja was himself a tribal and hence the princely state was able to maintain its sway over tribes, living in hilly areas.

The purpose of notifying some areas as wholly and others as partially excluded areas was two-fold. First, it was felt that the stage of development of the inhabitants of interior hills was such that the method of representation and administration prevalent elsewhere was totally alien to these communities. Secondly, the tribal communities, fearing loss of identity and livelihood, wanted protection and freedom to pursue their traditional way of life according to their customary laws and practices.[33]

Some elites among the ethnic groups aided and inspired by colonial rulers, started advocating autonomy in the wake of independence. In this context provision of constitutional safeguards for the administration of tribal hill areas of the North-East was examined and debated by the Constituent Assembly. A sub-committee headed by G. Bordoloi, Chief Minister of Assam, recommended the maintenance of cultural identity for those people where the protection of the communities of the region was necessary, and bringing them into the mainstream of the country.

The areas inhabited by different scheduled tribes within an autonomous district were divided into autonomous regions. The Lushai (Mizo) Hills Autonomous Council was dissolved with the granting of Union Territory status to Mizoram in 1972. However, the Chakma, Mara and Lai Autonomous district Councils in Chimptuipui district of Mizoram continued. Similarly, through the Forty Ninth Constitutional Amendment Act of 1984 an autonomous district council under the Sixth Schedule of the Constitution was constituted covering the tribal areas of Tripura. Thus at present, there are nine autonomous district councils under the Sixth Schedule of the Constitution in the North-Eastern India.

The Naga leaders, dissatisfied with the above mentioned provision of the Sixth Schedule for Naga hill districts did not accept this as they were aspiring for the independence of Nagaland from the Republic of India. The Naga National Council, after a decade long intense insurgency, negotiated the resolution of the Naga problem within the

Constitution of Nagaland and opted for the formation of a separate state of Nagaland in 1963.

The enactment of the 73rd Constitution Amendment in 1993 had already been operating in some parts of North-East India from 1950 – "The need for the establishment of local educational authorities at the district level" was emphasized in Kohan Commission's Report.[34] The 73rd and 74th Amendments to the Constitution constitute a new chapter in the process of democratic decentralization in India. In terms of the Amendments, the responsibility for taking decisions regarding activities at the grassroot level which affect peoples lives directly would rest upon the elected members of the people themselves. The basic function was to develop plans for local needs.[35] What was provided in the Sixth Schedule of the Constitution was, in fact, more than what had been attempted in the 73rd Amendment. While the ethos of the 73rd Amendment is devolution of executive power only, the Sixth Schedule provided autonomy and self-governance in all spheres, which is closer to the spirit of Article 40 of the Constitution, which says that the third tier should be able to function. As Professor Roy Burman pointed out in 1994, a study of the two constitutional provisions would, however, show that while in some matters the autonomous councils have greater scope, in some others the Panchayati Raj under the 73rd Amendment scores over them.

Arunachal Pradesh adopted the Panchayat system in spite of the recommendation of the Dying Ering Committee (1965), for recognizing the traditional village councils as Gram Panchayats. The system, therefore, consists of the *Gram Panchayat* at the village level, *Anchal Samiti* at the block or area level and *Zilla Parishad* at the district level.

Assam presents a spectacle of complexity because of the multiplicity of institutions and their concomitant patterns and provisions, such as, the Panchayati Raj and Autonomous Council, Borad and Autonomous Councils and other institutions. Way back in 1925, under the Government of India Act of 1919, Assam introduced the Panchayati System which since 1984 has been in the forefront of experimenting with panchayat raj with the Acts of 1959, 1972, 1986 and 1994. The 1972 act provided for the creation of the Panchayats at two levels: (i) *Gaon* Panchayat at the cluster level and (ii) *Muhkuma* Parishad at the sub-division level. Unlike other states in Assam, the sub-division (*muhkuma*) has an effective tier of administration. Most of the functions of the district were performed by the sub-divisional officers, who were authorized to communicate directly with the State Government. After 1986, when the three-tier system was introduced, the *muhkuma parishad* retained its position as the apex body, with *anchalik panchayat* (block level) as the intermediate tier, and *gaon* panchayat as the basic unit. After the 73rd Amendment, the Zilla Parishad constituted the apex body, and hence the *muhkuma parishad* was abolished.

Due to prolonged tribal agitation demanding autonomy to preserve their ethnic identities, the two hill districts of Assam - Karbi Anglong and North Cachar hills have been enjoying autonomous status.

There are many tribal groups living in the Brahmaputra valley, possibly from pre-historic times, claiming to be original settlers and now pushed into the fringe areas known as the plain tribes of Assam; among whom the prominent are the Bodo, Lalungs, Rabha - Hasong and Mising. The Boros, numerically the strongest, are concentrated in the Kokrajhar district as well as the districts of Darrang and Sonitpur. The Boros are still struggling for Bora Land, though the Bodo Autonomous Council Act has been passed by Assam Legislative Assembly, under Article 246 of the Constitution, framing autonomy for the social, economic, educational, ethnic and cultural advancement of Boros residing in notified areas. Shortly following this, the year 1995 witnessed a series of accords and legislations for constituting autonomous councils for Lalung, Mising and Rabha - Hasong plains of Assam under the State Act, but with the difference that these tribal councils will not have any specified territory but will have jurisdiction over the entire state. A distinctive feature of this Act is that it provides the formation of village councils for each block of villages which have 50 or more per cent tribal population. The state has to synthesize the provisions of the Sixth Schedule and the 73rd Panchayati Raj Amendment Act by constituting Tribal Autonomous Councils and Village Councils.

Manipur, like Assam has also different forms of local self-government institutions in the valley and the hills. The hills are two tier: (i) Autonomous District Councils at the district level, and (ii) Village Authorities at the village level. In 1955, the Circle authorities were abolished at the circle level. The district councils and village authorities were not mutually inter-related, as in the case of the Sixth Schedule where village authorities came under the direct control of the district councils. In the valley districts, the Panchayati Raj prevails.

The District Councils were introduced in Manipur hills by the Manipur Hill Areas District Council Act 1971 passed by Parliament in 1972. For this purpose the hill areas were divided into six District Councils.

(i) Manipur North
(ii) Manipur South

(iii) Manipur Sadan Hills
(iv) Manipur East
(v) Manipur West and
(vi) Manipur Tenguopal. The DCs consist of 20 members of whom 18 are elected through adult franchise and two nominated by the Governor. They in turn elect a chairman and a vice-chairman from amongst themselves.

The village authorities comprising of the Village Chief as Chairman and elected/ nominated members have been created in all the hill villages of Manipur by extending legal status to the traditional village self-governing institutions under the (Manipur State Hill Peoples Regulation 1947). These village authorities have their linkages with their tribal and hence the village authorities vary from community to community as for example Nagas and Kukis. Unlike the District Councils, the village authorities enjoy much respect among the people and are entrusted with more developmental responsibilities. They are institutions of local self-government.

The two-tier Panchayati Raj system in the three-valley districts account for 10 per cent of the area but 54 per cent of the population. The Panchayati system in Manipur can be traced to the emergence of the Darbar in Manipur in 33 AD - later modified by the British in 1891-92 as a single-tier rural panchayat. This system continued till 1966. After granting statehood to Manipur in 1972, the Manipur Panchayati Act 1975 introduced the three-tier structure of the Panchayats. However, the zilla parishad or the district panchayat was never constituted because of political reasons. In 1994, under the Manipur Panchayat Act, a two-tier system of Zilla Parishads and Village Panchayat were established, abolishing the block level panchayat.

In Meghalaya, a combination of traditional and modern (statutory) self-government institutions at the village, intermediate (cluster) and district levels exist. Under the Sixth Schedule, a measure of autonomy was provided to the three Autonomous District Councils of Khasi, Garos and Jaintias, with a view to provide autonomy to the tribal communities to preserve their own custom and manage their affairs according to tribal customary laws and practices.

Amongst the Garos, the village head is the husband of the traditional heiress of the clan called Nokma. As a custodian and manager of the village land, he wields considerable authority.

The traditional village darbar exists among the Khasis and Jaintias for each village presided over by an elected headman. The headman is helped by a number of executive members nominated by them. There also exists clan councils for the management of clan affairs. As the land belongs to the community and clan (Re-raid and Re-Kynti), the darbars and the clan Councils important role in managing community and clan lands and forests.

At the intermediate (area) level, there were Khasi Kings called Syiems or Sardars who controlled all the village heads and darbars within their jurisdiction. Now these Syiems or Sardars are elected and appointed by the district councils. Though enjoying judicial and executive powers within their jurisdiction, they no longer control village darbars and village heads who are elected and appointed by the district councils. In Garo hills, village courts have been set up at the cluster level presided over by the Laskars who are also appointed by the district councils. The ADCs which functioned like District Governments when Meghalaya was a part of Assam, representing the tribals today have had problems with the result that primary education has been temporarily transferred to the State Government.

Mizoram, the erstwhile Lushai hill district of undivided Assam, was ruled by several local tribal chiefs before the annexation of the state by the British in 1890. The British made chieftainship hereditary to ensure political stability and loyalty of the chiefs to the government. Each Chief or Lal was allotted a certain area to administer. Thus, Chiefs became representatives of the British Government in their own land. They owned all that was in the village. In village administration, he was assisted and advised by a Council of village elders who were men of the chief's choice. The chief was entitled to many privileges from the villagers as a token of respect for being head of the village administration.

Upon the recommendation of the North-East Frontier Tribal and Excluded Area Sub-Committee of the Constituent Assembly, the then Lushai Hills district was incorporated in part 'A' of the Sixth Schedule of the Constitution. The Mizo Union which won the district councils elections in 1953 enacted the Lushai Hills District Act abolishing special privileges of the chiefs. Presently the three autonomous district councils of Mara, Lai and Chakma exist.

The Village Council Acts prescribed democratically elected Village Councils. A village council is headed by a president who is chosen either unanimously or by a majority of the elected members. After 1987, the Village Councils came under the Department of Local Administration. In Chimptuipui district, the Village Councils function under the control and supervision of Mara, Lai and Chakma Autonomous District Councils.

They are endowed with administrative and judicial functions and powers. All the land in the village, excepting homesteads, belong to the village council. Even in urban areas of Mizoram, like Aizawl, there exist village councils.

Nagaland has introduced the innovative model of decentralized participatory rural development in the form of Village Department Boards (VDBs), which is an offshoot of the Village Council. Traditionally, the Nagas were organized into strongly regimented village government consisting of village councils comprising of clan elders or *gaonbura* chosen by consensus. The British found such traditional institutions an effective means of local governance and recognized them by notifying Rules for the Administration of Justice and Police in the Naga Hills District. In 1906, under this Act, the responsibility for settlement of all village disputes was vested with the village council.

After Independence, the Nagaland Traditional Provisions Regulation Act of 1961, provided for the creation of a three-tier tribal councils – consisting of council, range council and the tribal council for each tribe. In 1963, after obtaining statehood, the above Act was modified to retain only two-tier area councils within specific administrative, judicial and political functions.

The Nagaland village and area Council Act 1979 was the first step towards decentralization of rural development. It provided for the constitution of the village councils in all the recognized villages comprising of members chosen by all permanent residents of the village. The hereditary chiefs, Gaonbura and others are ex-officio members of the village council. The village council selects a member as its chairman.

The village council has been given wide ranging administrative, executive and judicial functions and powers. One of its functions was to constitute the Village Department Board (VDB) as the executive wing of the village council. By the Act of 1989 the area councils were abolished and were replaced by range level comprising of area inhabited by specific tribes. The financial soundness of the local body, the VDB is largely because public funds are channelized to the VDBs.

Tripura has two types of local self-government, viz. (i) Panchayati Raj in the non-tribal dominated plains and (ii) Autonomous District Council under the Sixth Schedule in the predominantly tribal hilly areas. The Panchayati Raj system run largely along the lines of the Panchayati Raj of West Bengal in which standing committees constituted at the Panchayati Samiti and Zilla Parishad levels have been given prominent role in planning and implementing rural development programmes. The Deputy Commissioner (District Magistrate in Tripura) is the ex-officio

Chief Executive Officer of the Zilla Parishad and the Additional Chief Executive Officer. District Planning Committees have also been constituted with a Minister in the State Government as Chairman and the District Magistrate/Chief Executive Officer of the Zilla Parishad as Secretary. The State Finance Commission has been constituted after the 73rd Amendment of the Indian Constitution.

The Tripura Tribal Areas Autonomous District Council (TTAADC) was formed in 1985, under the Sixth Schedule, replacing the ADC constituted under the Seventh Schedule in 1982. The ADC consists of 30 members of whom 28 are directly elected and two are nominated by the Governor of the 28 elected members, 24 are STs and 4 non-STs. These members in turn elect one of them, as Chairman of the Council, who also acts as speaker of the Assembly. A Vice Chairman is also elected. There is an Executive Committee of seven members who constitute a kind of Cabinet with one member selected as a leader designated as Chief Executive Member (CEM).

On official order there is one Chief Executive Officer, who is a Senior Grade IAS Officer on deputation from the State Government. Besides, there is one Additional Chief Executive Officer, One Deputy Chief Executive Officer and One Executive Officer, all deputed by the State Government and paid out of ADC funds. The ADC has four zonal development officers, one in each district headquarter and 20 sub-zonal offices, positioned in block headquarters and other central locations, whose main purpose is to implement and co-ordinate developmental activities.

In Arunachal Pradesh, of the 71 items functioning under the gram panchayat, as per the Panchayat Bill of 1994, one is education. Similarly, the *Anchal Samiti* looks after primary and secondary schools, as does Zilla Parishad.[36] Thus, at all the three levels, elementary education is looked after by the local bodies.

In Assam as per the Act of 1986, gram panchayats look after elementary education. The *Anchalik* Panchayat also performs the same function especially at the middle school level. Zilla Parishads assist in district level planning. In the Autonomous District Councils in the hill districts, the district council "may establish, construct and manage primary schools". They also levy taxes for maintenance of schools.[37]

The Manipur hill areas, through the Manipur State Peoples' Regulation of 1947 made the local authorities in-charge of lower and upper primary education.[38] Further, according to the Manipur Village Authorities Act (in Hill Areas) of 1956, the village authorities were to manage government primary schools within the village.

In the Autonomous District Councils, enacted by the Act of 1971, the Chief Executive Officer is responsible for establishing, managing and maintaining primary schools, education being one of the six subjects under the Council. In the 73rd Amendment, the Zilla Parishads have been given more power and hence the ADCs have lost a great deal.

Under the Manipur Panchayat Act of 1975 education at community and adult levels became the responsibility of the gram panchayats and more specifically, the management and administrative control of primary schools became a part of the functions of the Panchayat Samitis.

In Tripura, under the Panchayat Raj Act of 1993, education is looked after by the Panchayat Samiti as well as the Zilla Parishad. Apart from this the Tripura Tribal Areas Autonomous District Council (TTAADC) is a unique system where there are no clear demarcation of villages within and outside the ADCs.

The Panchayat bodies are supposed to promote one hundred per cent enrolment in primary schools, reduce drop-outs from schools, supervise primary schools, high schools and promote a total literacy campaign.

References

1. B.C. Smith, *Decentralization: The Territorial Dimension of the State* (London, George Alen and Unwin, 1985), p. 1.
2. Nasir Ahmad, 'Decentralization - A Case for Administrative Federalism' *Journal of Rural Development and Administration*, Volume XXIII, No.2 (Spring, 1991), p. 26.
3. Iqbal Narain, 'The Idea of Democratic Decentralization' *Indian Journal of Political Science* (April-June, 1960), pp. 184-185.
4. Shriram Maheshwari, *Local Governments in India* (New Delhi: Orient Longman, 1976), p. 29.
5. Rakesh Hooja, *District Planning: Concept, Setting and State Level Applications*, (Jaipur: Aalekh Publishers, 1986), p. 193.
6. Hanumantha M. Rao, 'Decentralised Planning: An Overview of Experience and Prospects', *Man and Development*, Vol. XI, No.3 (September 1989), p. 17.
7. V. Venkata Rao, *A Century of Tribal Politics in North East India 1874-1974* (New Delhi: S. Chand and Company, 1976), p. 186.
8. *Ibid.*, pp. 194-195.
9. *Ibid.*, p. 195.

10. *Ibid.*, p. 196.
11. *Ibid.*, p. 281.
12. *Ibid.*, pp. 281-282.
13. *Ibid.*, p. 282.
14. *Ibid.*, p.284.
15. *Ibid.*, p. 300.
16. *Ibid.*, pp. 301-302.
17. *Ibid.*, p. 308.
18. *Ibid.*, P. 216.
19. *Ibid.*, pp.238-239.
20. *Ibid.*, pp. 238-239.
21. *Ibid.*, p. 244.
22. *Committee on the Relationship between State Governments and Local Bodies in the Administration of Primary Education 1951*, New Delhi, Ministry of Education, 1954, p.7.
23. *Ibid.*, p. 7.
24. *Ibid.*, pp. 7-8.
25. *Ibid.*, p. 8.
26. S. Bhatnagar, *Rural Local Government in India* (New Delhi: Light of Life Publishers, 1978), pp. 23-25.
27. *Ibid.*, p. 36.
28. *Ibid.*, p. 37.
29. The Kher Committee recommended that local bodies should be associated with the administration of primary education. Quoted in D.S. Kothari, *Report of the Eduction Commission and National Development* (New Delhi: 1966), p. 447.
30. B.P. Maithani, ed., *Local Self-Government System in North- East India: An Appraisal* (Hyderabad: NIRD. 1997).
31. S.N. Misra, "Property Rights and the State of Development of North-Eastern Region, Mimeo", 1987 cited in B.P. Maithani, *op. cit.*, pp. 2-3.
32. B.K. Roy Burman, *Towards Poverty Alleviation in Manipur and Nagaland*, (New Delhi: Mithal Publications, 1983).
33. B.N. Bordolai, "Traditional Self-Governing Institutions in Hill Districts of Assam," mimeo in B.P. Maithani, *op. cit.*, p. 6.
34. D.S. Kothari, *Report of the Education Commission – Education and National Development*, *op. cit.*, p. 460.
35. Government of India, MHRD, Deptt. of Education, *CABE Committee on Decentralizatied Management of Education*, New Delhi, p. 2.

36. A.C. Jena, "Local Self-Government Institutions in Arunachal Pradesh" in B.P. Maithani, *op. cit.*, pp. 34-76.
37. Jacob George, "Local Self-Government Institutions in Assam" in B.P. Maithani, *op. cit.*, pp. 105-106.
38 S.C. Srivastava, "Local Self-Government Institutions in Manipur", in B.P. Maithani, *op. cit.*, p. 144.

5

Case Study: Mizoram - A Description of the State

Historical Background

The word Mizoram originates from word "Ram" and "Mizo" which mean land of the Mizos, they are from the nearby states and from Bangladesh. The state is bounded by Bangladesh and Tripura on the west and by Chin Hills of Myanmar (Burma) in the east and south. In the north, Mizoram shares a common boundary with Manipur and the Silchar district of Assam. The state was formerly known as 'Lushai Hills District' of Assam and commanded an important strategic position. It was named "Mizo Hills District" of Assam in 1954. On January 21st, 1972 the Mizo Hills District was separated from Assam and given the status of a Union Territory. In 1987 Mizoram gained its statehood.

There is no record of the early history of the Mizos. Ethnically Mongolian, it is believed that they came from the Chin Hills of Myanmar. According to the folk literature of the Hmars (a sub-tribe of the Mizos), they originally inhabited the Shan Plateau of Myanmar. During the 18th century, the Mizos were dislodged and arrived at their present habitation.

The Mizos constitute a multi-clan ethnic group and replaced the original inhabitants of the area, such as the Hrangkhols, Biates and the Thadous. Their early history is replete with inter-tribal and inter-clan feuds. Among the important Mizo tribes are the Lushai, the Ralte, the Hmar and the Pawis or the Lai. Though each tribe speaks a different dialect, the lingua franca of Mizoram is the dialect of the Lushai sub-tribe. It is written in the Roman script, which was introduced by the missionaries. It is called the "Duhlian".

During British rule, the different Mizo tribes created problems for the British by attacking the tea estate of Alexanderpur in Cachar in 1871-72. Subsequently the British annexed their territory in 1891. They divided the area into two districts namely, North Lushai Hills and South Lushai Hills with Aizawl and Lunglei as their headquarters. By 1898, both these districts were brought under the state of Assam, with the district officer designated as the Superintendent. In 1930, the southernmost part (now Chhimtuipui district), inhabited by the Lakhers, was also brought under this district. The British Superintendent was only the *dejure* administrator while the *defacto* administrator was the 'Lal' or Chieftain whose office was hereditary.[1]

British annexation of Mizoram was followed by the arrival of the Christian missionaries. Apart from propagating their faith these missionaries spread literacy and elementary education. The work of the Serampore Baptist Mission in Assam was followed by efforts made by the American Baptist Mission. The Presbyterians who moved to the Surma valley had a impact on the Mizos. Mr. J.H. Lorrain and F.W. Savidge established the first centre at Aizawl. They translated the Lushai language into the Roman script and started preaching in the local dialect. Boarding schools were next established, and by 1950s, several Mizo girls had also passed out of the nursing schools. The Presbyterian ethos was to impart a work-oriented school education; a feature which exists even today in Mizo school education and teacher's training programmes. Records from the educational experiment (1920-1930's), made by the Baptist Mission in South Lushai Girls' School, reveal that vocational courses, such as, weaving including the processing of cotton from seed; dying; needle work; basket work; simple pottery; baby welfare; infant care including first-aid and invalid cooking; knitting and crochet work; gardening and farming were introduced, in depth, along with other curricular courses. They were related to the tribal environment and economic activity.[2]

In 1935, the Mizos were made to come under the Governor's rule by an Act, and the 'Inner Line' was extended to the area. The post-independence era saw the continuation of the policy. The implementation of the 'Inner Line' had prevented the layout of roads and tracts, which have isolated the Mizos from the mainstream of Indian economic life, allowing for the continuation of a primitive economy based on shifting cultivation. A famine broke out in Mizoram in 1989, when upon the failure of the central and state governments to bring about famine relief, the

Mizo youths under the chairmanship of Laldenga's Famine Relief Front, rendered considerable service by bringing food to the people. As a result of the government neglect and the consequent angry reactions to it, there grew some political consciousness which led to the formation of the Mizo National Front, aiming at achieving independence and a sovereign status for the Mizo Hills.

The original aim of this new political front was to establish a Chin State comprising people of Chin origin living in Manipur, Bangladesh and Myanmar. The front which confined its objective to the attainment of independence of Mizoram did not have an educational policy or agenda.[3] Its military wing now became the Mizo National Army under the command of Lalmunwawia. In 1966, the Mizo National Front rose in an armed rebellion against the Indian government, surrendering in 1987 when Laldenga became the first Chief Minister of the State.

According to 1981 data, the state of Mizoram had an area of 21,108 square kilometres. There are three administrative districts namely, Aizawl, Lunglei and Chhimtuipui and twenty-two educational blocks (circles). In 1986, 571 villages were inhabited by persons. The total population in 1991 was 6,90,000. See Table 5.I.

Table – 5.1

Districts, Educational Blocks, Inhabited Villages and Habitations

			Mizoram	*India*
1	Area in sq. kms.	1981	21087	3287263
2.	No. of Districts	2001	8	593
3.	No. of Educational Blocks	1991	22	7098
4.	No. of Inhabited Villages	1991	699	579148
5.	No. of Villages having Population less than 500	1981	502	270795
6.	No. of Habitation	1991	785	981864
7.	Percentage of Rural Population	2001	50.5	72.2
8.	Population below poverty line	1999-2000	19.47	26.10

Source: A.K. Sinha, Indicators of School Education, Unpublished Draft, NIEPA, 1994.
Directorate of Economics and Statistics, Mozoram at a Glance, 2001.
Ministry of Finance, Govt. of India, Economic Survey, 2001-02.

Physical Setting

The State of Mizoram runs lengthwise from north to south with a narrow width. It consists of six ridges of hills running south to north. The highest peak is the 'Phawngpui' or the 'Blue Mountain'; about 2,165 metres above sea level. The hill regions are separated from each other by streams flowing from the north to the south. Numerous brooks also cut deep gorges at many places. Mizoram also has some lakes such as the Palah situated in the southern part. On the whole, Mizoram has a very pleasant climate. The Tropic of Cancer passes through it and hence the region is neither too hot nor too cold. Between May and September, it witnesses heavy rainfall amounting to 250 cm. Mizoram is known for its numerous trees, plants, bushes, creepers, and grasses. Bamboos grow in abundance. Of late, pine cultivation has begun at Champai. Important forest products are timber, bamboo, cane and 'agar'.

Economy

Agriculture is the mainstay of the Mizos. Shifting or 'jhum' cultivation is still in vogue, though efforts are being made to introduce terrace rice cultivation. Rice, maize, pumpkins, beans, cucumbers, brinjals, chillies, tobacco and cotton are the main agricultural products. Increase in population has, however, led to its decline in self-sufficiency in rice cultivation. Special attention is being paid to the cultivation of fruit products, and food-processing plants have been set up at Variangte and in Lunglei district (MIFCO). Fisheries have been also developed in Aizawl district. However, attempts to develop the state's economy have been thwarted by the shortage of power and water during the dry season. In order to avoid soil erosion cash crops such as coffee, cocoa, rubber, cardamom and cashew have been introduced. Discovery of oil in the southwest can boost the state's economy in the future. Mizoram supplied bamboo pulp to a paper mill in Silchar district (Assam). The Mizos are famous for their handicrafts and consequently there are several rural weaving and carpentry centres. The Khadi and Village Industries Commission is trying to industrialize these units. Among the other minor occupations of Mizos are, blacksmithy, tailoring and knitting. At some places sericulture has also been introduced. In each of the three censuses of 1951, 1961 and 1971 the concept of work was changed. In 1981, a person who has worked for 183 days or six months was considered to be a "main worker" and others as non-workers. Work was defined as participation in any economically productive activity. Such participation could be physical or mental in nature; the worker could be full-time or seasonal. The person who has worked for 183 day but may not be performing one activity only, will still be considered as a main worker. is he/she had worked for 183 days or six months. Secondary or marginal work was applied to those workers who had worked for less than the period of main workers. For example, he/she may have been a cultivator, or an agricultural labour or worked in an industry for only one season, which is less than 6 months. The non-worker is defined as a person occupied in activity not considered economically productive.

The percentage of main workers shows that both in 1971 as well as in 1991, the state had a larger share of cultivators, as compared with the all-India figures. However, the state's percentage of agricultural labourers and workers engaged in household industry is smaller, when compared with the all-India figures. Mizoram's increase in the number of workers engaged in 'other occupations' has been substantial in the past two decades. From 15.78 per cent in 1971 it has risen to 34.14 per cent in 1991, which is above the all-India percentage of 31.47. This factor is significant to understand the demand for education in the state (see Table 5.2). The expansion of the service sector since 1972 has created an increased demand for educated persons, a unique feature throughout the state unlike in the rest of the North-East. Given the stature and desire for education among the Mizos, both government bodies and parents play a participatory role in school education. This is reflected in the provisions of superior infrastructural facilities available even in rural areas, resulting in comparatively low drop out rates at the lower primary stage.

Table 5.2

Percentage of main workers in Cultivation, Agricultural Labour, Household Industry and Other Work to Total main workers for Mizoram and India: 1971 to 1991

Percentage of Categories of Workers to main workers

Categories	*1971*	*1981*	*1991*	*2001*
Cultivators	83 53 (43.08)	70.63 (41.58)	60.89 (38.75)	53.9 (31.1)
Agricultural Labourers	0.37 (26.69)	2.49 (24.94)	3.73 (26.15)	5 9 (26 7)
Household Industry	0.32 (3.57)	0.85 (3.47)	1.25 (3 63)	1 4 (4.1)
Other Workers	15.78 (26.66)	26.03 (30.01)	34.14 (31.47)	38.8 (37.7)

Note: Figures in bracket are for India excludes Assam for 1971 and 1981 and excludes J & K for 1991.

Source: Census of India 1991, Series - 17, Mizoram, Provisional Population Totals.

There is no substantial disparity between the male and female workers except in the category of 'other workers', and which indirectly reveals the status of women workers. While the Mizo women enjoy a comparatively higher egalitarian status than women of other eastern states, their preoccupation with domestic chores and cultivation in farms, keep them away from participating in other forms of labour. Hence no matter the professions, by way of entrepreneurship and service sector, are available – the percentage of women partaking in these is somewhat less than the men (see Table 5.3).

Demographic Characteristics

Mizoram has shown a decline in the growth rate of its population between the years 1981-91. However there exists inter-district disparity in its growth rates. Chhimtuipui district with 50.03 per cent has the highest growth rate followed by Aizawl (39.84) and Lunglei (26.59). The annual potential growth rate is only 3.40 (1981-91). Population density shows thirty-three persons per square kilometres (1991) as compared with only four way back in 1901. The sex ratio in Mizoram was above the national average in 1971 but from 1981 till 1991 it has gone below the national average (921 female to 1000 males, 1991). The percentage of rural population was 53.91 in 1991. The percentage increase in the population of new towns in 1991 was 33.55 per cent. Majority of its population who are Christians (nearly 95 per cent) belong to the Scheduled Tribes (see Table 5.4). The Scheduled Caste population is almost negligible although there exists a small percentage of upper caste Hindu population belonging mainly to Bangladesh, West Bengal, Assam, and other Indian states. The Nepali speaking population is fast decreasing in the state.

Education

Literacy

The phenomenal growth of literacy and elementary education in Mizoram may be explained primarily by socio-economic and political factors operating in the state during the past three decades. Basically an egalitarian society, Mizoram saw the rise in the demand for educated manpower due to the rapid expansion of government jobs since 1972. The economic benefits accruing from education served a political purpose; that employment should be restricted to 'sons of the soil'. This was related also to the insurgency movement, which demanded a state manned by the Mizos and not 'vais' (outsiders). The literacy rates of the three decades of development in the state as given in Table 5.5 indicate this increased demand in literacy.

District-wise progress of literacy rates for the years 1981-1991 is given in Table 5.6. Inter-district variation of literate persons as percentage of the total population shows that Chhimtuipui is performing better than Lunglei in 1991 as compared to 1981 data.

Table 5.3
Percentage of Different Categories of Workers to Total Main Workers for Males and Females Mizoram, 1981 and 1991

Categories of Workers	*Cultivators*			*Agricultural Labourers*			*Working in Household Industries*			*Other Workers*		
	1981	1991	2001	1981	1991	2001	1981	1991	2001	1981	1991	2001
Persons	70.64	60.89	53.9	2.48	3.73	5.9	0.85	1.25	1.4	26.03	34.13	38.8
Males	61.38	52.59	48.8	2.67	3.96	4.9	0.74	1.24	1.2	35.21	42.21	45.1
Females	86.31	73.83	60.5	2.16	3.38	7.1	1.05	1.25	1.7	10.48	21.54	30.8

Source: Census of India 1991, Series - 17 Mizoram, Provisional Population Totals.

Table 5.4
Selected Demographic Indicators

		Mizoram	*India*
1. Population	2001	891	1027015
2. Annual Exponential Growth Rate	1901-2001	2.55	1.95
3. Population Density (Per sq. kms.)	2001	42	324
4. Sex Ratio (per 1000 males)	2001	938	933
5. Percentage of Rural Population	2001	50.5	72.22
6. Percentage of SC Population	1991	0.10	16.33
7. Percentage of ST Population	1991	94.75	8.08

Source: A.K. Sinha, Indicators of School Education, Draft, NIEPA, 1994.
Census of India, 2001.

Table 5.5
Literacy Rates in Mizoram : 1961-1991

Year	*Persons*	*Males*	*Females*	*Gap between male and female literacy*
1961	51.24	62.25	40.34	21.91
1971	62.71	70.15	54.75	15.40
1981	74.26	79.37	68.60	10.77
	(69.90)	(74.77)	(64.53)	(10.24)
1991	81.23	84.06	78.09	5.97

Note 1 Literacy rates for 1961 and 1971 relate to population aged 5 and above. The rates for the year 1981 and 1991 relate to population aged 7 and above in 1981 have shown in bracket.

Note 2. In 1991 census all children below 7 years age have been treated as illiterates. In 1961, 1971 and 1981 censuses all children below age 5 years were treated as illiterates. The population aged 7 and above in 1991 is not based on actual count, but on estimated proportion and is therefore provisional.

Source: Census of India 1991, Series-17. Mizoram, Provisional Population Totals.

Table 5.6
District-wise Break up of Literates as percentage of Total Population

	1981			*1991*		
	Male	*Female*	*Persons*	*Male*	*Female*	*Persons*
Mizoram	66.0	52.6	59.5	54.3	45.7	67.4
Aizawl	69.6	58.4	64.2	53.4	46.6	72.3
Lunglei	65.3	49.0	57.4	55.8	44.3	64.3
Chhimtuipui	47.5	26.4	37 3	58.7	41.3	47.3

Sources: 1. Census of India, 1981, Series-31, Mizoram
2. Census of India, 1991, Series-17, Mizoram.

According to 1991 census the literacy rate for Mizoram is 81.23 per cent with male and female literacy rates being 84.06 per cent and 78.09 per cent respectively. The literacy rate of India was only 52.11 per cent with 63.86 per cent males and 39.42 per cent females. Though in 1991 Kerala registered the highest literacy rate of 90.59 per cent, among all the Indian states and Union Territories, Mizoram which had ranked 3rd in 1981 came up to the second position. Further the gap between the male and female literacy is also the least in Mizoram (5.97 per cent) followed by Meghalaya (6.75 per cent points) and Kerala (7.52 per cent points). This was despite the fact that Mizo tribes are both patriarchal and patrilineal. An interesting observation made by a traveller to Mizoram was, that, "There exists a primary school besides every church".[4] Though the majority of primary schools are run by the government or fall into the category of those receiving grant-in-aid.

Table 5.6.1
District-wise Literacy Rates, Mizoram

	2001			*1991*		
	Total	*Male*	*Female*	*Total*	*Male*	*Female*
Mizoram	88.49	90.69	86.13	82.27	85.61	78.6
Mamit	80.09	84.04	75.66	67.98	73.61	61.56
Kolasib	90.49	91.5	89.37	86.24	89.12	83.07
Aizawl	96.64	97.2	96.06	93.14	94.17	92.01
Champhai	91.88	94	89.64	87.98	91.76	84.11
Serchhip	96.16	97.24	95.02	90.44	92.82	87.94
Lunglei	84.2	87.36	80 74	77.73	82.37	72.58
Lawngtlai	56.45	65.13	46.68	42.71	51.3	32.79
Saiha	82.43	86.28	78.39	79.24	84.98	73.06

Sources: 1. Census of India, 2001
2. Census of India, 1991, Series-17, Mizoram.

The close relationship between the church and the school is apparent in the assemblies held on Sundays and week days which both teachers and students attend specially the Sunday service. This link between religion and education is not only unique, but also cuts across political parities in Mizoram.

Characteristics of Elementary Education

According to the Sixth All India Educational Survey data as furnished by the Directorate of School Education, Government of Mizoram, 1993, there existed 667 rural habitations out of which 586 had primary schools within their habitations. Three hundred and sixty rural habitations had upper primary schools, whereas only 151 of this habitation were provided with secondary schools. Higher secondary schools are almost negligible in the state, and hence only 3 habitations have those provisions within their habitation (as on 30th September 1993). However what is common is the existence of school complexes in the state.

According to Ministry of Human Resource Development, Annual Report, 1994-95[5], there existed 1082 primary; 609 middle; 294 high school/ higher secondary/ intermediate/pre-degree/junior colleges; 16 colleges for general education and one institution of professional education and no universities. However, the North Eastern Hill University (NEHU) has a campus at Aizawl. The enrolment ratio in both Classes I-V and Classes

VI-VIII of schools for general education, indicate a higher ratio for the state when compared with the all-India average. See Table 5.7.

Table 5.7

Enrolment Ratio in Classes I-V and VI-VIII of Schools for General Education : Mizoram and India, 1994-95 and 2001-02

		Mizoram		*India*	
		1994-95	*2001-02*	*1994-95*	*2001-02*
Classes I-V (6-11 years)	Boys	138.6	132.14	115.3	105.29
	Girls	132.3	106.67	92.9	86.91
	Total	135.6	119.07	104.5	96.30
Classes VI-VIII (11-14 years)	Boys	111.7	81.45	79.3	67.77
	Girls	103.2	78.45	55.2	52.09
	Total	107.5	79.95	67.7	60.20

Source: Annual Report, Ministry of Human Resource Development 1994-95.

The completion rates of five years of schooling in Mizoram when compared with other northeastern states show a relatively higher level of achievement. This is also true with the all-India average which was 63.45 for boys and 43.88 for girls (see Table 5.8 for details).

Table 5.8

Completion Rates of Schooling at the Primary Level in the North East

State	*Completion Rates of Five Years of Schooling (in %), 1991-92*	
	Primary Level	
	Boys	Girls
Arunachal Pradesh	84.90	33.55
Manipur	-	-
Meghalaya	29.23	19.27
Mizoram	67.13	64.22
Nagaland	-	-
Sikkim	32.59	30.44
Tripura	44.41	44.88

Source: Sinha, A.K. Indicators of School Education, Unpublished Draft, NIEPA, 1994.

District-wise data on educational facilities shows that Aizawl has the highest average density of educational facilities, followed by Chhimtuipui and Lunglei. Chhimtuipui's progress at the primary stage is largely attributed to the process of decentralisation started in 1972 in which the three Autonomous District Councils namely, Lai, Mara and

Chakma had initiatives in providing these facilities. For elementary schooling facilities per sq. km. see Table 5.9.

Table 5.9
Elementary Schooling Facilities per sq. km; in Mizoram, 1993

Districts	*Primary School*	*Middle School*
Aizawl	19.57	30.33
Lunglei	25.48	47.74
Chhimtuipui	16.35	38.04

Source: Mizoram School Statistics, Directorate of School Education, Aizawl, 1993.

Teachers' Training

It may be mentioned here that besides the two District Institutes of Education and Training (DIETs) situated at Aizawl and Lunglei, teacher training is offered in different teacher training colleges. Though Chhimtuipui has no training facilities, their teachers are sent for training to other districts by Autonomous District Councils.

Table 5.10
Number of Teachers, Percentage Trained and Teacher Pupil Ratio as on 30th September, 1993

Stage	*Number of Teachers*						*Percentage Trained*		*Teacher Pupil Ratio*	
	Male		*Female*		*Total*					
	1993	*2001*	*1993*	*2001*	*1993*	*2001*	*1993*	*2001*	*1993*	*2001*
Hr. Sec./Jr. College	48	271	12	214	60	485	26	38	16	19
High School	1477	2190	362	663	1839	2853	88	64	11	15
Middle School	2932	4048	806	1699	3738	5747	75	80	15	9
Primary School	2034	2715	1810	2714	3844	5429	48	82	30	21

Source: Selected Education Statistics, Department of Education, Ministry of Human Resource Development, New Delhi, 1993-94.

The positive effects of decentralised planning and management can be more clearly seen in the efforts made to train primary school teachers by the Autonomous District Councils from the sub-divisional data in Table 5.11.

Table 5.11

Sub-division-wise Number of Teachers by Sex in Mizoram

Name of Sub-division	Total Teachers Teachers	% of Female	Trained Male	Trained Female	Teacher Total
1. Aizawl East	1177	52.76	451	515	966
2. Aizawl West	839	57.09	353	479	832
3. Champhai	358	37.08	202	126	328
4. Kolasib	400	47.17	166	131	297
5. Lunglei	630	43.17	334	265	599
6. Lai Dist. Council	271	41.70	112	87	199
7. Mara Dist. Council	254	35.04	138	60	198
8. Chakma Dist. Council	114	12.28	5	1	6

Source: Mizoram School Statistics, Directorate of School Education, Aizawl, 1993.

Structure and Administration of School Education

The structure of education in the state is the 10+2 system. At present the entry point is generally at the Class I stage, although some Anganwadi centres and private nursery schools exist. Upon the completion of Lower Primary Stage (i.e., class IV) the students are required to sit for a Board Examination. So far there existed only the Mizoram Board of School Examination, however the Lai Board of School Education started conducting their own examinations from 1995. The Upper Primary stage which consists of Classes V to VII terminates in the "Middle School Leaving Certificate" when meritorious students are able to receive scholarships for high school education. Efforts are now being made to introduce the plus-two-stage in selected High Schools in the state. However, at present the post-high school education; (upon the successful completion of High School Leaving Examination), is given in the form of pre-university degrees in intermediate and other colleges.

At the secretariat level, the Secretary of Education and Human Resource Development, look after the education for the state under the Ministry of Education. He is assisted by one Deputy Secretary and two Under Secretaries. At the Directorate level, Director School Education is the person in-charge of elementary, secondary, higher secondary, teacher education, adult education, promotion of science education, Hindi Education, State Council of Educational Research and Training and pre-matric scholarships. He is assisted by four Joint Directors who look after Secondary, Elementary, Adult Education and the State Council of Educational Research and Training (SCERT). These Joint Directors are assisted by seven Deputy Directors.

At the district level in 1995 there were four District Education Officers looking after Aizawl East; Aizawl West; Lunglei and Chhimtuipui districts in 1995. There also existed an Assistant District Education Officer to look after non-government schools. At the sub-divisional level, there were 7 officers looking after elementary education. These officers are assisted by 27 Circle Education Officers. The three Autonomous District Councils of Chhimtuipui namely, the Lai, Mara and Chakma look after primary education in their areas. Details of the powers and functions of these District Councils have already been discussed in the previous chapter.

Financing of Primary Education

The approved outlay for Eighth Five Year Plan (1992-97) showed that Mizoram had Rs.23.02 crores for primary education out a total of Rs.45.35 crores for total education. The percentage of the budget of the Education Department to Net Domestic Product for the years 1990-91 was as much as 14.0 for Mizoram, as compared with 3.8 for all-India (1992-93). As stated in the Annual Plan 1995-96 the main strategies adopted in Mizoram are Universal Elementary Education, eradication of illiteracy and bringing forth an uniform and high standard of need-based education including vocational education. Schemes like Operation Blackboard, Science Education, Teachers' Training, Integrated Education of Disabled Children were also given importance in the state.

Chhimtuipui District

Chhimtuipui or the "South Sea" is located in the extreme south of Mizoram state bordering with Myanmar and Bangladesh. Though an economically backward district, it is no longer lagging behind in the development of its elementary education. To a large extent its progress between 1971 and 1991 can be attributed to the role played by its Autonomous District Councils, particularly, the exemplary role of Lai Autonomous District Council. More so since the population of the Lai Autonomous District Council consists of several linguistic groups, such as, the Lai, Mizo, Mara, Chakma, Bru and Riang.

The Fifth All India Educational Survey data reveals that Chhimtuipui had 192 rural habitations with an estimated 63683 population. Though this report refers to Lawngtlai as a semi-urban settlement, in view of its fast growth, yet 1991 census mentions to it as a village. This is because the district is lagging far behind in urbanization. Thus, the only municipality area in the district is Saiha, its administrative headquarter. Chhimtuipui had six educational circles. It had 823 rural schools and 182 urban schools making a total of 1005 primary schools. For the upper primary stage it had 369 rural and 88 urban schools making a total of 457.

As much as 89.58 per cent of the rural habitations are served by lower primary schools within the habitation and 97.70 per cent within one kilometre. The rural habitation served by upper primary schools within the habitation is 59.77 per cent whereas 69.42 per cent of the rural population have these facilities within the distance of three kilometers.

The significant feature of this district is that there is no schedule caste student enrolled in government schools for Classes I to V. This along with other statistical data go to show that the "vais" (outsiders to state population) either send their children to Aizawl and Lunglei districts for education or are enrolled in private institutions.

The girl's enrolment in Classes I to V was 43.30 percent. The gross enrolment ratio for Classes I to V was 99.55 for the district. The age specific (6-11 years) enrolment ratio for the district 55.36 (boys) and 48.65 (girls) out of a total of 52.05. The total enrolment of girls in Classes VI to VIII was 45.96 per cent according to the same report. The age specific (11 to below 14 years) enrolment ratio is 54.0 (boys) and 42.30 (girls) out of a total of 48.34 in 1995.

There were only 52 single teacher schools located in farflung areas. All lower primary schools have Assam type buildings with tin roofs, bamboo or brick walls. Efforts are now being made to construct pucca buildings. There is not a single lower primary school without a classroom.

Table 5.12
Subdivision-wise Enrolment in Primary Schools by Management, 1993

Name of Sub-division or Dist. Council	*Government*			*Aided*			*Private*			
	Boys	*Girls*	*Total*	*Boys*	*Girls*	*Total*	*Boys*	*Girls*	*Total*	
Aizawl East	13197	12723	25920	-	-	-	864	743	1607	48.92
Aizawl West	9649	9064	18713							48.44
Champhai	5804	5384	11188	-	-	-	-	-	-	48.12
Kolasib	4629	4129	8758	-	-	-	928	878	1806	47.40
Lunglei	6760	6243	13003							48.01
Lai Dist. Council	2701	2493	5194	495	268	.763	-	-	-	46.35
Mara Dist. Council	3409	3218	6627	444	412	856	-	-	-	48.51
Chakma Dist.	341	178	519	1619	704	2323	!25	49	174	30.87
Grand Total	46490	43432	89922	2558	1384	3942	1917	1670	3587	47.70

Source: Mizoram School Statistics, Statistical Wing, Directorate of School Education, Mizoram, Aizawl, 1993.

Moreover only 20 per cent of these have one room, the general pattern being one/two rooms or a hall partitioned by bamboo matting to accommodate different classes.

The enrolment pattern of Chhimtuipui indicates that the majority of primary school students are enrolled in government and aided schools except in the Chakma Autonomous District Council where the Chakma community and Christian missionaries have started many private schools. The percentage of girls enrolled in this Autonomous District Council is only 30.87 as compared to other subdivisions (See Table 5.12 for details).

The number of primary trained teachers in government schools in the same District is very few when compared with the other two districts. For the Upper Primary level, there were no trained teachers in the Chakma Autonomous District (1993 data) (see Tables 5.13 and 5.14 for details). Enrolment data for the Upper Primary stage shows that as compared to the Lower Primary stage, more students have been enrolled in private schools (1993). It is important to mention here that the management of Upper Primary schools has been handed over only as late as 1994 to the District Councils and hence no quality improvement could be made in government or aided schools for this level which would attract student enrolment. For details (see Table 5.15).

The administrative headquarters of the district is located at Saiha, which is also the headquarter of the Mara Autonomous District Council. The other sub-divisional headquarters are at Lawngtlai and Chawngte (now Kamlanagar) (see map for details). The District Education Officer located at Saiha looks after the administration of the whole revenue district assisted by two sub-divisional education officers. Since 1975 the administration of lower primary schools were looked after by the education officers of the three District Councils. However, since 1994-95 these officers have also inspected and supervise upper primary education.

Among the numerous languages taught in the district (i.e., Lai, Mara, Chakma) the medium of instruction is Mizo (state language) for the Lai and Mara Autonomous District Councils and Bengali for Chakma Autonomous District Council.

Lawngtlai - The Study Sample

Lawngtlai, which is inhabited by "Lai people", also has Mizo, Chakma, Mara, Bru and Riang tribes and a small percentage of population belonging to other Indian states employed in Central and State government services. It is the centre of trade between Chhimtuipui district and Myanmar, Bangladesh and Mizoram. The first-settlers of Lawngtlai may have come from Sangru village to the present site but no historical

Table 5.13
Subdivision-wise Teachers in Primary Schools by Management, Training and Sex-wise

Name of Subdivision or Dist.Council	Government Trained Teachers			Aided Trained Teachers			Private Trained Teachers			Total Teacher
	Male	Female	Total	Male	Female	Total	Male	Female	Total	
Aizawl East	447	509	956	-	-	-	4	6	10	117
Aizawl West	353	479	832	-	-	-	-	-	-	839
Champhai	202	126	328	-	-	-	-	-	-	358
Kolasib	164	130	294	-	-	-	2	1	3	400
Lunglei	334	265	599	-	-	-	-	-	-	630
Lai Dist Council	110	86	196	2	1	3	-	-	-	271
Mara Dist Council	124	55	179	14	5	19	-	-	-	254
Chakma Dist. Council	5	1	6	-	-	-	-	-	-	114
Grand Total	1739	1651	3390	16	6	22	6	7	13	4043

Source: Mizoram School Statistics, Statistical Wing, Directorate of School Education Mizoram, Aizawl, 1993.

Table 5.14

Subdivision-wise Enrolment in Middle Schools by Management

Name of Sub-division	*Government Trainded Teachers*			*Aided Trained Teachers*			*Private Trained Teachers*			*Total*		
	Male	*Female*	*Total*	*Male*	*Female*	*Total*	*Male*	*Female*	*Total*	*Male*	*Female*	*Total*
Aizawl East	3826	3553	7381	2038	1983	4021	362	288	650	6228	5824	12052
Aizawl West	3483	3218	6701	1392	1593	2985	397	251	648	5272	5062	10334
Champhai	1078	1016	2094	1359	1256	2615	79	71	150	2516	2343	4859
Kolasib	1255	1188	2443	937	861	1798	305	302	607	2497	2351	4848
Lunglei	1684	1457	3141	1531	1359	2890	-	-	-	3215	2816	6031
Lawngtlai	531	393	924	705	588	1293	759	514	1273	1995	1495	3490
Saiha	447	428	875	530	471	1004	124	95	219	1101	994	2095
Grand Total	12306	11253	23559	8492	8111	16603	2026	1521	3547	22824	20885	43709

Source: Mizoram School Statistics, Statistical Wing. Directorate of School Education, Mizoram, Aizawl, 1993.

Table 5.15

Subdivision-wise Training of Middle School Teachers by Management and Sex

Name of Sub-division	Government			Aided			Private		
	Total Tch.	Trained Tch.		Total Tch.	Trained Tch.		Total Tch.	Trained Tch.	
		M.	F.		M.	F.		M.	F.
Aizawl East	484	344	108	404	2 09	78	65	6	3
Aizawl West	442	334	88	257	152	49	74	12	4
Champhai	149	103	29	245	139	35	20	-	-
Kolasib	181	142	27	181	73	22	42	-	-
Lunglei	266	198	45	341	180	52	-	-	-
Lawngtlai	71	57	10	138	100	8	125	-	-
Saiha	86	78	4	160	115	12	13	1	-
Grand Total	1679	1256	311	1726	968	256	339	19	7

Source: Mizoram School Statistics, Statistical Wing, Directorate of School Education, Mizoram, Aizawl, 1993.

record is available to specify the exact place of their settlement.[6] The tribe commonly known as "China" in Chin Hills of Myanmar speak the Lai dialect. It has been said that Chief of Lawngtlai was a vassal of foreign warlords and in 1899 Captain John Shakespear had found the "Lai" (then Pawi) people engaged in cultivation and not hostile.[7] Most of them speak Mizo as well as "Lai" but fear that if they will be "assimilated" into the majority Mizo culture, and lose their cultural identity.[8] According to 1991 census Lawngtlai had a population of 29,098 of which 15,475 were males and 13,623 females. The percentage of total workers were 53.31 (56.85 males and 49.30 females).

The percentage of main workers were 50.20 (54.78 males and 45.00 females). The marginal workers were as little as 3.11 (2.07 males and 4.30 females). Out of total 14,607 main workers (8,476 males and 6,131 females) the percentage of cultivators was 76.46 (65.85 males and 91.14 females). Agricultural labourers constitute only 3.01 per cent (2.78 male and 3.33 female). Nobody is engaged in household industry, which is a unique feature of the village where urbanization has been considerable. However, 20.53 percentage fall into the category of 'other workers' (31.37 males and 5.53 females'. This percentage is above that other rural development blocks in the district except for Saiha town, the Chhimtuipui district headquarters. Lawngtlai, therefore, has all the characteristics of a semi-urban town with people engaged in trade and commerce and have a large per cent of contractors.

Situated on the top of two hillocks at a distance of 317 kilometres from Aizawl, the nearest railway station is Silchar in Assam at a distance of 503 kilometres[9]. In the southern part of the town, a number of Assam type houses are situated in the slopes of these hillocks, which are a part of the Mizo hill ranges. The softness of the rock accounts for various problems faced by the people, like landslides, soil erosion and scarcity of water. During the dry season water is distributed to people in trucks and despite efforts made by the public health engineering department to construct pipes, two-thirds of its population still depend upon water supply from springs. River "Tuipui" (Kolodyne) flows nearby and the highest mountain peak in Mizoram, Phawngpui Tlang (Blue Mountains) situated at a distance is visible during clear days.

Difficulties of transport and communication have been partly solved by the construction of National Highway 54, which connects the town with Lunglei and Saiha. However, most commodities used daily have to be transported from a distance and cost twice as much.

Yet there is no semblance of poverty as can be seen in parts of Assam, Tripura and Manipur. The Lai people who are well known for their hard work make the best of their disadvantaged circumstances. It is felt that proper supply of electricity and drinking water would boost the already thriving commercial activity in the town as well as increase agricultural production. The change in the pattern of shifting cultivation to wet terrace cultivation is already taking place and cash crops like coffee, rubber and ginger are being introduced. Recently effort has been made to start mining. These initiatives, taken by the local people to develop the economy of the district, are some of the positive features that strike a visitor.

Equally impressive are the literacy rates and quality of primary schools. In 1961 the literacy percentage was only 42.4 which rose to 61.7 in 1981. The re-study report published in 1988 shows 79.4 per cent literacy with female literacy as high as 73.7 per cent[10]. Whereas there were only three primary schools in 1961 the figure had risen to 104 in 1995. Of these 76 are government primary and 28 aided. The number of primary school teachers are 343 (207 males and 136 females). Data from the years 1991-93 shows a 4 per cent increase in enrolment in lower primary schools and a 41percentage increase in their trained teachers. The 63 per cent increase in trained female teachers is an indication of the efforts being made by the education authorities in the Lai Autonomous District Council to upgrade the quality of primary school teaching. Despite being situated in a remote and backward area Lawngtlai has substantial amount of qualified and trained primary school teachers which has enhanced enrolment in government primary schools (see Table 5.16).

Table 5.16

Qualification of Government Primary School Teachers, 1992

No of Teachers			*Matriculates*			*Trained Teachers*		
M	F	T	M	F	T	M	F	T
134	92	225	52	37	89	115	85	200

Source: Lai Autonomous District Council, 1992.

In addition, there are 50 teachers (26 males and 24 females) in aided primary schools. The salaries of above mentioned teachers are paid out of the District Council Funds. Moreover, there exist ten teachers out of the O.B. scheme, two Resource Teachers, five officiating teachers and 60 additional teachers. This increase in staff strength has reduced the teacher pupil ratio from 22.1 in 1991 to 17.1 in 1993. In 1992 there were 6427 students enrolled in the 100 government and aided primary schools out of which there were 3529 boys and 2898 girls.

The priority given to primary education both by Mizoram state and the Lai District Council is evident from the Annual Plan allocations of 1994-95 and 1995-96. According to plan Budget 1994-95, Lai Autonomous District Council has sanctioned Rs.56.30 lakhs for education. It provided for one Controller of Examinations and one Accountant and maintenance of teachers. Rs.37.06 lakhs were provided for primary education though only Rs. 0.30 and 18.94 for adult and middle schools respectively.[11] For the current year 1995-96, a sanction of Rs.477 lakhs (plan) and Rs.400 lakhs (non-plan) has been made towards the different expenses of the Lai Autonomous District Council. Out of sanction for the social sector education has been allotted as much as Rs.68.30 lakhs plan and Rs.220.00 lakhs non-plan expenditure making a total of Rs.288.30 lakhs more than any other item of expenditure in its budget. The breakup of expenditure for the education sector given below shows that teachers' salaries constitute the priority area.

Table 5.17

Lai Autonomous District Council Education Budget 1995-96

Education Grants-in-Aid (in Lakhs of Rupees)

1	*Salary*	*Plan*	*Non-Plan*	*Total*
(a)	Pay	16.00	100.00	116.00
(b)	D.A.	20.00	92.00	112.00
(c)	Other Allowances	9.30	25.00	34.30
	Total Salary	45.30	217.00	262.30
2	Wages	9.00	-	9.00
3	Travelling Expenses	1.00	-	1.00
4	Building	4.00	-	4.00
5	Qualitative Improvement	5.00	-	5.00
6	Textbooks	3.00	-	3.00
7	Other Charges	1.00	3.00	4.00
	Total	68.30	220.00	288.30
	Total LADC Budget	477.00	400.00	877.00

Source: Lai Autonomous District Council, Office of the District Council Affairs, Aizawl, 1995.

The Draft Annual Plan of the Lai Autonomous District Council 1995-96 has demanded this increase in its educational expenditure in view of expenses being incurred not only for the Primary School Teachers but also since it will now have to provide salaries for the middle school teachers. This is above the additional costs of building and furniture.

The importance attached to primary schools by District Council authorities reflects their keenness to impart quality education and develop Lawngtlai along state norms.

References

1. Jayashree Roy Jalali, "Universalization of Elementary Education: A Case Study of the Mizoram" NIEPA, UNESCO Sponsored National Workshop on Universal Primary Education, Disadvantaged Areas, *Report*, New Delhi, NIEPA, 1988.
2. Jayashree Roy Jalali, "An Approach to the Development of the Educational Plan for North Eastern Region" NIEPA, Mimeo, 1995.
3. Interview with Mr. Zoranthanga, Chairman, Mizo National Front, now the Chief Minister of the State, Aizawl, September, 1993.
4. In an interview with N. Somorendro Singh, Ph.D. Research Student, JNU, New Delhi, Aizawl, 1995.
5. Government of India, Ministry of Human Resource Development, Department of Education, *Annual Report 1994-95*, New Delhi, 1995.
6. Interviews with C. Thanghluna, Chief Executive Member, Lai Autonomous District Council, Lawngtlai, May, 1995.
7. Census of India 1981, Part XC, Series 31, Mizoram, Survey Report on Restudy of Village Lawngtlai, p. 5.
8. Interviews with B. Rualchhinga, Executive Member, In-charge of Education, Lai Autonomous District Council, Lawngtlai, May 1995.
9. Census of India, 1981, Series-31, Mizoram, District Census Handbook; Chhimtuipui District.
10. Survey Report on Re-study of Village Lawngtlai, *op. cit.*
11. Government of Mizoram, Annual Plan 1994-95, Planning and Programme Implementation Department, Aizawl.

6

Quality of Lower Primary Schools in LADC in Mizoram

All the sample lower primary schools have semi-pucca buildings, consisting of walls made from either bricks or bamboo mats with tinned roofing. Eighty per cent have two class rooms, whereas only twenty per cent have a large hall partitioned into four class rooms with bamboo mats or bricks. Every school has a Head Teacher's room which is shared by other staff members. Sixty per cent have their own playgrounds, although the remaining forty per cent share this facility with a middle and high school, situated within the school complex. Though school buildings are fitted with electric wires, yet the acute shortage of electric supply during the day time, made the respondents give me a 'negative' picture of the situation. It may be mentioned here that electricity is generally available between 5-12 p.m. on most days. The classes, however, function with kerosene lanterns when required.

The schools have a make-shift toilet arrangements which consists of tin or bamboo walls with mud holes dug as pits; a mat curtain is hung on its entrance. Such temporary toilets are constructed outside the school and are used both by staff and students (boys and girls). It may be mentioned here that no modern type toilet consisting of seats and flush, is available in these rural primary schools. The ten per cent response on toilet facilities in the questionnaire was with reference to a modern toilet. Drinking water has to be fetched from nearby wells. Despite the existence of pipelines, the area has acute shortage of running water, specially in the dry seasons when water is supplied by trucks,

Table 6.1
Physical Facilities provided by Lai Autonomous District Council

S.No.	*Facilities*	*Percentage of Schools*
1.	Semi pucca buildings	100
2.	School having 2-3 rooms	100
3.	Electricity during school hours	0
4.	Toilet	10
5.	Drinking water	20
6.	Separate playground	60
7.	Desks	100
8.	Benches	100
9.	Staff furniture	100
10.	Cupboards	60
11.	Racks	50
12.	Brooms	100

Source: School Questionnaire.

was observed by the project team. The twenty per cent schools which have drinking water are located near tubewells, water is fetched in steel buckets and stored during schools hours. The schools often have to get water from nearby springs, and from the children's and teachers' homes or depend on the supply from trucks.

Though the electricity, drinking water and toilets are lacking in the sample schools, reflecting the general pattern of facilities available in rural schools in the district, other items such as furniture, desks, benches, staff furniture consisting of tables, chairs, cupboards and racks are sufficiently provided by the district authority. Thus, every class room in the school visited by the investigator consisted of a head teacher's desk and chair and one or two long desks with chairs for other staff members. There were also sufficient number of desks accompanied by benches for the students. No student sits on a mat to do his/her studies, like in some other rural Indian schools. The superior infrastructural facilities provided by the district councils make the teaching-learning situation comfortable. The brooms provided are generally used by both teachers and students to clean their buildings before the first period. A school day hence begins with all the children, accompanied by class teachers, sweeping floors and dusting furniture. This exemplary practice inculcates a sense of hygiene but more important a sense of pride and belonging to the school.

The physical facilities which have been provided by district council authorities has come about because of a sense of affinity which the people have towards their school and a desire to improve what "belongs" to them.

Academic Inputs

Though the provision of physical facilities is the sole responsibility of the district authorities, the academic inputs have been shared by both state and district authorities with some help from the parents of the students or local community. Table 6.2 gives details on the provision of academic facilities by the state government, district authorities and community.

Table 6.2
Provision of Academic Facilities

S.No.	*Facilities*	*Percentage of Schools Provided by*		
		State Govt.	*LADC*	*Parents*
1	Text Books	-	50	50
2	Stationary	-	100	-
3	Blackboards	-	100	-
4	Chalks	-	100	-
5	Dusters	-	100	-
6	Maps	-	100	-
7	Charts	-	100	-
8	Globes	-	100	-
9	Science Kits	90	10	-
10	Radio	60	40	-
11	Reference Books	-	-	40
12	Musical Instruments	-	10	10
13	Physical Education Equipments	-	10	-
14	Teacher Guides	-	-	-

Source: School Questionnaires.

An analysis of the school data reveals that both parents and district authorities share the responsibility of providing textbooks to students (fifty per cent by parents and fifty per cent by LADC). It has been repeatedly pointed out by the Headmasters, when interviewed, that "all students require free distribution of textbooks". So far the LADC supplies free textbooks to the economically disadvantaged students. At an interview held with the Education Officer of the Lai Autonomous District Council, revealed that the district authorities "supply textbooks to schools after making an assessment of their needs". The paucity of district council funds does not allow them to provide every child with free textbooks. The Education Officer, as well as the members of the Lai Board of Primary Education, felt that the community did not come forward to supply textbooks, stationary or mid-day meals and other incentives as they, perhaps, felt that the sole responsibility of providing such facilities rested with state government or the district authorities. This was despite their identification with the school as a part of their community. Hence the urgent need to hold parent-teacher meetings.[1]

Most of the other academic facilities like stationary, blackboards, chalks, dusters, maps, charts, globes are provided by the district council authorities (See Table 6.2). Only ten per cent of Science Kits was provided by the council, the remaining ninety per cent was given by the state government. Similarly, other facilities such as radios were provided by the state government (which was sixty per cent), while forty per cent was given by the Council in the sample schools. Forty per cent of the reference books for the sample schools were provided by the parents, and ten per cent of physical education requirements by the council. The musical instruments are shared, ten per cent provided by the council and 10 per cent by the parents in the sample schools. It may be mentioned here that though music is a compulsory subject in the primary schools, most students sang only songs like hymns, and did not learn musical instruments because of their non-availability.

Teaching Staff

There has been a total of thirty-five per cent increase in the trained staff strength between the years 1991 and 1995 in the sample school. Out of this, the percentage increase of trained female teachers has been sixty-three per cent. All the teachers have a High School Learning Certificate and eighty-five per cent of the sample school teachers also posses a Certificate/Diploma or Degree in Teachers' Training from Teachers Training Colleges/Institutes, situated either at Aizawl or Lunglei districts. The district council authorities feel an acute need of having a teachers' training college in their district so that they are able to send more of their teachers for in-service training in the future. The Council authorities expressed this desire by stressing that "funds for the establishment of a Teachers' Training cum Research Institute had to be allotted to the District Authorities".[2]

About seventy per cent of the primary schools have five to six teachers per school including the Head Teacher. Thirty per cent of these sample schools have between 6 and 7 teachers which allows for subject specialization even at the primary level - a feature unique in rural Indian schools (See Table 6.3 for details).

The Mizo Language is taught by one single teacher "TS" for all the classes and sections. Similarly, English is restricted to teacher "NG" for

Table 6.3
Staff Strength in Sample Schools, 1995

S.No.	*Number of Teachers*	*Number of Schools*
1	Less than 5	0
2	Between 5-6	7
3	Between 6-7	3
4	More than 7	0
	Total	10

Source: School Questionnaire.

Classes III and IV, Lai Careel in Lai language is taught by teacher "D" in Classes II and III. Thus, the increase in staff strength has added to specialised language teaching at this level of school education. The science subject is taught by teacher "S", only in that school, for Classes II, III and IV. Specialized teaching has no doubt improved the quality of teaching at the lower primary schools, thereby having a positive effect on the pupils' achievement. For example, about seventy per cent of the children successfully complete their lower primary schooling and continue with middle school which is above the State average which was sixty-eight per cent for the same year (1994-95).

Table 6.4
Use of Teaching Aids

Sl. No.	*Lists of Aids*	*Percentage Use by Teachers*
1	Text Books	100
2	Black Boards	100
3	Maps	100
4	Charts	90
5	Globes	90
6	Science Kits	80
7	Reference Books	40
8	Musical Instruments	10*

*N.B. There are very few musical instruments in these schools. Only 10 per cent of the sample schools had guitars and drums.

While observing the teaching-learning in the ten sample schools we found teachers using textbooks while teaching. In work education locally available material —such as mud and bamboo were made use of to make useful school items such as clay pots, pencil containers and animal figures for Class I and II children by children of Classes III and IV. In some schools, the students prepared teaching-aids like charts and local maps. At two schools, attempts were made to prepare a globe and political maps of India apart from the map of Mizoram state. Each class has a blackboard, chalks and duster. The project team while observing classroom teaching, found the class/subject teachers using blackboards especially for mathematics and language teaching. The investigator observed the conduct of class tests in subjects like Science and English language for Class IV students, and the correction of children's examination papers by teachers, as well as their homework. The teachers were found to give much time and to take pains to correct students' mistakes.

While interviewing teachers and Head Teachers we discovered that they preferred to remain posted in the schools which came under the district authorities rather than state government, because the latter involved frequent transfers outside their home districts. The transfer of power to local authorities has certainly had a positive effect on the quality of the primary schools and has improved the teaching-learning situation. Since the teachers are locally recruited and generally posted near their homes (villages), they tended to spend most of their time with students. While interviewing the teachers, the investigators found that on average, the school teacher was present in his/her school from 8.30 am. to 4.30 p.m., attending to both teaching as well as administrative work. There was a sense of greater commitment to the school among them as they belonged to the same neighbourhood and could understand the problems of individual students and their parents. Interviews held with district council authorities revealed that in Chakma dominated area, they generally posted a Chakma as their Head Teacher, since teaching is imparted in the mother tongue. In fact, Lai Autonomous District Council imparts education for this level in Mizo and Lai, Mara and Chakma for each ethnic minority group, in grant-in-aid schools or government schools. The members of the council also consist of members belonging to Bru, Riang, and Chakma ethnic minorities along with the Lai majority group (see photograph for details).

All the respondents indicated that recruitment, posting, and transfer policies were now being done by district council authorities. The cases of transfer and posting are in the hands of District Council. Hence "there is no interference by the State Government in this regard".[3] Despite political interference in the appointment and transfer of some teachers, it was observed that, accountability of their work performance had improved substantially due to decentralization of management. In the ten per cent sample school teachers interviewed (out of 343), through structured questionnaires, it was revealed that schools were being supervised more frequently by the education officers belonging to the District Council rather than the Circle Education Officers appointed by the State Government as was done previously. Moreover, the salary of the teachers was paid on time and their demand for better working conditions such as pension facilities along the lines of the State Government Servants were adequately met by the Lai Autonomous District Council. The community's sense of identification with educational development has no doubt grown as a result of the transfer of responsibility to local bodies. A significant aspect of it all is that the locally recruited teachers now interact with and are directly accountable to their local representatives and not with a remote authority in distant Aizawl. Majority of the teachers are in the entry pay scale of Rs.1200-30-1380 EB-30-1560-EB-1800-EB[4]-40-2040, however the Head Teachers who had served for more than 15 years of service (some as much as 25 years) were on a Rs.3000 basic. In a few schools the temporary 6th or 7th teacher was on a fixed pay of Rs.900.

Inspection and Supervision

Discipline is strictly maintained in the schools, and Head Teachers are required to adhere to conduct rules as per the circular issued by the council authorities. All the respondents indicated that inspection of schools done by district council authorities was more frequent than before. On an average, a school was inspected every quarter, though often informal visits by district council authorities was also common. The inspecting authorities checked both physical and academic facilities of these schools. Nine out of ten Head Teachers said that the reports of inspecting officers were discussed with them, both in the school premises, as well as, in meetings held at the District Council Office. But all respondents (Head Teachers) opined that these inspecting reports had not been discussed with state level authorities, and felt that their problems could also be conveyed to State Government. The fact was that monitoring of the academic and administrative aspects of lower primary schools was being done solely by District Council Authorities.

Another distinguishing feature of the Lai Autonomous District Council is to involve the Village Board of School Education in maintaining discipline in primary schools and ensuring that quality education is being imparted. One of the main functions of the Board is to "keep a close watch" on the working of primary schools. They are to see that discipline is maintained, teacher's attendance is regular and suggest measures to improve the teaching-learning situation. In addition to district authorities, this Board also monitors the academic progress of primary schools by keeping its own records on each school which are submitted to District authorities. The Board is also entrusted with the responsibility of organizing seminar/conferences for schools, at least once a year, to encourage parents, village members and educationists to share experiences and give suggestions for school improvement.

All teachers are expected to obey and respect the proposal or suggestion made by the Village Board of School Education for their schools, for building up their pupils' character and conduct in their social and academic life. The Board has the "power of recommendation" for the approval of E.O.L for the period of six months at a time to those teachers who are "negligent" of duty and "irregular" in attending the school. The Board recommended to the authority "grant notice" to such teachers. For the improvement of the quality of primary education and to achieve excellence in pupils' studies, as well as, in their performance, the teachers, particularly the Head Teacher, have been given a number of responsibilities. The Head Teacher has to ensure punctuality, regularity, and prevent teachers from getting intoxicated by drinks. He has to ensure that rules and conduct, as far as leave days and absence from duty by the teachers are concerned, are properly adhered to. In all cases of unauthorized absence from duty or in continuation of leave rendered the employees liable to disciplinary action. The Board is to make sure that the staff meeting in the schools was conducted, at least, once in a month, for the purpose of maintaining cooperation between Head Teacher and the staff. Moreover, the Head Teacher of each school has to submit Monthly Reports to the Office of the authority concerned. As the stipulation was that "If the Monthly Report was not submitted before 25th of every month, salary of staff of the school concerned should be withheld". Thus, strict discipline and rules of conduct are made for improving the management and supervision of school education. The respondents were satisfied with the working environment and management of primary schools despite such rules and regulations. Thus, the conclusion that the quality of primary education has improved considerably with the process of decentralization in education and the powers delegated to the Lai Autonomous District Council is more than justified. The respondents were not certain about whether District Council authorities have the same power and authority over their primary schools.

Curricular Innovations

Administrative decentralization has led to curricular innovation in the Lai Autonomous District Council. Lai District in Primary Education

Board which functions under the Council has introduced Social Studies II in Classes III, IV and Lai Careel (Language) in Classes II, III, IV. These are in addition to the already existing subjects such as Mizo, English, Social Studies I, Science, Maths, Physical Education and Work Education. The Work-Education consisting of teaching local handicrafts, drawing and music along with science, maths, English and social studies I, follows the syllabus of the State Government. Prescribed by them Social Studies II and Lai Careel are prepared by Lai District Primary Education Board. The Lai Careel is an attempt to revive the Lai language in the Roman script. According to linguists this language resembles a Thai dialect its origin still uncertain, is spoken across the border by a small group of people living in Myanmar. The members of Planning Board attended conferences in Manila trying to trace the linguistic origin of this language. In Social Studies II, history and geography of the Lai people, their customs and traditions are taught.

The Lai District Primary Education Board, a village Board set up by the Council, plays a crucial role as far as curriculum and conduct of examination are concerned. The Executive Member in-charge of Education and Human Resource Department of the Council is the Chairman. There is a Vice Chairman and other members who are educational experts and teachers both from Primary and High Schools. The Board prescribes the textbooks after they are approved of by the Executive Committee of the Council. So far, the Board has been implementing the recommendation of the Mizoram Board of School Education. However, it has the power to add new subjects, formulated and prepared by the Board itself. Thus, Social Studies II for Class III and IV and Lai Careel (Language) for Class II, III and IV, have been added in the already existing textbooks. The Board however still requires the approval of the Education Department of the Government of Mizoram in regard to changes in Primary School curriculum. The Board also conducts the annual exam for the Class IV. According to the terms and conditions of the transferred schools, the Education Department (Government of Mizoram), still continues to be the "appropriate authority for approval of syllabi, curriculums and textbooks in the recognized Lower Primary Schools" in the Lai Autonomous District Council. In other words, the Council needs the approval of the Government of Mizoram in this regard. We found out from the respondents that the Council does not have the freedom of choosing the medium of instruction without the permission of the State Government. So far Lai language which is "preferred for teaching in primary schools is accepted as one of the subject only". However, the general feeling among the respondents is that "Mizo language is being used as medium of instruction because language assimilation from the British era still prevails in Mizoram". The books of "Lai Careel" for Class II, III and IV are being introduced as one of the compulsory subject which teaches their local language using the Roman script. The respondents expressed that "there lies deep feeling in the minds of the people that local language requires study for the new generations and is taught with a view to gradually impart knowledge to students until the time comes when our own language can be used as medium of instruction which may however take sometime".[5] Thus, curricular innovation relevant to local history, culture and environment, a unique feature in rural Indian schools, has been a distinguishing feature of primary education in the Council. In addition, State Government curriculum and textbooks are implemented in the primary schools.

Conclusion

In a multi-cultural society such as India, a state like Mizoram's regional needs and aspirations assume importance. These have to be attended to through decentralization. Autonomy and accountability are interrelated phenomena and form an essential ingredient of a federal state. The Lai experiment is an important indicator of the productive relationship that can exist between the state and the local body which enhances educational development in a backward region and provides us with an example which can be adopted for future strategies elsewhere.

The rationale behind transfer of power for planning and management of primary education to district or village councils was based upon the premise that it will give them more autonomy which would enhance their accountability. By fostering the spirit of freedom and self-government, these 'local managers' would be able to assume more responsibility and conduct their affairs without any interference by the state government. They are thus accountable to their local community as well as to the Governor of the State, who has the power to annul any act of the Council. However, such autonomy also has some disadvantages when it comes to Lai Autonomous District Council, particularly relating to primary education.

As per the modification on the "Terms and Conditions of Schools Transferred to Autonomous District Councils in Mizoram", all government schools are now given the status of non-government aided primary schools but under the "general patterns of education in primary schools as laid down by government from time to time."

Hence it is not a picture of total exercise in autonomy, in opening and upgrading institutions prior to obtaining government sanction. The services of teachers transferred without any deputation allowance, are now under the direct control of the district authorities. However, with regard to the 'prescription of academic and training qualification', the state government retains its authority. Similarly, the syllabi and textbooks prescribed by the state government are used by the district council. This is in addition to the council's freedom to introduce additional subjects and textbooks, as already mentioned. But the class IV Board Examination in 1995 was restricted to testing the students of the Mizo Board. Since the formation of the Lai Board it has become possible to include Lai Careel and Social Studies II in the class IV examination. The Lai Autonomous District Council (LADC) is not free to set its own standard in examination and award of scholarships, to its meritorious students; therefore, scholarships are awarded by the State Government only. Even class promotion rules are done with the approval of the State Government.

The effectiveness of school has been assessed in terms of academic, administrative and financial aspects of ten per cent grant-in-aid schools in Lawngtlai educational circle. The major findings of this study, indicate how innovative practices initiated by the autonomous functioning of the district council, as well as, its cordial relationship with the state government have led to changes in the condition of primary schools.

Autonomy and Infrastructural Facilities

1. As far as infrastructural facilities go, cent per cent of the sample lower primary schools consist of one/two large semi-pucca rooms partitioned by bamboo walls/brick walls into class rooms; and one Principal's room including provision for sitting accommodation for three to four other staff members.
2. One hundred (100%) per cent of these schools had furniture for staff including racks and cupboards, dusters and adequate school textbooks for the staff. Ten per cent of the schools have other reference books while cent per cent (100%) of the schools have charts, maps, globes and other teaching aids provided to them by the District Council through funds obtained from the State Government. All students sit on benches and have desks and blackboards in all their classrooms. Even if the room is partitioned in the middle, every class has its own blackboard, chalk, duster and room duster. On enquiry it was found that though there is little

electricity in the area, yet classes go on with lanterns during frequent power cuts. Most of these facilities had existed prior to 1990, but since 1992 the Lai Autonomous District Council has made every effort possible to provide facilities out of its education budget which accounts for more than fifty per cent of its budgeted expenditure on education.

3. Seventy per cent (70%) of the lower primary schools are situated next to upper primary schools and hence share the facilities of a common playground. About fifty per cent (50%) of primary schools (lower and upper) are constructed in a school complex consisting of a high school, and often an Anganwadi centre.
4. Though the local government provided the above facilities, the children's uniform, textbook, stationary, including their work education items, are provided by the parents. It may be mentioned here that though the Lai people practice primitive form of agriculture and are economically backward, they are not living below the poverty line. On enquiry, it was found that children do not drop out of lower primary schools despite their participation in domestic and agricultural workforce. This is primarily because education is seen as the best means of upward mobility in a state where the service sector has expanded rapidly even since Mizoram became a separate union territory in 1972, and more so since it obtained statehood in 1987. This is a unique feature throughout the state, unlike the rest of the North-East. Given the stature and desire for education among the Mizo people, both government bodies and parents play a greater participatory role in school education which is reflected in the provision of superior infrastructural facilities even in rural areas, which in turn has resulted in a comparatively low dropout rate in the lower primary stage.

Curricular Innovations

Administrative decentralization has led to the formation of Lai Board of School Education which has introduced Lai Chareel (Language) and Social Studies II in Classes I-IV in addition of the already existing subjects such as Mizo, English, Social Studies I, Science, Maths, Physical Education and Work Education. The work education consists of teaching local handicrafts, drawing and music. A school day begins with all the children, accompanied by class teachers, sweeping the floors and dusting the furniture. This exemplary practice inculcates a sense of hygiene, but more important a sense of pride and belonging to the school. Except for Lai Careel and Social Studies II, all other textbooks used belong to the Mizo Board of School Education. The introduction of courses imparting knowledge of history and culture has increased the relevance of the primary curriculum. Efforts are now being made to bring out locally produced science textbooks comprising of local ecology for Class I +II (A+B).

Pupil Evaluation

Pupils are evaluated internally by school authorities at the end of each term, and annually between Classes I and III, but at the end of their lower primary cycle (i.e., Class IV) they have to appear for a board examination. So far there existed only the Mizo Board of Examination, but since the beginning of 1995, Lai Autonomous District Council has constituted its own board which will in the future examine students of their own locality. The norms followed by the Lai Board confirm to the standards set by the Mizo Board. This is being done consciously so as not to deviate from state norms. It may be mentioned here that all students appear for a State Board Examination at the end of Class VIII and hence if standards are not kept uniform within the state, then the Lai people may find it difficult to compete with others.

Teacher Accountability

Despite political interference in the appointment and transfer of some teachers, it was observed that accountability of their work performance had improved substantially since decentralization of management. Out of the ten per cent (10%) head teachers interviewed (out of 343), through structured questionnaires, it was revealed that their schools were being supervised more frequently by the education officers belonging to the district council.

Despite a partial improvement in inspection and supervision of schools, it was found that only the attendance register of students, teachers, stock of furniture and students' achievements in Class IV examination (by the project) that school records were incomplete.

Community Participation

Community participation has grown substantially as a result of the transfer of power from the state to the Local Body. This was evineed by the fact that often parents of the school children helped to provide the school with infrastructural inputs such as jute mats, raw material for craft classes, extra teaching aids like books, maps, charts instead of depending upon the government bodies. In fact, parents often went to the extent of repairing buildings, building fences and providing water during scarcity. Thus, community involvement is not only confined to providing educational and other inputs but in imparting quality education (which needs to be further strengthened by the V.E.C.). Their keen sense of involvement and desire to improve the schooling facilities stem from the feeling that the school 'belongs to us', a sentiment expressed repeatedly by both parents and teachers to the project team. Another unique feature of community participation is the role of the Young Lai Association which is a Voluntary Organisation of the local youth.

Sharing of Responsibility

This case study shows the growth of effective management of primary schools by local bodies for deprived groups such as the Lai through a healthy partnership between the state government and local body. At the planning stage the State grants the Autonomous District Council a total sum of money under specified heads out of which the educational expenditure is met. The Local Body is then free to incur expenditure according to its own priorities as long as it satisfies the targets set by the State Government. Seldom is there a misunderstanding between these two bodies. On the contrary this happy partnership is reflected in the sharing of physical and human inputs in order to impart quality education. Hence what one observes is that schooling facilities provided initially by the State Government has been considerably improved upon and managed efficiently by the Local Body.

Despite innovations and some positive developments which the case study has revealed there are also some shortcomings as a result of decentralization, noted by the team. One major concern is the tendency to encourage separatist feeling which can lead to the disintegration of states. It can give rise to unhealthy ethnic problem. If must be remembered that although the 'Lai people' are a somewhat separate ethnic group, yet they are one of Mizo sub-tribes and have as a result of the process of assimilation into culture, have lost some of their original characteristics. As a part of Mizoram state in which they enjoy complete freedom to remain a district identity, it would be against their interest if through decentralization they were to move away from the mainstream Mizo life. Thus, decentralization need not foster a kind of autonomy encouraging divisiveness but rather for effective planning and management of local affairs.

Another feature observed by the team is the personal bias or prejudice used in the posting and transfer of teachers. Invariably favours were made to these teachers who were more familiar with the council members. Hence a proper assessment made on the institutional requirements must be made available so that posting of teachers is not made on the basis of individual preference. The suggested tool for school base information may provide answer or teacher requirements in remote areas.

The study which was limited to random sampling of ten schools in semi-urban Lawgtlai educational circle did not deal with schools in remote areas of the Lai Autonomous District Council due to the paucity of time and the lack of transport facilities. Thus, the superior infrastructural facilities and teaching staff claimed in this report may not generally hold true of all primary schools located within that district council. However, since the salaries of the teaching staff has been increased and preference is being given to the local teacher, it is very possible that quality improvement will take place in the teaching-learning situation in the future especially as the teaching profession has now assumed a relatively higher status. Another drawback is that the council spends most of its funds of primary education on teacher's salaries and does not pay sufficient attention to infrastructural facilities, text-books, building up of school libraries and holding seminars. One suggestion is to hold awareness campaigns and seminars for enlisting community participation. Moreover the centre needs to open a Teacher Training Institute in Chhimtuipui district for elementary school teachers, such as the District Institutes of Education at Aizawl and Lunglei.

References

1. H.C. Lalghinga, Lawngtlai, 1995.
2. Headmaster's Questionnaire.
3. C. Thanghluna, Chief Executive Member, Lai Autonomous District Council, Lawngtlai, May 1995.
4. Efficiency Bar.
5. C. Thanghluna, Chief Executive Member. Lai Autonomous District Council.

7

Case Study II: Nagaland - A Description of the State

It should be mentioned at the outset, that unlike the case study on Mizoram which was done over a period of five visits to the state, the case study on Nagaland could not be accomplished in a similar fashion on account of the on-going insurgency movement. I could visit Nagaland only once in 1990, for collection of primary data, and I have had to depend on secondary data, available both at New Delhi and in the North Eastern Council, Shillong (Meghalaya) in 1996, for upgrading my knowlege. I have had to rely also on data in dissertations guided by me, for the sample district of Kohima, which I have duly acknowledged.

As pointed out by Monirul Hussain, "The repeated reorganization of Assam since the early '60s, the substantial reduction of its territory over the years, the vicious threat of reorganization, the perpetual inter-state boundary disputes, erupting in periodic violence, the long drawn out armed struggles of the Nagas and the Mizos for secession . . ." have contributed to the similarities between the states of Mizoram and Nagaland. Historically speaking the hill areas were neither a part of pre-colonial Assam nor a part of pre-colonial India. They were tribal and feudal[1]. Along with the Khasis of the now Meghalaya state, the Nagas and the Mizo also had a very small but distinguishable group of western educated leaders largely on account of their exposure to Christianity and western education, who played a significant political role in establishing the demand for separate statehoods. Conscious of their distinct identities they felt (after 1947), that "India should give them sovereignty and recognize them as friends rather than as a part of India." It was this feeling, fuelled by their incomplete integration with India, that led to the rise of insurgency in the Naga hills during the early 50s and in the Lushai (Mizo) hills during the mid-60s. In order to meet the aspiration of the hill tribals, the Sixth Schedule of the Indian Constitution was introduced, which granted some autonomy in the form of Autonomous District Councils. (See Introductory Chapter for further details on the insurgency movement).

On December Ist, 1963, Nagaland became the sixteenth state of the Indian Union with Kohima as its capital. Prior to this as a district of Assam it was known as "Naga Hills". After 1947, the area, was renamed as 'Naga Hills District' which later was converted to 'Naga Hills Tuensang Area' thereby merging the erstwhile North East Frontier Agency (presently the State of Arunachal Pradesh).

Essentially a hill state, Nagaland is situated in the north-eastern part of the country consisting of 16,579 square kilometres. It lies between 2506' and 2704' latitude north of the Equater and between 93020' E and 95015' E.[2] Its only international boundary lying in the east, is with Myanmar. Arunachal Pradesh (east), Assam (north and west) and Manipur (south) are its borders with neighbouring North Eastern States of India. Topographically varied, the state is broken up into hill ranges. Its altitude varies between 194 and 3,048 metres.

Agriculture is the mainstay of the Naga tribes comprising of 7,233 persons out of 1,209,546 population (as per 1991) data. As in Mizoram, 'Jhum' or shifting cultivation characterizes its agricultural mode of production, thus making the state similar to others in the North East region of India. However, recent efforts have been made to adopt terrace cultivation in Nagaland.[3] Apart from rice, its other agricultural products and cash crops are cereals, pulses, spices, cardamom, fibre, sugar and bamboo. There is nonetheless a shortage of foodgrains in the state.

As per 1991 census data, Nagaland had 42.29 per cent of its population as main workers out of which 45.40 were females. The concentration of main workers was around the rural areas. Cultivators constituted 72.65 per cent of Nagaland's working force. The percentage of female cultivators was 51.84 per cent. Only 1.41 per cent of the state's population was agricultural labourers, consisting mainly of men. In household industry, manufacturing, food processing, servicing and repairing only 0.38 of its population participated, though the percentage of females was as high as 55.00. Besides these figures the percentage of 'other workers' was only 17.19, which include weavers, blacksmiths, people employed in handicrafts, domestic industries and in the private and public sector enterprise.[4] This percentage of 'other workers' is marginal if compared with states likes Assam and Meghalaya. However, Nagaland and Mizoram have by and large the same percentage of main workers, cultivators, agricultural labourers, engaged in household industry, manufacturing, food processing, servicing and repairing as well as in the category of 'other workers'. The British in India had felt the need for creating only a single type of work forces skilled in running an imperial administration. After Independence, India, inherited this system, and for a number of years not enough was done to bring about a change. One of the main reasons being the state of the Indian industry, during the fifties was still in its nascent stage of development. Secondly, even the government which created a large network of state owned enterprizes did not find it necessary to develop trained labour force, as the managerial needs of these enterprizes were fulfilled by administrators. That the government of that day did not have work-oriented education as one of its priorities, can be seen in the Industrial Policy Resolution of 1956. This resolution – the blueprint for Indian industrial development – though far-sighted in its approach, neglected training of a labour force.

The nexus between education, work and employment varies not only between different states in India, but also between the districts and circles in each state. Since my argument concludes with the situation in the eighties, I have obtained the sector-wise distribution of the workforce of Nagaland from the 1981 census.

Despite physical and human inputs there still exists of that time, disparity in educational development among seven districts, Kohima being the highest in literacy and educational development. Tuensang and Mon were considered as educationally backward. Besides these, three more sub-divisions were also declared as backward, such as, Aghunato, Mehimi, Penen. Several reasons have been cited for having declared these sub-divisions as backward. Most of the villages situated in these parts vary in altitude from 194 to 3048 metres, and are both inaccessible and socio-economically backward. Inter-village communications are often interrupted due to heavy monsoons and landslides (See Table 7.1 for details).

This table clearly shows that literacy is high in both Kohima and Mokukchung and lowest in Mon. Female literacy though very high in Mokokchung (57.18) is also relatively high in Kohima (38.69) as

Table 7.1
District-wise Breakup of Male/Female Literacy in Percentage in Nagaland

Sl.No.	*District*	*Total Literacy*	*Male Literacy*	*Female Literacy*
1.	Kohima	68.94	61.3	38.69
2.	Phek	37.99	74.73	25.27
3.	Wokha	45.60	65.18	34.82
4.	Zunheboto	45.59	61.90	38.10
5.	Mokokchung	61.78	42.82	57.18
6.	Tuensang	30.89	76.68	23.32
7.	Mon	19.89	87.65	12.35
8.	Total	42.57	66.11	33.89

Source: Census 1981

compared with the dismal picture of Mon (12.35%). High female literacy is also an indicator of educational development of the districts.

Table 7.1.1
District-wise Literacy Rates, North East

State	2001			1991		
	Total	*Male*	*Female*	*Total*	*Male*	*Female*
Nagaland	67.11	71.77	61.92	61.65	67.62	54.75
Mon	42.25	46.7	37.12	36.02	41.9	29.1
Tuensang	51.3	55.97	46.12	48.39	53.98	41.98
Mokokchur	84.27	86.14	82.2	77.85	80.52	74.88
Zunheboto	69.73	73.43	65.8	64.36	70.76	57.63
Bokha	81.28	85.69	76.46	73.92	81.06	65.99
Dimapur	78.15	82.16	73.34	68.65	73.64	62.42
Kohima	74.28	81.44	66.64	69.58	77.24	60.6
Phek	71.35	78.97	63.08	62.59	72.28	51.34

Sources: 1. Census of India, 2001.
2. Census of India, 1991.

There are 21 scheduled tribes in the entire state. Among these tribes some are educationally forward, but most are educationally backward. Angami and Ao's tribes are educationally forward as compared to other tribes in the state. Kohima district is dominated by Angami tribes and Mokukchung district is dominated by Ao's tribes. The illiteracy position of these tribes are given in Table 7.2.

Table 7.2
Percentage of Illiterate ST with their Total Rural/Urban Population in Nagaland

Sl.No.	*Name of Tribe*	*Rural*	*Urban*
1.	Garo	56.0	25.1
2.	Kachari	64.9	25.1
3.	Kuki	46.19	28.7
4.	Mikir	86.0	46.6
5.	Naga	61.8	35.7
6.	Angami	57.7	38.5
7.	Ao	38.3	26.0
8.	Chakhesang	63.9	43.8
9.	Chang	71.0	36.5
10.	Chirr	85.0	50.5
11.	Khienungan	85.5	45.0
12.	Konyak	87.8	50.2
13.	Lotha	56.1	31.5
14.	Makwara	74.4	70.0
15.	Phom	69.4	18.2
16.	Rengma	59.0	27.2
17.	Sangtam	64.2	36.1
18.	Sema	56.5	33.1
19.	Tikhir	74.4	40.0
20.	Yimchungra	75.7	42.7
21.	Zeliang	66.4	41.2
22.	All Tribes	62.49	30.57

Source: Census 1981.

Table 7.3
Sector-wise Distribution of Workforce in Nagaland in Percentages

District	*Primary*			*Secondary*			*Territory*		
	M	*F*	*T*	*M*	*F*	*T*	*M*	*F*	*T*
Kohima	35.6	40.9	76.5	3 2	0.8	4.0	16.0	3.4	19.4
Phek	37.0	50.2	87.2	1.4	0.2	1.6	09.8	1.2	11.0
Wokha	34.5	48.3	82.8	1.8	0.3	2.1	13.2	1.6	14.8
Zunheboto	35.5	47.4	82.9	1.6	0.3	1.6	12.4	2.3	14.7
Mokokchung	35.6	42.8	78.4	3.4	0.4	3.8	14.0	3.4	17.4
Tuensang	41.8	48.3	90.1	0.7	0.0	0.7	08.1	0.8	08.9
Mon	46.1	47.2	93.3	1.0	0.0	1.0	04.8	0.5	05.3

Source: Census 1981.

Table 7.3 shows that in the district which are educationally backward, the labour force is more engaged in the primary sector. For example district Mon is most educationally backward, and in which 93.3 per cent of its labour force is engaged in the primary sector. An educationally forward district, like Kohima, has only 76.5 per cent labour force engaged in the primary sector. From this table it may be assumed that there is a relationship between education and employment mobility. This is true not only of the Kohima and Mokokchung districts, but also of the tribes such as Angami and Aos, who inhabit such districts, though the overall tendency among the 'Naga' tribes is to resist any occupational change, that may disrupt their traditional self-sufficient agricultural economy. Yet an access to modern education, industrial development and modernization of agriculture has offered alternative occupations. One can safely summarize the aforesaid phenomena, and say, that whatever nascent industrial growth taking place in Nagaland, has been largely due to the efforts of the Aos of Mokokchung and Angamis of Kohima districts. It is, therefore, not surprising to find more workforce engaged in the tertiary sector of these districts than in the others.

The educational level of marginal workers and non-workers and their activity at state level is given in Table 7.4 and Table 7.5. For the sample Kohima district, Tables 7.6 and 7.7 provide the educational status of the marginal and non-marginal workers.

Distribution of Marginal Workers and Non-Workers of Scheduled Tribes by the Activity and Level of Education in percentages in Nagaland

Table 7.4
Marginal Workers

Sl.No.	*Educational Level*	*Total*	*Full time Students*	*Households Duties*	*Dependant and Infants*	*Others*
1.	Total	4775	3715	864	58	94
2.	Illiterate	18.0	5.6	64.5	77.5	40.4
3.	Literate (without edn.level)	36.6	42.7	15.3	25.8	6.3
4	Primary	24.0	28.9	10.8	3.4	10.6
5.	Middle	11.4	12.6	5.4	1.7	30.0
6.	Matriculation/ Secondary	6.0	6.9	2.5	6.8	4.2

Contd

Sl.No.	*Educational Level*	*Total*	*Full time Students*	*Households Duties*	*Dependant and Infants*	*Others*
7.	Higher Secod-nary/ Intermediate/ Pre-University	0.1	2.2	0.6	-	6.3
8.	Non-tech. Dip. or certificate not equal to degree	-	—	-	-	-
9.	Tech. Dip. or certificate not equal to degree	0.0	0.0	-	-	-
10.	Graduate & above	0.7	0.7	0.4	5.1	1.0

Source: Census 1981

Table 7.5 Non Workers

Sl No.	*Educational Level*	*Total*	*Full time Students*	*Households Duties*	*Dependant and Infants*	*Others*
1.	Total	340031	161860	20917	154617	1578
2.	Illiterate	52.9	11.1	51.3	97.1	30.4
3.	Literate (without edn.level)	25.6	49.9	60.6	1.7	15.0
4.	Primary	12.0	22.1	18.6	0.5	1.0
5.	Middle	5.5	10.0	8.9	0.2	20.0
6.	Matriculation/ Secondary	2.7	4.9	3.8	0.1	12.8
7.	Higher Secondary/ Institute/Pre-University	0.7	1.2	0.6	0.0	13.3
8.	Non-tech.Dip. or certificate not equal to degree	0.0	0.0	0.0	-	2.5
9.	Tech. Dip. Or certificate not equal to degree	0.0	0.0	0.0	0.0	-
10.	Graduate & above	0.2	0.3	0.3	0.0	0.0

Source: Census 1981

Table 7.6

Kohima District : Schedule Tribe Workers

Marginal Workers

Sl.No.	*Educational Level*	*Total*	*Full time Students*	*Households Duties*	*Dependant and Infants*	*Others*
1.	Total	2659	2173	363	27	59

Contd.

Sl.No.	*Educational Level*	*Total*	*Full time Students*	*Households Duties*	*Dependant and Infants*	*Others*
2.	Illiterate	13.9	4.8	57.0	44.4	42.3
3.	Literate (without edn. level)	35.8	40.1	16.5	22.2	3.3
4.	Primary	25.5	28.4	12.9	3.7	15.2
5.	Middle	12.5	12.9	7.9	3.7	33.8
6.	Matriculation/ Secondary	7.9	8.8	3.0	11.1	3.3
7.	Higher Secod nary/ Interme-diate /Pre-University	2.9	3.2	-	-	3.3
8.	Non-tech.Dip. or certificate not equal to degree	-	-	-	-	-
9.	Tech. Dip. or certificate not equal to degree	-	-	-	-	-
10.	Graduate and above	1.1	1.1	0.5	11.1	-

Source: Census 1981

Table 7.7
Kohima District : Non-Workers

Sl.No.	*Educational Level*	*Total*	*Full time Students*	*Households Duties*	*Dependant and Infants*	*Others*
1.	Total	89060	43336	7959	36652	636
2.	Illiterate	50.5	11.9	51.1	96.5	25.3
3.	Literate (without edn. level)	26.3	49.5	15.1	1.8	11.7
4.	Primary	11.6	19.8	16.6	0.7	16.5
5.	Middle	6.0	9.9	9.2	0.4	22.0
6.	Matriculation/ Secondary	3.8	6.2	5.5	0.3	15.7
7.	Higher Secondary/ Intermediate/Pre-University	1.1	1.9	0.9	0.0	3.7
8.	Non-tech.Dip. or certificate not equal to degree	-	-	-	-	-

Contd

Sl.No.	Educational Level	Total	Full time Students	Households Duties	Dependant and Infants	Others
9.	Tech. Dip. or certificate not equal to degree	0.0	0.0	0.0	-	-
10.	Graduate and above	0.3	0.5	0.0	0.0	4.7

Source: Census 1981.

It is a clear from the tables VII.4, VII.5, VII.6 and VII.7, that, there was educational disparity between marginal workers and non-workers and also in the type of activity they performed. For example, at the state level, the marginal workers were 18% illiterate and 5.6% were full-time students, whereas the non-workers were 52.9% illiterate and 11% full time students. At the district level (Kohima) 13.9% were illiterate marginal workers, 4.8% were the full time students, and the non-workers were 50.5% illiterate and 11.9% full time students. Among the non-workers it has been found that both at the state as well as at the district level the percentage of illiterates was very high i.e. (Nagaland 52.9%) and Kohima 50.5%). It is well known that the traditional self-sufficient economy does not require the knowledge of modern education, more so in Nagaland, where the land is extremely fertile and crops grow without much effort. In fact, the paucity of market economy is largely due to the simple life-style of the Nagas, for whom locally available fruits and vegetables are sufficient to meet their daily requirements.

The illiterates, dependents and infants at both the state and the district levels for the categories of the marginal and the non-worker is glaring. For example in Nagaland 77.5% (marginal workers) and 97.1% (non-workers) fall into this category. These figures if compared with Kohima, an educationally forward district, indicate that only at the level of the marginal workers (44.4) there is a disparity between the percentage of illiterate dependant and infants, but not at the level of the non-workers. As many as 96.5% of non-workers in the district fall into the category of illiterate, dependent and infants. The high percentage of dependants can be attributed to the fact that even when educated (in Kohima – 11.1% marginal workers had attained the graduate and above level), they did not participate full time in the labour force, since the fertility of the land required only a few members of the family to work on it, on a regular basis. Further since modern education does not help improve agricultural productivity it is irrelevant to the local needs of the Naga tribes.

As per the 1981 census, there were 17 circles in Kohima district. The largest concentration of population was in Dimapur Sadar, i.e., 35,085. The Scheduled Tribe population in terms of the percentage of the total population was 56.45 per cent. Main workers as percentage to the total population was 38.11. In the circle of Dimapur town, out of total percentage of population 34,340, the scheduled tribe population, as percentage of the total population, was 56.32. Literates were 64.68. The percentage of main workers in relation to the total population was 34.79. Nsong circle had a total population of 99.82 per cent. The literates belonging to the same circle in terms of percentage of the total population was (20.76%). The main workers of the total population was 59.59 per cent. Circle-wise distribution of main workers is given in Table 7.8.

Table 7.8
Literate, Workers, Main Workers, Scheduled Tribe Population in the District Kohima

Sl.No.	*Name of Circle*	*Total Population*	*ST Pop. to Total Pop.*	*Percentage*	
				Literate to Total Pop.	*Main Workers to Total Pop.*
1.	Tenning	4343	96.73	29.93	54.48
2.	Nsong	1705	99.82	20.76	59.59
3.	Pedi	5507	96.06	38.31	48.85
4.	Jaluke	14883	79.29	43.03	44.43
5.	Dhansiripar	9059	60.00	21.00	37.23
6.	Dimapur Sadar	35085	42.68	56.45	38.11
7.	Nihokhu	15278	70.13	34.74	56.86
8.	Ghaspani	18773	63.75	49.51	44.54
9.	Zubza	7815	85.91	49.37	51.57
10.	Jakhama	18104	93.80	35.35	54.25
11.	Chielphobozou	21380	92.73	46.16	50.59
12.	Tseminyu	15209	96.07	42.11	52.46
13.	Pughoboto	6382	98.06	45.88	51.11
14.	Ghathashi	4976	97.55	43.45	49.40
15.	Peren	4388	90.15	40.22	48.97
16.	Kohima Town	34340	56.32	64.68	34.79
17.	Dimapur Town	32878	15.88	61.82	38.37
18	District Total	250105	65.53	48.94	44.69

Source: Census 1981.

An analysis of data based on secondary data, interviews and field-visits highlight some peculiar characteristics of the relationship between education and employment in Nagaland. In general, districts with high literacy like Kohima and Mokokchung, have less percentage of main workers than Mon, the district with the lowest literacy rate and yet with the highest number of main workers. A major factor contributing to this inconsistency is the inability of many of the 21 Naga tribes to develop primers in their native language, which hinders their prospects of continuing education. Therefore, they tend to remain in their traditional occupations. The reasons why Kohima and Mokokchung have the highest literacy is because they are dominated by Angamis and Aos, who do not suffer from this handicap. However, most of the other Naga tribes do not continue beyond the primary level, because of their inability to comprehend an alien language, and also because the syllabus is not relevant to their occupations. This is not the case with the Angamis and Aos, where modern education has made them want to get out of their traditional occupations. But in the absence of technical and professional education in the state, and of alternative employment opportunities, their aspirations for occupational mobility are denied to them, within the state. Further, Nagaland has not been developed industrially to absorb its technically and professionally trained people.

As discussed in the previous chapters, Mizoram's success in employing its educated youth in the service sector, has led to the growth in the demand for education, a unique feature of the region.

The only means of transport in the state is roadways. Dimapur, however, is linked both by rail and air services. Private transport, which is well developed, is restricted to the urban areas only.[5] Since transport facilities, economic and educational development is restricted to certain districts and more specifically to urban areas, the state has an iniquitous distribution of the social service sector and is educationally backward in the rural areas.

The predominant ethnic composition of the state consists of the 'Naga', recognized as a Scheduled Tribe. There are sixteen Naga Tribes, each speaking a different language, and having arrived in Nagaland from Arunachal Pradesh, China, Burma, Manipur and other parts of South East Asia, which may be traced by studies conducted on Naga languages and their varied customs, costumes, dances and jewellery. Their link with South-East Asia is seen in the frequent use of sea shells and coral. What is even more curious is the resemblance between Naga and the Red Indians in their use of colours and in the design of their handloom products. According to the 1981, census the population of Nagaland was 774,930. This figure rose to 1,215,573 in the 1991 census, but this growth is not significant as compared with that in the period 1971-81. The highest growth rate of 69.92 per cent was in Tuensang district, while the lowest 35.04 per cent was in Zunheboto district between 1981-91.[6] As per 1991 census, out of 1,215,573 persons there were 643,273 males and 572, 300 females. The total growth rate of the population between 1981-1991 was 56.86 per cent.

Table 7.9
Selected Demographic Indicators

			Nagaland	*India*
1	Population (,000)	2001	1988	1027015
2	Annual Exponential Growth Rate	1991-2001	5.09	1.95
3	Population Density (per sq. kms.)	2001	120	324
4	Sex Ratio (per 1000 males)	2001	909	933
5	Percentage of Rural Population	2001	82.2	72.22
6	Percentage of SC Population	1991	NA	16.33
7	Percentage of ST Population	1991	87.11	8.08

Source: A.K. Sinha, *Indicators of School Education* (New Delhi: NIEPA, Draft Unpublished Report, 1994).
Census of India, 2001.

The sex ratio which was females 863 per 1000 males in 1981 rose to 890 in 1991. The density of population per square kilometre was 47 persons in 1981 and had risen to 73 by 1991. Both Kohima and Mokokchung, comprising largely of Angami and Ao tribes, have the greatest density that is 98 (Kohima) and 97 (Mokokchung). The decennial growth rate of population, for the years 1971-81, was +50.03 which rose to +56.86 between the years 1981-91. However, Kohima district had shown an increase of +96.09 per cent between 1971-81 but declined to 65.10 between 1981-1991, making its position lower than Mokokchung, which rose from 44.56 (1971-81) to +69.92 between 1981-91. The reasons for this decline in Kohima's population has been attributed to the on-going insurgency movements and the state of continuous curfew in these years.[7]

The traditional form of education which had prevailed among the Nagas was the 'Morang' or a dormitory for boys, who joined the 'Morang' after their puberty. The 'Morangs' taught them life skills and refinement of heart and discipline which were its ideals. It became the duty of the senior in the 'Morang' to review the education which a boy received at home. Hence vigorous tests were conducted often leading to harassment of the juniors by their seniors. The 'Morangs' served as reformatory schools as they taught manners and etiquette. They also made the boys respect elders in society, learn hunting; their Naga tribal language and native religion. Each tribal population had, therefore, its own 'Morang'.

This traditional system of education gradually lost its importance with the arrival of the Christian missionaries in the nineteenth century. Its pioneer was an American Baptist missionary called Rev. E. W. Clark who had settled in Anguri, (present day Assam state), a Naga village in the 19th century, (the exact date is not known). He converted the surrounding villages, but there did not exist any primary school prior to 1876. In 1876-77 at Samaguting (now Chumukidima), at the foot-hills in Kohima division near Dimapur, the British Government had opened the first primary school for the children of its government servants. This was followed by two more primary schools started by Rev. E.W. Clark at Molungyimsen village in 1878. The Impur Baptist Mission Centre started imparting literacy and primary education from 1882, but the Government's initiative to open primary schools only took place from 1884 onwards. From 1893 the government started encouraging the Nagas to open their own schools and thus by 1931 there were 94 primary schools in the Naga Hills, out of which 40 per cent were run by missionaries.

Table 7.10

Nagaland Districts, Educational Blocks, Inhabited Villages and Habitations

		Year	*Nagaland*	*India*
1	Area in sq. km.	1981	16579	3287263
2	No. of Districts	2001	8	593
3	No. of Educational Blocks	2000-01	28	7098
4	No. of Inhabited Villages	2000-01	1216	579148
5	No. of villages having population less than 500	1981	680	2707795
6	Percentage of Rural Population	2001	82.24	72.22
7	Population below poverty line (%)	1999-2000	22.67	26.10

Source: A.K. Sinha, *Indicators of School Education*, New Delhi, NIEPA, Draft Unpublished Report, 1994.
Census, 2001, Planning Commission.

During 1939-40 the Government Middle School in Kohima became recognized as the Government High School. Similarly, the Government Middle School Mokokchung, established in 1941, became a Government High School in 1948. The Angami Nagas dominating Kohima district, therefore, benefited from education, as much as, the Ao Nagas of Mokokchung district, due to the initiatives taken by the new government of Assam and the missionaries. By 1948, the Naga Hills had as much as 161 Government Primary Schools, 3 Government Middle Schools and 2

Government High Schools and 1 Junior Technical School situated in Kohima.

Literacy

In 1991, the literacy rate of the state was 61.30 per cent as against 52.11 per cent for the whole of India. Table 7.11 shows the literacy rates for the age-group 5 and above, both for 1961 and 1971. However, the literacy rate for the population of age-group of 7 and above have been taken into account for 1981 and 1991.

Table 7.11
Literacy Rate in Nagaland in Percentage : 1961-2001

Year	*Persons*	*Males*	*Females*
1961	20.43	27.21	13.04
1971	31.32	39.65	21.56
1981	50.20	58.52	40.28
1991	61.30	66.09	55.72
2001	67.11	71.77	61.92

Source: Census of India, 1991 Series 18, *Nagaland, Provisional Population Totals, Paper I of 1991*, Kohima, 1991.
Census, 2001, Planning Commission.

Quite similar to Mizoram, the literacy rate in Nagaland has been gradually rising for both the sexes from 1961 to 1991. Though in Mizoram the growth rate was faster due to both identity consciousness, and the economic benefits which the service sector could provide, after it attained statehood in 1987, in Nagaland the growth of the service sector was slow, and hence one finds non-Nagas manning several government jobs even in the 1990s. Moreover, the insurgency movement in Nagaland instead of leading to a 'Naga consciousness' became fragmented between several groups and has, therefore, adversely affected the literacy movement. In this context we may observe that the growth of ethnic consciousness leading to the 'Mizo' identity, encouraged by the Mizo National Front, was absent in Nagaland, an aspect explained earlier in this thesis.

As per 1991 census, Kohima district had the largest number of literate persons and the lowest gap between male and female, followed by Mokokchung. Both these districts had the largest percentage of literacy due to the efforts made by the missionaries and the advanced tribal groups such as the Angamis and Aos.

A district-wise break up of literate population in Nagaland also indicates that Mon, Zunhebato and Phek districts have low literate population with the gap between male and female literates widest in Mon and Phek districts.

Table 7.12
District-wise Literate Nagaland Population by Sexes

District	*Persons*		*Males*		*Females*	
	1991	*2001*	*1991*	*2001*	*1991*	*2001*
Nagaland	621.048	1.146.523	360.526	645.860	260.522	500.716
Kohima	221.500	200,137	128,036	113.205	93,464	86.932
Phek	52,539	87.008	32,817	50,132	19.722	36,876
Zunhebato	51,757	90,864	29.121	49.205	22.636	41,659
Wokha	48.909	113,704	28,261	62,565	20,648	51,139
Mokokchung	107.060	172,208	58.090	92,188	48.970	80,020
Tuensang	94.431	183,513	55.954	105.249	38.477	78,264
Mon	44.852	93,859	28,247	55,586	16,605	38.273
Dimapur		205,230		117.677		87,553

Source:Census of India 1991, Series 18, *Provisional Population Totals. Paper I of 1991*, Kohima 1991.
Census. 2001, Planning Commission.

Characteristics of Elementary Education

In the eighties, it was found that, out of a total of 997 habitations, 98.85 per cent were served with a primary school within their habitation, and 99.45 per cent within 1.0 km. For the upper primary stage, 43.25 per cent of the children were served with a school within their habitation, and 6.15 per cent within 1 km. of it. About 66.41 per cent of the habitations were served with a school within a distance of 3 km. According to the Fifth All India Education Survey of NCERT, New Delhi, 1989, only 60 out of 1131 primary schools were located in the towns. At the upper primary level as much as 225 schools were located in the rural areas, and only 36 in urban areas. Thus, most of the Naga schools at the elementary level are found in the rural areas.

According to data obtained from the Education Department of Nagaland, in its Annual Administrative Report 1995-96 the schooling facilities expanded further by the nineties. By 1995-96, there were 1247 government primary schools (Classes I-IV), and 83 private primary schools making a total of 1330. This gap between government and private schools is less at the upper primary level (Classes V-VIII), that is, 230 government schools as against 139 private schools. Nevertheless there is growth in the demand for private schools, as was explained to the investigator when conducting the village education survey of Phesama village in Kohima district in 1990.

The parents ana school teachers explained at length that compared with government upper primary schools, the private upper primary schools were better equipped with teaching aids and taught the English language better, which met the requirement for entering high school. This was despite the active Angami community participation to provide better infrastructural facilities to the government schools, by providing playgrounds, furniture and extra class rooms.

Nagaland has adopted the New Education Policy of 1986 and, therefore, formal education begins at the age of 6. The sixteen Naga sub-tribe languages or dialects have been recognized as medium of teaching at the primary level. Efforts have been made to develop 'Nagamese', a mixture of Assamese, several north Indian languages and Naga words, used originally for trading. English is taught from Class I and Hindi from Class V. Beyond the primary stage, English remains the medium of instruction.

The class-wise enrolment of boys and girls, as per the data obtained from the Department of Education, Government of Nagaland on 30th September, 1995, was 53.59 per cent boys as compared to 46.41 per cent girls, between the pre-primary to Class IV. However, for the middle school the enrolment of girls has increased to 49.49 per cent whereas the boys' enrolment is reduced to 50.51 per cent. (Classes V-VIII)

According to the data on government schools for 1993, as furnished by the Statistical Cell of the Directorate of School Education, Nagaland, there existed 480 Government schools in Kohima district, followed by 317 in Tuensang and 230 in Mokokchung. Next came Zunhebato with 166 followed by Mon district (161), Phek (127) and Wokha (121).

The number of teachers in government schools was also the highest in Kohima district (5243) followed by Tuensang (2319) and Mokokchung (2300). Zunheboto had as many as 1463 teachers, followed by Wokha (1432), Phek (1431), and Mon (1270).

There were 4535 male and 2088 female teachers in government primary schools and 3263 male and 1258 female upper primary teachers during 1995-96.

Table 7.13
Government Primary and Middle Schools in Nagaland

S. No.	*District*	*Primary Schools*		*Middle Schools*	
		1993	*2001-02*	*1993*	*2001-02*
1.	Kohima	399	259	53	86
2.	Phek	87	115	27	52

Contd.

S. No.	District	Primary Schools 1993	Primary Schools 2001-02	Middle Schools 1993	Middle Schools 2001-02
3.	Wokha	108	118	16	35
4.	Zunheboto	132	148	23	46
5.	Mokokchung	179	198	35	64
6.	Tuensang	255	281	47	81
7.	Mon	126	159	26	50
8.	Nagaland	1296	1499	227	479
9.	Dimapur		221		65

Source: Directorate of School Education, Government of Nagaland, Statistical Cell, Kohima. 1993.

Teachers' Training

According to the 10+2 Higher Secondary pattern, the percentage of trained teachers in Nagaland was 50 with 1:11 Teacher-Pupil ratio in 1990. Data available for the same year shows that 30 per cent were trained teachers in high schools, which had a 1:27 teacher pupil ratio. For the middle school, the percentage of trained teachers was 29 with 1:21 teacher-pupil ratio. The figure for trained teachers increases in the primary schools to 48 per cent with 1:19 teacher-pupil ratio.

As in most of the North Eastern States of India, Nagaland also (till the late 1980s) emphasized more on general rather than technical, professional and higher education. In fact, the latter type of institutions were encouraged to develop region-wise and not state-wise.

The only University, a branch of the NEHU campus exists in Kohima, offering B.A., M.A., M.Phil, and Ph.D. courses. In 1992, there existed 16 Art/Science and Commerce Colleges, and one Agricultural College, but no Engineering, Medical and Veterinary colleges. Only one Teachers' Training College existed.

However, there existed five Junior colleges for the plus-two stage. There were four Teacher Training Schools which by the mid-nineties have been upgraded to DIETs (District Institute of Education and Training) for the elementary school teachers and are located in Kohima, Tuensang and Mokokchung and other districts. In 1992, there was only one Polytechnic and three Technical and Industrial schools.

According to the Fifth All India Educational Survey of NCERT, the percentage of trained primary school teachers in 1986 was 87.6, and 50.6 for the middle school level. Despite a comparatively good teacher-pupil ratio at the elementary level, the standard was very low, especially in

Table 7.14

District-Wise Teacher-Pupil Ratio in Government Schools in Nagaland in 1993

S. No.	*District*	*Primary Schools*		*Middle Schools*	
		1993	*2001-02*	*1993*	*2001-02*
1.	Kohima	1:18	32	1:12	15
2.	Phek	1:21	35	1:16	11
3.	Wokha	1:13	33	1:25	7
4.	Zunheboto	1:14	32	1:12	12
5.	Mokokchung	1:11	30	1:12	13
6.	Tuensang	1:18	26	1:19	13
7.	Mon	1:26	26	1:18	13
8.	Dimapur	36			20
9.	Nagaland	1:17	31	1:15	14

Source: Directorate of School Education, Government of Nagaland, Kohima, 1993.

Table 7.15

Number of Students in Educational Institutions in Nagaland

S.N.	*Type of Institution*	*1986-87*	*1987-88*	*1988-89*	*1989-90*	*1990-91*
1.	University (NEHU Campus)	12	24	47(R)	37	91
2.	Colleges for general education	6,275	6,234	7,473	8,439	28948
3.	Higher professional education of Education					
	(a) Nagaland College	91	193	193	102	94
	(b) Agricultural College	-	-	244	228	239
	(c) Theology	-	-	378	463	611
4.	Schools for General Edu.					
	(a) High School	49,123	51,457	54,662	71,407	82166
	(b) Middle Schools	68,922	72,194	76,691	76,270	68256
	(c) Primary Schools	147,345	154,340	163,953	115,747	1345655
5.	Schools for Profe-ssional Education					
	(a) Polyechnic	222	240	278	301	385
	(b) Basic Trg. Inst. (JTTI)	86	87	254	69	41
	(c) Industrial Trg. Instt.	303	277	358	423	349

Contd.

S.N.	Type of Institution	1986-87	1987-88	1988-89	1989-90	1990-91
6.	Law College	229	251	308	329	298
	Total	272,608	285,297	304,839 (R)	273.815	296002

Source: Directorate of Higher & Technical and School Education, Government of Nagaland, Kohima not dated.

Table 7.15.1
Number of Educational Institutions, Nagaland

	1991-92	1992-93	1993-94	1994-95	1995-96
1	121	121	120	131	135
2	10833	11679	12320	13617	13742
3					
A	107	77	82	83	124
B	241	235	235		
C	885	891	1051	1119	1183
4					
A			3687	3835	3536
B	102062	103324	110049	111665	113739
C	74273	77215	75483	75781	75243
D	126781	124931	121264	121606	133101
5					
A	365	328	352	361	375
B	35	40	36	23	17
C	297	311	313	310	319
6	309	389	466	478	510
Total	316309	319541	325458	329009	342024

Source: Statistical Handbook of Nagaland, 1996.
Directorate of Economics and Statistics, Govt. of Nagaland, Kohima.

subjects like Science and Mathematics.[8] The language is another factor affecting the development of elementary education. Since as many as sixteen Naga dialects have been officially recognized as the mother tongue at the primary stage, textbook preparation and procurement of sufficient number of language teachers are problems that exist even today. Moreover, often the child is the first generation learner and hence has no academic support at home. Further, the Naga language teachers are often untrained, quite unlike in Mizoram, where, the Lai language teacher is trained even in its educationally backward district such as Chhimtuipui.

The dependence on science and mathematics teachers from outside the state has lowered the level of science and mathematics teaching, as most of them ('outsiders') are employed at the high school level. Thus, at the elementary stage, we find science and mathematics being taught

Table 7.16

Number of Teachers in Educational Institutions in Nagaland

S.No.	Type of Institution	1986-87	1987-88	1988-89	1989-90	1990-91
1.	University (NEHU Campus)	18	18	18	21	21
2.	Colleges for general education	28	295	272(R)	297	305
3.	Higher professional education					
	(a) Nagaland College of Edu.	11	13	13	10	10
	(b) Agricultural College	-	-	37	39	39
	(c) Theology	-	-	35	36	37
4.	Schools for General Edu.					
	(a) H.S.S.					
	(b) High School	2.429	2.437	2.507	2.928	3.122
	(c) Middle Schools	3.245	3.267	3.279	3.248	3.598
	(d) Primary Schools	6.497	6.499	6.533	6,572	62.325
5.	Schools for Professional Education					
	(a) Polyechnic	14	13	17(R)	17	39
	(b) Basic Trg. Inst.(JTTI)	22	22	22	22	22
	(c) Industrial Trg. Instt.	30	49	47	48	48
6.	Law College	12	11	11	12	12
	Total	272.608	285.297	304,839 (R)	273,815	296002

Source: Directorate of Higher & Technical and School Education. Government of Nagaland. Kohima not dated.

Table 7.16.1

Number of Teachers in Educational Institutions in Nagaland

S.No.	Type of Institution	1991-92	1992-93	1993-94	1994-95	1995-96
1.	University (NEHU Campus)	23	26	27	27	28
2.	Colleges for general education	323	378	404	412	414
3.	Higher professional education					
	(a) Nagaland College of Edu.	11	11	11	11	12
	(b) Agricultural College	39	39	39		
	(c) Theology	65	64	74	83	88
4.	Schools for General Edu.					
	(a) H.S.S.			53	153	156
	(b) High School	3666	3809	4314	4342	4451
	(c) Middle Schools	3651	3651	5429	4281	4468
	(d) Primary Schools	6425	6443	8677	6600	6749
5.	Schools for Professional Education					
	(a) Polytechnic	38	41	39	40	41
	(b) Basic Trg. Inst.(JTTI)	22	26	26	26	13
	(c) Industrial Trg. Instt.	49	48	47	51	51
6.	Law College	13	13	13	21	23
	Total	14325	14569	19153	16047	16494

Source: Statistical Handbook of Nagaland, 1996.
Directorate of Economics and Statistics, Government of Nagaland, Kohima.

by Arts Graduates, under graduates, social science teachers and sometimes even a Hindi language teacher. This is a feature, which Mizoram had gradually done away with, having developed subject specialization even at the elementary level.

Elementary education in Nagaland, which is by and large unrelated to its environmental needs, is also less attractive to the Naga as compared to the Mizo. The Naga economy though primitive is more self-sufficient than that of the Mizos. Unlike Mizoram where market economy has developed – increasing the demand for education; and communication with people outside the state, the Naga's spirit of economic self-help and self-reliance kept them away from the need to communicate with the outside world. It has reduced the demand for education. Thus, despite a similar progress of literacy and elementary education in both Mizoram and Nagaland, between 1980-1990, their exists a gap between these states because of the economic development, the role of their respective churches, development of ethnic consciousness and the differing political experiences.

These factors taken together have had an effect on the demand for education. Whereas by the eighties and more so by the nineties, we find Mizos predominating the service sector, especially in government jobs and school education; in Nagaland, several government departments had non-Nagas even till 1990. Not only did these 'outsiders' dominate teaching at the tertiary level, but they were found in several middle and high schools also.

Yet another important difference between these two states is the disparity between the educational developments of tribes. Whereas in Mizoram, there is comparatively less difference between the educational achievement of a Lushai and a Lai, Bru, Riang, Chakma and Mara, in Nagaland, the Ao, Angami, Lotha, Sangtam are far ahead of other tribes who live in Mon, Phek and Tuensang districts.

Further most of the benefits accruing from education have been confined to a few tribes, leaving the majority outside the pale of development. Hence, even if he is a Naga government officer, he is most likely to belong to one of the major educationally advanced tribes.

According to the 1981 census, out of 21 Scheduled Tribes living in Nagaland, the percentage of illiteracy was as high as 87.8 among the Konyaks in rural areas followed by Khienungan (85.5) and Chirr (85.0). Compared with these we find only 57.7 per cent of Angamis were illiterate–illiteracy being the lowest among the Aos (38.3). The pattern of rural illiteracy among the tribes as mentioned above is also similar in the urban areas.

The involvement of the Mizo and Naga churches in education has also been different. Whereas the former demanded state recognition of their denomination schools, the latter has been concentrating more on preaching Christianity. One does not find a school located next to each church in Nagaland common to Mizoram. In Mizoram, the church is an integral part of society. Christianity having unified the Mizos cut across the ideological differences between the political parties. Moreover, the role of the Church in Nagaland is largely confined to the spread of Christianity and has no impact on the political movements in the state. The church has not helped to unify the different political groups in Nagaland after Phizo's death contrary to the rise of Mizo consciousness under Laldenga.

Structure and Administration of School Education

After adapting the National Policy on Education, 1986, Nagaland has merged its classes A and B into a single pre-primary class of one years' duration. Thus, primary education starts from Class I and terminates in Class V. This is different from the pattern of primary education in Mizoram, which terminates in Class IV, with a board examination. However, due to the shortage of middle school teachers, some Naga primary schools terminate at Class IV. Middle schools often start at Class V terminating at Class VIII. Classes IX and X, the High/ or Secondary School, terminates with a board examination. The Higher Secondary stage comprising of Classes XI and XII is only offered in selected high schools, mainly in urban areas. High schools are concentrated in educationally advanced districts like Kohima (44) and Mokokchung (27). Mon district only has 11.

Altogether there were 1247 Government Primary Schools, 230 Middle Schools, 107 High Schools, and 4 Higher Secondary Schools, supervised by the Directorate of School Education, as indicated in its Annual Administrative Report of 1995-96. According to the same Report, there existed in Nagaland 83 Private Primary Schools, 139 Middle Schools and 169 High Schools. The reasons for the increase in the demand for private schools, beyond the primary sector, has already been mentioned earlier. However, there existed an equal number of both government and private High Schools, which were 4 each respectively.

At the Secretariat level, administration of school education is looked after by a Secretary-cum-Commissioner; who is generally an IAS Officer. He is assisted by one Additional Secretary, one Joint Secretary, one Deputy Secretary and one Under Secretary. At the Directorate level, there are four Directors each looking after Higher and Technical Education; Sports and Youth Resources; School Education and the State Council of Educational Research and Training separately.

Director of School Education looks after pre-school, elementary, secondary, adult and non-formal education in the state. He was assisted by 2 Joint Directors; 3 Deputy Directors; 5 Assistant Directors; 1 Senior Accounts Officer; 1 Registrar; 1 Research Officer in charge of planning; 2 Assistant Research Officers; 1 Vocational Guidance and Counseling Officer; One Programme-cum-Script Writing for Educational Technology; 1 Special Officer for Work Experience; 1 Secretary Education; 6 Language Officers; 1 Junior Accounts Officer; 1 State Survey Officer; 1 Assistant State Survey Officer, and 5 Superintendents. An engineering division, headed by one executive engineer also looked after the construction work of the department and also had four sub-divisional officers under him. All of these officers were the under Director of School Education in 1995-96.

In Nagaland, the concept of district administration took shape in December 1st 1963, upon its attaining statehood. Originally, the state had been divided into nine educational sub-divisions, each headed by one Deputy Inspector of Schools, responsible for inspection and supervision of middle schools, all of which had been working under the Inspector of Schools in the State's Directorate of Education. However, inspection and supervision of high schools was done by the State Level Inspectorate. Inspection and supervision of primary schools was undertaken by the Deputy Inspectors of Schools who were, in turn, assisted by Sub Inspectors. This system prevailed in the state till 1979, after which Zonal Inspectorates were created, headed by Inspectors of Schools for each of the zones such as Kohima, Mokokchung and Tuensang. Due to the inability of the zones to provide effective supervision because of topographical variation in the state, in 1980 these three Zonal Inspectorates were converted into District Inspectorates. In Mon district a new Inspectorate was set up. Separate Inspectorates were also set up for Phek, Wokho Zunheboto districts by deploying the existing officers and staff of the Directorate of School Education. By 1996, there were seven Inspector of schools assisted by twenty Deputy Inspectors. These Deputy Inspectors were assisted by Sub Inspectors.

The Sub Inspector looks after primary schools only, whereas middle schools are generally supervised by the Deputy Inspector. Each Inspector of schools has directly under him a Science Supervisor who is responsible for improving the quality of science education at the school level - a feature that does not exist in some other states of India.

Financing of Elementary Education

In the Eighth Five Year Plan (1992-97) of Nagaland, the approved outlay for elementary education was 38.93 per cent less than what Mizoram had of, that is 50.76 per cent. It is also less than the All India percentage for the same sector which was 45.59. During the sixties (1963-67), Nagaland had spent as much as 63.39 to 60.76 per cent on elementary education, out of its total expenditure on education from its revenue account. However, from 1967 to 1975 this figure had declined from 60.76 per cent in 1966-67 to 58.88 per cent in 1974-75. The expenditure somewhat picks up during 1975 and 1994 to around little above 60 per cent.

During 1992-93 Nagaland had received 7.84 lacks Rupees from the centre for the scheme of Operation Blackboard, which was meant for quality improvement of primary schools. However, Mizoram had received as much as 13.42 lacks Rupees for the same years. Unlike Mizoram, Nagaland was unable to bargain from the centre for assistance in improving the quality of its primary schools.

For example, in the scheme for Non-Formal Education, Nagaland had received no money since 1990, whereas Mizoram had received as much as 2.6 lack rupees which was increased to 8.58 in the years 1993-94.

Thus, Mizoram was able to improve its elementary education, by taking advantage of these centrally sponsored schemes. It also managed to train its elementary teachers through the Teacher Programme and Pre-service Education Scheme.

Kohima District

Quite unlike Mizoram's Chhimtuipui district which had been declared as economically and educationally backward between the sixties and the early nineties, Kohima district of Nagaland was considered advanced. As pointed out by the Angami Nagas (Shilo Ao. 1995), what had transformed Nagaland was the spread of Christianity. The first effort to convert the Nagas was done by Rev. M. Brousan in 1834-40. Although, the then government of Assam approved of a few schools it was unable to attract Naga children to enroll into them. During 1876-77, a school at Chumunkedima Headquarters was attended only by children of the government officials. The missionaries who had started their pioneering work among Ao Nagas in Mokokchung district, later moved to Kohima and in 1878, Rev. C.D. King was deputed to Kohima to educate the Angami Nagas.

Thus, by 1884 the Angami Naga language was translated into the Roman Script and by 1911-12 Kohima district had 22 schools out of which 12 belonged to the Mission. Before 1947 a High School in Kohima was upgraded for a Middle English School. Despite efforts made both by the government and the missionaries the literacy rate of Kohima district (by 1991) was only 50.93 per cent, as against the state literacy rate of 60.59 per cent. One of the reasons for the low literacy rate in the district was the ongoing insurgency movement leading to frequent curfews. The other was the influence of labour from Bihar, U.P., Nepal and other parts of Northern India who did not participate in the literacy programmes.

In 1991, there were 647 educational institutions in the district which included a District Institute of Education and Training (DIET) for primary teacher-training.

Table 7.17
Enrolment of Children in Schools in the Kohima District by Stages in 1993

Stage of School Education	*Enrolment in 1993*		
	Boys	*Girls*	*Total*
Pre-Primary	15010	13149	28159
Primary (Classes I-V)	16468	16688	33156
Middle (Classes VI-VIII)	13012	1048	14060
Secondary (Classes IX-X)	19116	25699	54815
Total District	73606	56584	130815

Source: Directorate of School Education, Government of Nagaland, Statistical Cell, Kohima, 1993.

In 1993, Kohima district had 33156 primary schools, with an almost equal amount of distribution between boys (16468) and girls (16688) attending the schools. However, the girls seem to dropout at the middle school level (10.48 girls as against 13012 boys enrolled in 1993). This gender disparity gets less from the High School level (25699 girls as against 29116 boys).

Similarly, at the Higher Secondary level we find 218 girls as against 304 boys. This district had the highest enrolment of school students as compared with the other six districts of the state.

As for teachers in position, Kohima also had the largest number of teachers present for the primary stage (1816), though the male teachers out numbered the female teachers (1671 males as against 145 females). However, for the middle school stage, there were more female teachers (734) as compared to male teachers (466). This is also true of the High Schools (1619 females to 558 males); though there were no female teachers in the Higher Secondary Schools in 1993 (50 males only).

There are in total 4513 teachers in the district teaching at the different stages of school education. The total percentage of trained teachers was only 37.54 in 1993. In the district the teacher-pupil ratio was favourable for all stages, that is, 1:18 (primary), 1:12 (middle), 1:25 high school and 1:10 (Higher Secondary).

Administration of education in Nagaland is of recent origin. In 1995 at Kohima district there was one Inspector of Schools, followed a Science Supervisor. He is followed by four Deputy Inspector of Schools for the Sub divisions, namely; Kohima, Dimapur, and Peren. These in turn have Sub Inspectors of Schools. In 1995, there were 10 Sub Inspectors of Schools in Kohima; 8 in Dimapur and 6 in Peren.

Unlike Chhimtuipui district of Mizoram, which had sub-divisional level education autonomy, for the three autonomous districts namely, Lai, Mara and Chakma autonomous district councils in Kohima had no such parallel structures. In fact, since the entire state of Nagaland is inhabited largely by the Naga tribes, no need was felt to create autonomous district councils for ethnic minorities living in the state.

Though the southern boundary of Kohima has the Assamese population, and to a large measure of Bengalis, yet there was no educational autonomy for this minority population. Mokokchung and Tuensang districts consisting of Naga tribes did not have any such councils. The situation is similar in areas which form the boundary with Manipur in the south and Myanmar in the East, where different Naga tribes live, as described earlier. (See Map of Kohima district).

Climate of Kohima being temperate, the summers are relatively warm and winters cold. Kohima district has Japfu mountain at the centre, Kapamezu in the south-east and Saramati in the North East. Majority of the population in the district comprises of Angami Nagas. The five blocks of the district are Jalukie, Medziphema, Kuhubato, Tseminyu and Kohima. Jalukie comprises of Zeliangroug and Kuki tribes speaking Zema, Liangmei and Kuki dialects. This is by far the most educationally backward area of the district.

According to 1991 census the population of the district was 392,179 persons, out of which, there were 210,666 males and 183,513 females. Only 26.88 per cent of the population was urban, concentrating in Dimapur and Kohima towns. The Scheduled Tribe population was only 65.53 per cent which as compared with Chhimtuipui district of Mizoram is far less. The latter having above 90 per cent of such population. However, the density of the population in Kohima district was much more, which was 98 persons per square kilometre.

The major economic activities of the district comprised of agriculture. According to 1981 census, 76.5 of Kohima's population was engaged in the primary sector where the females (40.5 per cent) out numbered the male workers (35.6 per cent). Only 4 per cent of its workers were engaged at the secondary level (3.2 per cent males and 0.8 per cent females). At the tertiary level as much as 19.4 per cent of Kohima district's labour was engaged; out of which 16.0 per cent were males and 3.4 per cent females. Due to a tendency of the Naga tribes to resist change in their occupation, Kohima district though an educationally advanced district have majority of the Nagas who remain content with their self-sufficient economy. Despite education, minimal industrial development and the opening of the service sector, agriculture remains their predominant occupation; 'wet-rice' terraced cultivation as compared with Chhimtuipui's jhumming cultivation. The Angamis unlike the Lai people took to terrace cultivation long ago. The terraces leaned against stone walls, at different levels, were protected from soil erosion. In Dimapur, the local Nagas have made use of animals for paddy cultivation.

The principal crops of the district are arums, yams, rice, and sugarcane. The common vegetables are gourds, watermelon, melon, lentils, cucumbers, spinach, mustard, onion, chillies, garlic, pumpkins, brinjals, potato, tomato, radish, and carrot. There are plenty of fruits in the district out of which pineapples are especially cultivated at Ghaspani (Medziphema). Besides these, animal husbandry also exists; specializing in ducks, chicken, pig, and sheep breeding. The Mithun is also a great favourite of the Nagas. Cottage industry is the traditional industry of the district comprising of cane work; bamboo work; woodcraft; blacksmithy; clay pottery and handloom cloth/shawls.

Study Sample

The study sample covers of 10 schools, located in Dimapur sub-division of Kohima district. Dimapur has a mixed population, having had Kacharis serving side by side with the Naga tribes since long. It comes under a sub-divisional officer with two extra Assistant Commissioners, subordinate to the Medziphema Rural Development Block with its population of 73,677 persons. Dimapur town is connected by railways, roadways and air to Assam and is very central when compared with Lawngtlai. It is a place of worship for various communities living in the region; its Kali temple is famous. Apart from Hindu places of worship, there also exists a Jain temple, a mosque and a number of beautiful churches in Dimapur, which was the capital of the

Kachari Kingdom, attacked several times by the Ahoms. The Dhansuri River runs across the town, which boast of all the modern amenities. It has a mixed population. It is a thriving business centre for the entire state, and an important market of foreign goods transported from South East Asia through Burma. In short, Dimapur has all the infrastructure for educational development.

Quality of Lower Primary Schools

VEC and Infrastructural facilities

The Village Education Committee has played a good role in improving the quality of primary education. They have provided infrastructural facilities, such as, school building, playground, to school wall, furniture, seen in our visit to Phasema Village Education Committee in Kohima district in 1990. The concept of Village Education Committee (VEC) in Nagaland originated in 1989. The Naga villages traditionally had councils even prior to the foundation of the VEC. But the VEC is more effective in urban and literate areas than in their rural counterparts.

Previously, the VEC was called the Village School Managing Board, headed by a literate person in the village. Today, after its upgradation, it is headed by an Extra Assistant Commissioner (EAC) who is also in-charge of the administrative officers of the sub-divisional or block level. The Secretary of the VEC is nominated from among the committee members. In general, the VEC members are selected by the village general meeting usually held at the end of the year. Members consist of 5 to 7 persons. Their term in office varies from village to village, although normally, it is for 2 to 3 years. There are no proper rules and regulation as to how to improve the condition of schools, rather the members decide on what to do quite arbitrarily. Most of the time they concern themselves with improvement of school building and other infrastructure aspects, to the neglect of academic aspects different from the role played by the Lai Autonomous District Council of Mizoram.

Some of the duties of the VEC are:

1. Selection of a school site compound which is decided after the people in the village have had a meeting to decide about the site;
2. It is compulsory for the villages to collect money, material, labour and any other infrastructral affairs of the school;
3. The village authority approves and allows the committee to incur the genuine expenditure and submit the expenditure bills to the village funding authority. In case the fund is not immediately available, a loan can be obtained from rich families along with other contributors. An annual collection of money is made to repay the loan;

4. The villagers are compelled to spend many days away from their homes in order to complete the school work and after they spend their own money to build the school; which is adjusted on their returns;
5. A list of all required items of the school is submitted to the Village Annual General Meeting within the current year and they decide on the developmental activities for the next year;
6. Upon the visit of the Education Officer to the village, the VEC members organize a joint meeting of the village elders, officers and Board members to discuss school problems, and, try and find its solutions;
7. The VEC members and joint-members can visit the school any day to find out the disciplinary problems, irregularity of staff and teaching and take corrective measures;
8. Should the school be short of a teacher, the committee can approach higher authorities to deploy or re-deploy a teacher. If necessary the village can employ an educated member and pay him salary out of the village's collection.

Thus, it appears that both the location of the school and its functioning is carried out in a democratic manner. It reveals a village-level planning, which is non-existent in the Lai Autonomous District Council, which does not deviate from the state norms. The role of the Village Education Committee reveals larger community participation than in the autonomous district bodies. Though there is no scope of decentralizing the academic matters such as introducing new local specific curriculum as was done by the latter, the VEC's role though limited is yet substantial.

Location and Infrastructural Facilities

Most of the respondents felt the schools were located wherever necessary, however the members of the VEC felt that the schools should be located away from the main road which is noisy. About 54.82 per cent of the VEC members expressed their satisfaction with the school building, sitting arrangements. Only 45.16 per cent felt that these needed improvement. In general, the school buildings, drinking water, electricity, furniture and infrastructural arrangements are satisfactory in Kohima primary schools. Only 19 per cent of the VEC members were not satisfied with their facilities. About 75 per cent of the respondents said that the Village Education Committee had provided facilities such as material and labour for construction of the school building, furniture and hostel facilities for boys and girls. But they were able to do this for the urban schools only, and not for the rural schools. Thirty-eight respondents said that only a few urban schools had drinking water, electricity toilets, play ground and benches, cupboards, and 61.29 per cent were dissatisfied with these infrastructural facilities. The district authorities did not pay any attention to the lack of these facilities and the community was helpless to provide the schools with the latter. Only 20.90 per cent of the schools have teaching aids such as maps, charts, science kits (box), and most schools lacked these facilities, quite unlike the situation Lai. There was also a serious shortage of funds for providing the school with these facilities.

Since in Kohima district, 62.16 per cent of the schools were located in rural areas, the lack of proper facilities led to poor teaching-learning situation. The schools located away from the main road are generally poor in terms of infrastructural facilities, despite efforts made by the community to supply them with good quality buildings. The latter is reflected in our data that shows that 88.89 per cent of the schools had proper school buildings. This is in total contrast to the Lai experience, where despite the shortage of school buildings, other infrastructural facilities like maps, cupboards, teaching aids, globes and science kits (boxes) were in plenty. Most of the schools in Kohima district had their own buildings (54%) and about 40% per cent schools were located in rent-free buildings. About 32.45 per cent of the buildings were pucca and 59.46 katcha. Once again the number of pucca buildings in Kohima district is far more than the Lai area, where almost all buildings were katcha of the Assam type with thatched roofs.

Academic Facilities

The staff strength of primary schools in Kohima did not exceed beyond 4 to 5 teachers, in total contrast to the staff strength in Lai Autonomous District Council, which had an average of 5 to 6 staff members, thereby allowing for subject specialization. The rural schools had a shortage of staff and the urban schools a surplus. The VEC is actively engaged in improving the academic content of the schools. Its members help in teaching the students, especially in language teaching, in mother tongue. There exists numerous Naga dialects and no one Naga language (unlike Mizoram), and hence the VEC members have to often teach the children the first language, which the other school teachers may not know.

The curriculum is not local specific (like it is in Lai) nor has there been any attempt to decentralize it. Apart from mother tongue, and English Social Studies, Environmental Studies are conducted in English.

There is, therefore, a demand for quality English teachers. Here the language factor has much implication for understanding the achievement level of students.

Although the schools have Work Experience, or Work Education as part of curricula they do not teach useful work, as making school teaching aids. Generally these activities are confined to carpentry, more often to games, singing hymns, and playing musical instruments such as the drum. There is therefore much difference in work experience/ work education activities of Lai schools and schools in Kohima.

Most of the respondents were dissatisfied with the lack of teaching aids in the rural schools in Kohima, nor did the VEC members or community leaders did anything to improve them. Though there were sufficient black boards, desks, chairs, pencils and chalks.

Unlike Lai, the primary school teachers of Kohima were only 50 per cent trained and even when they were, they did not attend any refresher classes. One of the reasons could be that there is only one District Institute of Educational Research and Training (DIET) located at Kohima and hence far from Dimapur our study sample. Though there exists Basic Teacher Training Institutes near Dimapur, yet they are old fashioned and do not teach the latest pedagogical methods. The DIET in Kohima is far too new to train the backlog of untrained school teachers.

Despite the shortage of teaching aids, textbooks exist in all schools. VEC however, has made no effort to develop a primary school library or add reference books to schools. In general the urban schools have a few additional books. Unlike the Lai Autonomous Council which has its own textbook section and printing press, thereby providing reference books rooted in the local history, ecology of the people, although printing presses exist in Dimapur, reference books are only available in urban schools, since there is no local board of education and examination. Decentralization of educational curriculum as evinced in Lai would have helped to enrich the academic.

Administrative Aspects

The VEC is entrusted with the power to administer the primary schools. It was found that out of the 50 primary schools in the district, 96.77 per cent of the VEC members visited the schools in order to check attendance of the students and teachers so that the schools ran on a regular basis, and discussed problems faced by both the teachers and the students; 66.68 per cent of them visited the schools monthly; 16.66 fortnightly and 16.66 annually.

They also held regular meetings with teachers, parents, headmasters and the community every month, and conveyed the proceedings to the District Office, mentioning the practical difficulties in running the schools, or making decisions. These were shortage of teachers, poor academic performance of students and problems faced by the parents. VEC's also had half yearly and monthly meetings. Majority of the respondents were satisfied with the meetings and 87.10 per cent were happy with VEC's involvement in administering school affairs. The management of 87.16 per cent schools had also improved due to the active involvement of the VEC members.

The involvement of the VEC members is especially important, in view of the fact that no regular inspection of the schools was done by Inspectors or Sub-Inspectors, due to a shortage of vehicles. More than 96 per cent of the members complained about the irregular visit of the Inspectors of schools, thus the supervision of the schools was done solely by the VEC members. In fact, 25.87 per cent of the VEC members expressed their concern over the lack of academic supervision in schools – due to the irregular visit of Inspectors to classroom.

There is a provision for giving incentive to those children attending school regularly and a reward for the best student in a discipline, but these aspects were not attended to by the Inspectors, and therefore, as much as 74.19 per cent of the schools had not implemented these incentive schemes. There was however no provision for scholarships, stipends, free mid-day meals, uniform and textbooks stationary; which the Lai Autonomous District Council provided in Mizoram.

About 87.10 per cent of the VEC members felt that they had the freedom to approach the state and district authorities over the appointment and transfer of teachers in primary schools. However, the VEC members also felt they were not awarded any incentive for their contribution to academic supervision and inspection of schools. This is particularly so since, as much as 93.55 per cent of the VEC members, attended school functions regularly like the sports week or annual function.

There was however no substitution teaching done in the schools when a teacher was absent. The VEC members stated that the district and state authorities need to spend more time to improve the academic and administrative aspects of the schools.

Financial Aspects

The Village Education Committee has the power to utilize the school funds provided by the district and state authorities in any way they thought befitting. About 62.16 per cent of the VEC members stated that they received a certain amount of the Rural Development Fund for improvement of school building and repairing – for even providing electricity and a school approach road. Apart from this a substantial amount is contributed by the parents of the school children for maintenance of infrastructural facilities. These parents also provide locally available material to help build school furniture.

Private fund is raised by as many as 86.11 per cent of VEC members to arrange for private teachers wherever there is a shortage of teaching staff. The government from time to time also gives separate funds for school building, school office, toilets etc.

One may conclude that despite the existence of the Village Education Committee and powers given to them for ensuring quality improvement of primary schools in Nagaland, there has not been an effective intervention by them leading to improvement of infrastructural facilities and curriculum innovation. Decentralization of educational planning and administration, a policy commitment in the National Policy of Education 1986, has been more effective in Mizoram than in Nagaland. Mizoram as explained in earlier chapter is a more integrated state, extremely conscious of the need to compete with other states of India. In the desire to become a part of the Indian mainstream, it has availed of whatever funds it could for education, allotted by the Centre. In my meetings with the North Eastern States held with the Education Division of the Planning Commission, I became aware how Mizoram could argue its case and get funds allotted to it more effectively than Nagaland. Moreover, the community participation at the local level in Mizoram is also far greater than in Nagaland, the latter distracted, as it has been by fifty years of constant insurgency movement.

References

1. Monirul Hussain, "The nationality question", *Seminar*, 366, February 1990, New Delhi, pp. 38-39.
2. Directorate of Economics and Statistics, Government of Nagaland, *Statistical Hand Book of Nagaland*, 1987. (Kohima, 1987).
3. Sipra Sen, *Tribes of Nagaland* (New Delhi: Mittal Publications, 1987).
4. North Eastern Council Secretariat, *Basic Statistics of North Eastern Region 1995*, (Shillong: Ministry of Home Affairs, Government of India.)
5. R.B. Purkayastha, "A Diagnostic study of District Educational Administration in Nagaland - A Case Study of Kohima District", DEPA, dissertation, New Delhi, NIEPA, 1988-89. p. 3.
6. Census of India 1991, Series 18, *Nagaland, Provisional Population Tables*, Kohima, 1991.

7. Interviews with Jack Sekhose, Education Officer, SCERT, Kohima, at Kohima during June 4-9, 1990.
8. Planning Commission, Education Division, "Progress and Problems of Educational Development in the States and the UTs of North Eastern Region", Mimeo, New Delhi, 1985-86.

Appendices

Appendix I

North Eastern States Arranged in Descending Order of Literacy Rate Among Persons, Males and Females, 1991

State	*Literacy Rate (Total)*		*State*	*Male Literacy Rate*		*State*	*Female Literacy Rate*	
	2001	1991		2001	1991		2001	1991
Mizoram	88.49	82.27	Mizoram	90.69	85.61	Mizoram	86.13	78.60
Nagaland	67.11	61.65	Manipur	77.87	71.63	Nagaland	61.92	54.75
Tripura	73.66	60.44	Tripura	81.47	70.58	Tripura	65.41	49.65
Manipur	68.87	59.89	Nagaland	71.11	67.62	Manipur	59.7	47.60
Assam	62.78	52.89	Assam	71.93	61.87	Meghalaya	60.41	44.85
Meghalaya	63.31	49.10	Meghalaya	66.14	53.12	Assam	56.03	43.03
Arunachal Pradesh	57.74	41.59	Arunachal Pradesh	64.07	51.45	Arunachal Pradesh	44.24	29.69

Source: Ministry of Human Resource Development, Annual Report 1994-95, Part I, Govt. of India, Department of Education, 1995, pp. 205.

Appendix II

Literacy Rates 1991 North East

State	*General*			*Scheduled Castes*			*Scheduled Tribes*		
	Person	*Male*	*Female*	*Person*	*Male*	*Female*	*Person*	*Male*	*Female*
Arunachal Pradesh	41.59	51.45	29.69	57.27	66.25	41.42	34.45	44.00	24.94
Assam	52.89	61.87	43.03	53.94	63.88	42.99	49.16	58.93	38.98
Manipur	59.89	71.63	47.60	56.44	65.28	47.41	53.63	62.39	44.48
Meghalaya	49.10	53.12	44.85	44.27	54.56	31.19	46.71	49.78	43.63
Mizoram	82.27	85.61	78.60	77.92	77.54	81.25	82.71	86.66	78.70
Nagaland	61.65	67.62	54.75	-	-	-	60.59	66.27	54.51
Tripura	60.44	70.58	49.65	56.66	67.25	45.45	40.37	52.88	27.34

Source: Census of India 1991 Final Population. Total Paper 2 of 1992, p.206.

Appendix III

Literacy Rates of Scheduled Tribes 1991 Census in Descending Order

States	*Literacy Rates of Scheduled Tribes*
Mizoram	82.71
Nagaland	60.59
Manipur	53.63
Assam	49.16
Meghalaya	46.71
Tripura	40.37
Arunachal Pradesh	34.45

Source: Ministry of Human Resource Development. Annual Report 1994-95, Part I, Government of India, Department of Education, 1995. p. 208.

Appendix IV

Rural Habitations with and without Primary Sections in North East, 1965

State/ Union Territory	*Item of Information*	Habitations with Primary Sections as a distance of *within them*	*upto 0.5 mile*	*0.6 to 1.0 mile*	*1.1 to 1.5 miles*	*1.6 to 2 miles*	*more than 2 miles*	*Total*
Assam	No. of Habitations	16312	5370	4791	1644	1134	2220	31471
	their population	8890067	1249387	1111921	369552	192705	241523	1205.5155
	percentage	73.74	10.36	9.22	3.07	1.60	2.00	100.00
Manipur	No. of Habitations	1773	407	183	69	75	299	2806
	their population	679588	102244	28777	7955	7387	31863	857814
	percentage	79.22	11.92	3.35	0.93	0.86	3.71	100.00
Tripura	No. of Habitations	1296	1933	1019	472	327	730	577
	their population	603872	297444	139201	56562	32903	54609	1184591
	percentage	50.98	25.11	11.75	4.77	2.78	4.61	100.00

Source: Second All India Educational Survey, NCERT, New Delhi, 1967, pp. 118-120
Note: States of Nagaland, Mizoram Meghalaya were parts of the State of Assam.

Appendix V

Rural Habitations with/without Primary Schools/Sections in North East, 1973

State/Union Territory	Habitations with Primary Sections as a Distance of						
	within the Total Habitation	*upto 0.5 km.*	*0.6 to 1.0 km.*	*1.1 to 1.5 km.*	*1.6 to 2.0 km.*	*more than 2.0 km.*	
1	*2*	*3*	*4*	*5*	*6*	*7*	*8*
Arunachal Pradesh	A 546	15	23	10	24	2355	2973
	B 224312	3192	3664	1469	4230	246160	482827
	C 46.46%	0.66%	0.72%	0.31%	0.88%	50.97%	100.00%
Assam	A 17689	2744	5512	1152	1381	964	29442
	B 10705233	802454	1394276	303396	338437	201726	1374552
	C 77.80%	5.84%	10.14%	2.21%	2.46%	1.47%	100.00%
Manipur	A 1920	50	66	6	31	272	2345
	B 889143	20332	18857	971	4717	33.20%	967227
	C 91.93%	2.10%	1.95%	0.10%	0.49%	3.43%	100.00%
Meghalaya	A 2792	194	299	100	221	1235	4841
	B 752704	27084	4041	13436	24724	121971	980030
	C 76.80%	2.77%	4.09%	1.37	2.52%	12.45%	100.00%

Contd.

Contd.

1	*2*	*3*	*4*	*5*	*6*	*7*	*8*
Mizoram	A 214	-	-	-	-	1	215
	B 303177	-	-	-	-	731	303908
	C 99.76	-	-	-	-	0.24%	100.00%
Nagaland	A 1031	236	84	27	29	30	1431
	B 427573	50770	17266	8737	5298	5206	514850
	C 83.04%	9.86%	3.35%	1.69%	1 04%	1.02%	100.00%
Tripura	A 1616	715	1388	964	542	825	6050
	B 851354	155985	272859	126425	66313	81515	1554446
	C 54.77%	10.04%	17.55%	8.13%	4.27%	5.24%	100.00%

Source: Third All India Educational Survey. NCERT. New Delhi, 1979. pp. 144-148.
Note: A. No. of Habitations B. Their Total Population C. Percentage of their population to the total population in the State.

Appendix VI

Rural Habitations with and without Primary Schools/Sections in North East, 1978

State. Union Territory	Habitations with Primary Sections as a Distance of						
	within the Total Habitation	*upto 0.5 km*	*0.6 to 1.0 km.*	*upto 1.0 km.*	*1.1 to 1.5 km.*	*1.6 to 2.0 km.*	*more than 5 km.*
1	*2*	*3*	*4*	*5*	*6*	*7*	*8*
Arunachal Pradesh	A 832	49	132	1013	38	138	1928
	B 314204	9675	17249	341128	4372	18107	198484
	C 55.90	1.72	3.07	60.69	0.78	3.22	35.31
Assam	A 18561	2776	3423	24760	1428	1077	766
	B 12759143	959808	1058210	14777161	430411	295739	181883
	C 81.34	6.12	6.75	94.21	2.75	1.89	1.16
Manipur	A 2146	102	110	2358	16	47	110
	B 1047985	26988	32475	1107448	3935	7314	10342
	C 92.82	2.39	2.88	98.09	0.35	0.65	0.91
Meghalaya	A 3396	602	463	4461	202	374	675
	B 893671	86645	59025	1039341	23373	42805	68543
	C 76.12	7.38	5.03	88.53	1.99	3.64	5.84

Contd.

Contd.

1	2	3	4	5	6	7	8
Mizoram	A 256	-	1	257	2	6	320
	B 278286	-	350	278636	872	760	93074
	C 74.54	-	0.09	74.63	0.23	0.20	24.94
Nagaland	A 939	15	17	971	1	4	13
	B 630523	3935	3384	637842	754	492	1977
	C 98.35	0.61	0.53	99.49	0.12	0.03	0.31
Tripura	A 1738	758	1295	3791	401	685	1361
	B 951304	183180	269097	1403581	74228	118474	151784
	C 54.42	10.48	15.39	80.29	4.28	6.78	8.68

Source: Fourth All India Educational Survey. NCERT, New Delhi, 1982, pp. 226-231.

Note: A- No. of Habitations

B- Total Population of habitations in 'A'

C- Percentage of population in 'B' as of the total rural population in the State/Union Territory.

Appendix VI.1

Rural Habitations with and without Primary Schools/Sections in North East, 1986

State/ Union Territory	within Habitation	Habitations with a primary Section as a Distance of Upto 0.5 km.	0.6 to1.0 km.	upto 1.0 km.	1.1 to 1.5 km.	1.6 to 2.0 km.	Upto 2 km.	more than 2 km.	Total
Arunachal Pradesh	A1134	59	158	1351	52	178	1581	1656	3237
	B450338	16898	34379	501665	6393	23371	531429	152501	683930
	C65.85	2.47	5.03	73.35	0.93	3.42	77.7	22.3	100
	A22292	3072	3252	28616	1607	962	31185	618	31803
Assam	B16064902	1061451	1262865	18389218	705934	372268	19467420	185495	196952915
	C81.74	5.4	6.43	93.57	3.59	1.89	99.06	0.94	100
	A2151	103	126	2380	17	33	2430	184	63728
Manipur	B1078984	41643	47440	1168067	3901	5888	1177856	21466	45497113
	C89.97	3.47	3.96	97.39	0.33	0.49	98.21	1.79	100
Meghalaya	A3350	205	452	4007	145	412	4564	773	5337
	B117055	42563	81039	1320657	21111	49134	1390902	89308	1480210
	C80.87	2.88	5.47	89.22	1.43	3.32	93.37	6.03	100

Contd.

Contd.

State Union Territory	Habitations with a primary Section as a Distance of								
	within Habitation	*Upto 0.5 km.*	*0.6 to1.0 km.*	*upto 1.0 km.*	*1.1 to 1.5 km.*	*1.6 to 2.0 km.*	*Upto 2 km.*	*more than 2 km.*	*Total*
Mizoram	A579	6	-	585	-	2	587	29		616
	B420994	977	-	421971	-	538	422509	6863		429732
	C98.05	0.23	-	98.28	-	0.13	98.4	1.6		100
Nagaland	A955	10	9	974	3	11	988	9		997
	B757588	3257	1327	762172	484	2829	765485	923		766408
	C98.85	0.42	0.17	99.45	0.06	0.37	99.88	0.12		100
Tripura	A2388	902	1144	4434	495	590	5519	781		6300
	B1299236	292650	323997	1915883	125154	128774	2169811	107850		2277661
	C57.04	12.85	14.22	84.12	5.49	5.65	95.26	4.74		100

Source: Fifth All India Educational Survey, NCERT, New Delhi, 1986.

Appendix VI.2

Rural Habitations with and without Primary Schools/Sections in North East, 1993

State/ Union Territory	Habitations with a primary Section as a Distance of							Total
	within Habitation	Upto 0.5 km.	0.6 to1.0 km.	upto 1.0 km.	1.1 to 2.0 km.	Upto 2 km.	more than 2 km.	
	A1436	137	231	1804	327	2131	1703	3834
Arunachal	B563841	30393	31695	626129	48383	674512	129597	804109
Pradesh	C70.12	3.78	3.97	77.87	6.02	83.88	16.12	100
	A22448	7707	5145	35300	3808	39108	2071	41179
Assam	B14139361	2970975	1795157	18905493	1499102	20404595	930074	21334669
	C66.27	13.93	8.41	88.61	7.03	95.64	4.36	100
	A2489	296	174	2959	156	3115	254	3369
Manipur	B1159288	110031	57156		37060	1363535	45762	1409297
	C82.26	7.81	4.06		2.63	96.75	3.25	100
	A3677	573	753		675	5678	898	6576
Meghalaya	B1169620	105767	114039		85288	1474714	104695	1579409
	C74.05	6.7	7.22		5.4	93.37	6.63	100
	A605	7	8		7	627	78	705
Mizoram	B385341	4500	1543		1193	392577	16075	408652
	C94.3	1.1	0.38		0.29	96.07	3.93	100
	A1035	51	31		31	1148	129	1277

Contd.

Contd.

State/ Union Territory	Habitations with a primary Section as a Distance of							Total
	within Habitation	*Upto 0.5 km.*	*0.6 to1.0 km.*	*upto 1.0 km.*	*1.1 to 2.0 km.*	*Upto 2 km.*	*more than 2 km.*	
Nagaland	B1050243	14955	15537		2392	1093127	43943	1137070
	C92.36	1.32	1.37		1.09	96.015	3.86	100
	A2619	1071	1444		949	6083	719	6802
Tripura	B1372622	325112	407094		247460	2352288	123970	2476258
	C55.43	13.13	16.44		9.99	94.99	5.01	100

Source: Sixth All India Educational Survey, NCERT, New Delhi, 1993.

Appendix VII

Rural Habitations with/without Middle Schools/Sections in North East, 1973

State/Union Territory		*Habitations with Middle Sections as a Distance of*					
within the Habitation		*upto 1.0 km.*	*1.1 to 2.0 km.*	*2.1 to 3.0 km.*	*3.1 to 4.0 km.*	*4.1 to 5 km.*	*more than 5 km.*
Arunachal	A 74	9	5	11	7	12	2855
	B 55614	6894	2491	2022	1062	6321	408423
	C 11.52%	1.43%	0.58%	0.42%	0.22%	1.30	89.53%
Assam	A 2850	4121	6005	6124	3835	2648	3859
	B 2166986	21211001	2774551	2698257	1755134	1091349	1138244
	C 15.76%	15.43%	20.19%	19.63%	12.77%	7.94%	8.28%
Manipur	A 346	283	198	132	83	69	1234
	B 317009	181835	95800	63797	39001	18750	251035
	C 32.77%	18.80%	9.90%	6.60%	4.04	1.94	25.95%
Meghalaya	A 282	212	235	283	188	374	3267
	B 148904	53915	58.013	51911	37445	56972	578870
	C 15.20%	5.50%	5.92%	5.29%	3.82%	5.20%	59.07%

Contd.

Contd.

State/Union Territory	Habitations with Middle Sections as a Distance of						
	within the Habitation	upto 1.0 km.	1.1 to 2.0 km.	2.1 to 3.0 km.	3.1 to 4.0 km.	4.1 to 5 km.	more than 5 km.
Mizoram	A 157	-	-	-	-	-	58
	B 280725	-	-	-	-	-	23183
	C 92.37	-	-	-	-	-	7.63%
Nagaland	A 258	214	135	78	52	76	620
	B 155830	69226	49739	21765	14764	23346	180180
	C 30.26%	13.44%	9.66%	4.22%	2.86%	4.53%	35.03%
Tripura	A 307	601	706	756	657	544	2479
	B 300562	247365	239539	213615	152836	1001540	298989
	C 19.35	15.91	15.41	13.74	9.83	6.53	19.23

Source: Third All India Educational Survey, NCERT, New Delhi, 1979, pp.152-155.
Note: A No. of Habitations B. Their Total Population C. Percentage of their population to the total population in the State.

Appendix VIII

Rural Habitations with and without Middle Schools/Sections, 1978

State/ Union than Territory		Habitations with Primary Sections as a distance of						
	within the Habitation	upto 1.0 km.	1.1 to 2.0 km.	2.1 to 3.0 km.	upto 3.0 km.	3.1 to 4.0 km.	4.1 to 5 km.	more 5 km.
Arunachal Pradesh	A 130	69	71	80	350	52	67	2648
	B 101995	21075	17802	17352	158224	10668	14044	379155
	C 18.14	3.75	3.17	3.09	28.15	1.90	2.50	67.45
Assam	A 3437	4049	6692	6055	20233	3649	1922	2227
	B 3279299	2299803	3707824	3098020	12384946	1683880	877598	738770
	C 20.91	14.66	23.64	19.75	78.96	10.74	5.59	4.71
Manipur	A 402	313	267	265	1247	127	126	1037
	B 436088	188700	134874	103498	863160	35749	35031	195099
	C 38.62	16.71	11.95	9.17	76.45	3.17	3.10	17.28
Meghalaya	A 363	675	663	756	2457	609	561	2085
	B 184623	159398	136538	142071	622630	110785	100164	340483
	C 15.72	13.58	11.63	12.10	53.03	9.44	8.53	29.00

Contd.

State Union than Territory	Habitations with Middle Sections as a Distance of: within the Habitation	upto 1.0 km.	1.1 to 2.0 km.	2.1 to 3.0 km.	upto 3.0 km.	3.1 to 4.0 km.	4.1 to 5 km.	more 5 km.
Mizoram	A 170	4	10	14	198	17	27	343
	B 240125	2482	3352	5710	251669	3835	7265	110573
	C 64.32	0.66	0.90	1.53	77.41	1.03	1.94	29.62
Nagaland	A 298	68	75	76	517	57	63	352
	B 325124	40038	44061	46754	455977	25976	27904	131208
	C 50.72	6.25	6.87	7.29	71.13	4.05	4.35	20.47
Tripura	A 365	819	1007	819	3010	579	546	2103
	B 345927	327673	348695	235926	1258221	124221	89159	276466
	C 19.79	18.74	19.95	13.50	71.98	7.11	5.10	15.81
All India	33.47	13.10	17.78	14.48	78.82	7.90	5.37	7.90

Source: Fourth All India Educational Survey, NCERT, New Delhi, 1982, pp. 252-257.

Appendix VIII

Rural Habitations with and without Middle Schools/Sections in North East, 1986

State/ Union Territory	Habitations with a primary Section as a Distance of									Total
	within Habitation	Up to 1.0 km.	1.1 to 2.0 km	2.1 to 3.0 km.	Up to 3.0 km.	3.1 to 4.0 km.	4.1 to 5.0.	Up to 5 km.	More than 5.0 km.	
Arunachal Pradesh	A233	110	144	147	634	103	114	851	2386	3237
	B181138	38014	30994	38439	288585	27409	21940	337934	345996	683930
	C26.48	5.56	4.53	5.62	42.2	4.01	3.21	49341	50.59	100
Assam	A5456	5542	7848	6342	25188	3316	3316	1521	1778	31803
	B7454767	3487855	4534826	3591157	16368605	1779551	1779551	819311	688448	19652915
	C24.19	17.75	23.07	18.27	83.29	9.05	9.05	40.17	3.49	100
Manipur	A495	407	381	225	1508	131	131	93	882	2614
	B461451	251493	173810	74948	961702	38124	38124	25309	174187	1199322
	C38.48	20.97	14.49	6.25	80.19	3.18	3.18	2.11	14.52	100
Meghalaya	A600	574	718	808	2700	544	544	516	1577	5337
	B397396	187354	190429	186877	962056	109483	109483	103486	305185	1480210
	C26.85	12.66	12.86	12.63	64.99	7.4	704	6.99	20.62	100
Mizoram	A324	8	8	12	352	4	4	3	257	616
	B345066	4426	2231	4010	355733	597	597	911	72131	429372
	C80.37	1.03	0.52	0.93	82.85	0.14	0.14	0.21	16.8	100
Nagaland	A254	76	66	92	488	34	34	53	422	997
	B331449	47113	57686	72714	508962	28898	28898	30698	197850	766408
	C43.25	6.15	7.53	9.49	66.41	3.77	3.77	4.01	25.82	100
Tripura	A713	1334	1451	963	44.59	543	543	325	973	6300
	B587224	596535	520154	261986	1965899	119407	119407	60113	132242	2277661
	C25.78	26.19	22.84	11.5	86.31	5.24	5.24	2.64	5.81	100

Source: Fifth All India Educational Survey. NCERT. New Delhi, 1986.

Appendix VIII.2

Rural Habitations with and without Primary Schools/Sections in North East, 1993

State/Union Territory	*Habitations with a primary Sections as a Distance of*								*Total*
	within Habitation	*upto 1.0 km.*	*1.1 to 2.0 km.*	*2.1 to 3.0 km.*	*Up to 3.0 km.*	*3.1 to 4.0 km.*	*4.1 to 5.0 km.*	*more than 5 km.*	
Arunachal	A368	204	263	252	1087	193	242	2312	3834
Pradesh	B266373	54715	62757	53520	437360	38766	41604	286379	804109
	C33.13	6.8	7.8	6.66	54.39	4.82	5.17	35.61	100
Assam	A6237	12267	10898	5822	35224	2315	1459	2181	41179
	B4778238	5693442	5261098	2862118	18594896	1122215	639682	977876	21334669
	C22.4	26.69	24.66	13.42	87.16	5.26	3	4.58	100
Manipur	A717	732	453	348	2250	204	202	713	3369
	B524900	360728	163051	110307	1158986	53269	48906	148136	1409297
	C37.25	25.6	11.57	7.83	82.24	3.78	3.47	10.51	100
Meghalaya	A796	1264	1006	823	3889	636	666	1385	6576
	B403778	335071	205365	153524	1097738	111898	116789	252984	1579409
	C25.57	21.21	13	9.72	69.5	7.08	7.39	16.02	100
Mizoram	A369	37	26	22	454	19	27	205	705
	B317030	12258	6348	5097	340733	4910	6236	56733	408652
	C77.58	3	1.55	1.25	83.38	1.2	1.53	13.89	100
Nagaland	A347	234	87	68	736	40	83	418	1277
	B543028	174232	70622	59722	847604	31909	42785	213772	1137070
	C47.76	15.32	6.21	5.25	74.54	2.81	3.85	18.8	100
Tripura	A783	1825	1554	909	5071	477	325	929	6802
	B617124	702728	541337	265596	2126825	129579	67189	152665	2476258
	C24.92	28.38	21.86	10.73	85.89	5.23	2.71	6.17	100

Source: Sixth All India Educational Survey. NCERT, New Delhi, 1993.

Appendix IX

Statewise Percentage of Rural Population with and without Primary Schools/Sections

States	*Percentage of Population served by Primary Schools/Sections at a distance of*							
	within the habitations	*upto 0.5 km but not within habitation*	*0.6 to 1.0 km.*	*upto 1.0 km.*	*1.1 to 1.5 km.*	*1.6 to 2.0 km.*	*upto 2.0 km.*	*more than 2.0 km.*
Arunachal Pradesh	65.85	2.47	5.03	73.35	0.93	3.42	77.70	22.30
Assam	81.75	5.40	6.43	93.58	3.59	1.89	99.06	0.94
Manipur	89.97	3.47	3.95	97.39	0.33	0.49	98.21	1.79
Meghalaya	80.87	2.88	5.47	89.22	1.43	3.32	93.97	6.03
Mizoram	98.05	0.23	0.00	98.28	0.00	0.12	98.40	1.60
Nagaland	98.85	0.42	0.18	99.45	0.06	0.37	99.88	0.12
Tripura	57.04	12.85	14.22	84.11	5.50	5.65	95.26	4.74

Source: Fifth All India Educational Survey, A Concise Report. New Delhi, NCERT, 1990.

Appendix X

Statewise Percentage of Rural Population with and without Upper Primary Schools

States	*Percentage of Population served by Upper Primary Schools at a distance of*								
	within the habitation	*upto 1.0 km.*	*1.1 to 2.0 km.*	*2.1 to 3.0 km.*	*upto 3.0 km.*	*3.1 to 4.0 km.*	*4.1 to 5.0 km.*	*upto 5.0 km.*	*more than 5.0 km.*
Arunachal Pradesh	26.48	5.56	4.53	5.62	42.19	4.01	3.21	49.41	50.59
Assam	24.19	17.75	23.08	18.27	83.29	9.05	4.17	96.57	3.49
Manipur	38.48	20.97	14.49	6.25	80.19	3.18	2.11	85.48	14.52
Meghalaya	26.85	12.66	12.86	12.62	64.99	7.40	6.99	79.38	20.62
Mizoram	80.37	1.03	0.52	0.93	82.85	0.14	0.21	83.70	6.80
Nagaland	43.25	6.15	7.52	9.49	66.41	3.77	4.01	74.19	25.81
Tripura	25.78	26.19	22.89	11.50	86.31	5.24	2.64	94.19	5.81
All India	36.98	17.83	17.64	12.94	85.39	6.07	3.82	95.28	4.72

Source: Fifth All India Educational Survey, A Concise Report, New Delhi, NCERT, 1990.

Appendix XI

Educational Facilities in Rural Habitations

Number of Habitations having stages of schools

State	*Total Habitations*	*Primary*	*Upper Primary*
Arunachal Pradesh	3812	1319	332
Manipur	39933	25049	6167
Meghalaya	6533	3768	742
Mizoram	667	586	375
Nagaland	1233	1056	266
Tripura	6743	2648	786

Source: Sixth All India Educational Survey, Provisional Statistics, New Delhi, NCERT, 1995.

Appendix XII

Arunachal Pradesh - Data on Primary Schools Having Incentive Schemes

S.No.	*Particulars*	*1973*	*1978*	*1986*	*1993*
1.	Mid-Day Meals				
	(a) No. of Schools	7	215	841	899
	(b) No. of Pupils	58	N.A.	44633	52864
2.	Free Uniform Schemes				
	(a) No. of Schools	29	5	884	993
	(b) No. of Pupils	768	N.A.	40543	48130
3.	Free Textbooks				
	(a) No. of Schools	497	733	927	1087
	(b) No. of Pupils	24442	N.A.	42673	54922
4.	Scholarships Schemes				
	(a) No. of Schools	31	N.A.	N.A.	2
	(b) No. of Pupils	546	N.A.	N.A.	14
5.	Schools Having Integrated Programme for the Disabled	N.A.	N.A.	N.A.	N.A.

Source: Third, Fourth and Fifth All India Educational Surveys NCERT, New Delhi.

Appendix XIII

Assam - Data of Primary Schools Having Incentive Schemes

S.No.	*Particulars*	*1973*	*1978*	*1986*	*1993*
1.	Mid-Day Meals Schemes				
	(a) No. of Schools	438	754	1262	121
	(b) No. of Pupils	6663	N.A.	52286	4528
2.	Free Uniform Schemes				
	(a) No. of Schools	2457	11	1506	988
	(b) No. of Pupils	740	N.A.	21671	20681
3.	Free Textbook Schemes				
	(a) No. of Schools	109	815	25873	24608
	(b) No. of Pupils	4555	N.A.	2575959	530894
4.	Scholarships Schemes				
	(a) No. of Schools	9	N.A.	N.A.	164
	(b) No. of Pupils	154	N.A.	N.A.	745
5.	Integrated Programme for disabled				
	(a) No. of Schools	N.A.	N.A.	3	N.A.

Source: Third, Fourth and Fifth All India Educational Surveys 1957-1993, NCERT, New Delhi.

Appendix XIV

Manipur - Data of Primary Schools Having Incentive Schemes

S.No.	*Particulars*	*1973*	*1978*	*1986*	*1993*
1.	Mid-Day Meals Schemes				
	(a) No. of Schools	5	N.A.	N.A.	5
	(b) No. of Pupils	408	N.A.	52286	16
2.	Free Uniform Schemes				
	(a) No. of Schools	216	N.A.	N.A.	7
	(b) No. of Pupils	20	N.A.	N.A.	73
3.	Free Textbook Schemes				
	(a) No. of Schools	7	N.A.	39	10
	(b) No. of Pupils	207	N.A.	430	129
4.	Scholarships Schemes				
	(a) No of Schools	104	N.A.	N.A.	24
	(b) No. of Pupils	948	N.A.	N A.	264
5.	Schools having Integrated Programme for the disabled	N.A.	N.A.	3	N.A

Source: Third, Fourth and Fifth All India Educational Surveys 1957-1993. NCERT, New Delhi.

Appendix XV

Meghalaya - Data of Primary Schools Having Incentive Schemes

S.No.	*Particulars*	*1973*	*1978*	*1986*	*1993*
1.	Mid-Day Meals Schemes				
	(a) No. of Schools	12	15	178	0
	(b) No. of Pupils	253	N.A.	7120	0
2.	Free Uniform Schemes				
	(a) No. of Schools	332	4	N.A.	61
	(b) No. of Pupils	600	N.A.	935	932
3.	Free Textbook Schemes				
	(a) No. of Schools	56	50	419	559
	(b) No. of Pupils	834	N.A.	13476	14860
4.	Scholarships Schemes				
	(a) No. of Schools	4	N.A.	N.A.	11
	(b) No. of Pupils	44	N.A.	N.A.	121
5.	Schools having Integrated Educational Programmes for disabled	N.A.	N.A.	N.A.	N.A.

Source: Third, Fourth and Fifth All India Educational Surveys 1957-1993, NCERT, New Delhi.

Appendix XVI

Mizoram - Data of Primary Schools Having Incentive Schemes

S.No.	Particulars	1973	1978	1986	1993
1.	Mid-Day Meals Schemes				
	(a) No. of Schools	N.A.	N.A.	N.A.	41
	(b) No. of Pupils	N.A.	N.A.	N.A.	4953
2.	Free Uniform Schemes				
	(a) No. of Schools	424	35	126	57
	(b) No. of Pupils	115656	N.A.	1473	1002
3.	Free Textbook Schemes				
	(a) No. of Schools	181	154	86	40
	(b) No. of Pupils	6703	N.A.	802	595
4.	Scholarships Schemes				
	(a) No. of Schools	1	N.A.	N.A.	1
	(b) No. of Pupils	3	N.A.	N.A.	5
5.	Schools having Integrated Educational Programmes for disabled	N.A.	N.A.	4	N.A.

Source: Third, Fourth and Fifth All India Educational Surveys 1957-1993, NCERT, New Delhi.

Appendix XVII

Nagaland - Data of Primary Schools Having Incentive Schemes

S.No.	*Particulars*	*1973*	*1978*	*1986*	*1993*
1.	Mid-Day Meals Schemes				
	(a) No. of Schools	6	N.A.	1	0
	(b) No. of Pupils	136	N.A	193	0
2.	Free Uniform Schemes				
	(a) No. of Schools	38	N.A.	1	0
	(b) No of Pupils	145	N.A.	70	0
3.	Free Textbook Schemes				
	(a) No. of Schools	305	294	500	0
	(b) No. of Pupils	20604	N.A.	49699	0
4.	Scholarships Schemes				
	(a) No. of Schools	10	N.A.	N.A.	0
	(b) No. of Pupils	22	N.A.	N.A.	0
5.	Schools having Integrated Educational Programmes for disabled	N.A.	N.A.	N.A.	N.A.

Source: Third, Fourth and Fifth All India Educational Surveys 1957-1993, NCERT, New Delhi.

Appendix XVIII

Tripura - Data of Primary Schools Having Incentive Schemes

S.No.	*Particulars*	*1973*	*1978*	*1986*	*1993*
1.	Mid-Day Meals Schemes				
	(a) No. of Schools	4	N.A.	1790	1783
	(b) No. of Pupils	N.A.	N.A.	204510	183839
2.	Free Uniform Schemes				
	(a) No. of Schools	N.A.	1573	1469	1112
	(b) No. of Pupils	N.A.	N.A.	11132	38361
3.	Free Textbook Schemes				
	(a) No. of Schools	1536	1573	1859	1301
	(b) No. of Pupils	49679	N.A.	97960	134142
4.	Scholarships Schemes				
	(a) No. of Schools	11	N.A.	N.A.	1005
	(b) No. of Pupils	210	N.A.	N.A.	33619
5.	Schools having Integrated Educational Programmes for disabled	N.A.	N.A.	N.A.	N.A.

Source: Third, Fourth and Fifth All India Educational Surveys 1957-1993, NCERT, New Delhi.

Appendix – XIX

Statement showing the Scheduled Tribes with 10,000 and above population and their three major languages excluding Assam.

Scheduled Tribes with 1000 and above population		*Ist three major mother tongues with speakers strength*	
Name of ST	*Population*	*Mother Tongues*	*Speakers*
1	*2*	*3*	*4*
Arunachal Pradesh			
1. Adi	24,206	1. Adi	23,948
		2. Others	73
		3. Nissi/Dafla	65
2. Adi Gallong	36,366	1. Adi	36,276
		2. Others	34
		3. Nissi/Dafla	14
3. Adi Minyong	25,259	1. Adi	25,216
		2. Wancho	11
		3. Nissi/Dafla	10
4. Apatani	16,580	1. Nissi/Dafla	15,432
		2. Others	1,092
		3. Adi	7
5. Bangi	31,125	1. Nissi/Dafla	31,040
		2. Others	25
		3. Bengali	23
6. Monpa	21,619	1. Monpa	20,609
		2. Others	870
		3. Sautali	53
7. Nissi	56,107	1. Nissi/Dafla	55,946
		2. Adi	68
		3. Others	40
8. Nocte	19,606	1. Nocte	19,318
		2. Others	158
		3. Wancho	51
9. Tagin	27,122	1. Nissi/Dafla	26,675
		2. Adi	409
		3. (a)Monpa	10
		(b) Others	10

Contd.

1	2	3	4
10. Wancho	32,441	1. Wancho	32,350
		2. Others	42
		3. Nocte	20
Manipur			
1. Hmar	29,216	1. Hmar	28,432
		2. Lushhai/Mizo	273
		3. Others	203
2. Kabui	26,006	1. Kabui	25,744
		2. Manipuri/Meitei	69
		3. Thado	56
3. Kacha Naga	12,754	1. Kacha Naga	12,397
		2. Zemi Naga	161
		3. Kabui	126
4. Mao	56,715	1. Mao	49,730
		2. Others	695
		3. Naga	197
5. Maring	11,910	1. Maring	11,557
		2. Others	285
		3. Thangkul	18
6. Paite	30,959	1. Paite	29,841
		2. Thado	227
		3. Lushai/Mizo	192
7. Thangkhul	79,029	1. Thangkhul	78,076
		2. Thado	264
		3. Vaiphei	151
8. Thadou	56,467	1. Thadou	49,686
		2. Kuki	5,641
		3. Others	191
9. Vaiphei	15,463	1. Vaiphei	14,008
		2. Kuki	658
		3. Others	216
10. Zou	12,576	1. Zou	11,948
		2. Others	216
		3. Thado	155
Meghalaya			
1. Garo	405,449	1. Garo	404,301
		2. Khasi	544
		3. Assamese	296
2. Hajong	24,331	1. Bengali	22,394
		2. Assamese	296
		3. Garo	111
3. Khasi, Jaintia, Synteng	628,104	1. Khasi	623,188
		2. Mikir	2,780
		3. Garo	850
Mizoram			
1. Chakma	39,900	1. Bengali	9,280
		2. Mogh	304

Contd.

Contd.

1	*2*	*3*	*4*
		3. Others	164
2. Any Kuki Tribe	20,785	1. Tripuri	19,342
		2. Lushai/Mizo	654
		3. Others	318
3. Lakher/Mara	16,704	1. Lakher/Mara	15,925
		2. Lushai/Mizo	701
		3. Pawi	54
4. Any Mizo (Lushai)	351,340	1. Lushai/Mizo	348,886
		2. Paite	1588
		3. Hmar	305
5. Pawi/Lai	22,997	1. Pawi/Lai	11,511
		2. Lushai/Mizo	11,251
		3. Others	120
Nagaland			
1. Angami	62,555	1. Angami	40,539
		2. Others	21,412
		3. Ao	179
2. Ao	104,578	1. Ao	100,288
		2. Others	3,419
		3. Angami	185
3. Chakhesang	60,771	1. Angami	37,263
		2. Khezha	16,436
		3. Mao	3,362
4. Chang	22,375	1. Chang	21,910
		2. Ao	111
		3. Yimchungre	66
5. Khiemnungan	18,080	1. Khiemnungan	17,332
		2. Others	637
		3. Konyak	32
6. Konyak	83,652	1. Konyak	75,654
		2. Others	6,810
		3. Naga	560
7. Lotha	58,030	1. Lotha	57,442
		2. Sema	131
		3. Ao	91
8. Phom	24,427	1. Phom	4,195
		2. Ao	55
		3. Konyak	36
9. Rengma	15,313	1. Rengma	15,012
		2. Angami	89
		3. Sema	52
10. Sangtam	29,076	1. Sangtam	27,936
		2. Sema	420
		3. Thang khul	302
11. Sema	95,312	1. Sema	94,407
		2. Sangtam	198
		3. Angami	101

Contd.

Contd.

1	2	3	4
12. Yimchungre	22,054	1. Yimchungre	20,677
		2. Khiemnungan	407
		3. Gujarathi	312
Zeliang	21,085	1. Naga	12,524
		2. Zemi Naga	5,069
		3. Kacha Naga	3,191
Tripura			
1. Chakma	34,797	1. Bengali	34,392
		2. Tripuri	368
		3. Garo	28
2. Halam	28,970	1. Halam	18,221
		2. Tripuri	9,246
		3. Others	908
3. Jamatia	44,501	1. Tripuri	44,415
		2. Bengali	68
		3. Others	7
4. Mag	18,230	1. Mag	16,907
		2. Others	874
		3. Bengali	303
5. Riang	84,004	1. Tripuri	83,758
		2. Bengali	162
		3. Others	33
6. Tripura, Tripuri, Tippera	330,872	1. Tripuri	325,409
		2. Bengali	4,889
		3. Halam	331

Source: Census of India 1981, Series – I India, Part – IX (ii) Special Tables for ST on Mother Tongue and Bilingualism, pp. 13-23.

Appendix – XX

State-wise Scheduled Caste, Scheduled Tribe and Non-Scheduled Caste/ Scheduled Tribe Population (North East 1981-91)

State	*Percentage of Total Population 1981*				*Percentage of Total Population 1991*			
	Total Popu	*SC Popu.*	*ST Popu.*	*Non SC/ST Popu.*	*Total Popu.*	*SC Popu.*	*ST Popu.*	*Non SC/ST Popu.*
Arunachal Pradesh	100.00	0.46	69.82	29.72	100.00	0.47	63.66	35.87
Assam	NA	NA	NA	NA	100.00	7.40	12.83	79.77
Manipur·	100.00	1.25	27.30	71.45	100.00	2.02	34.41	63.57
Meghalaya	100.00	0.41	80.58	19.01	100.00	0.51	85.53	13.96
Mizoram	100.00	0.03	93.55	6.42	100.00	0.10	94.75	5.15
Nagaland	100.00	-	83.99	16.01	100.00	-	87.70	12.30
Tripura	100.00	15.12	28.44	56.44	100.00	16.36	30.95	52.69

Source: Census of India 1991, Series-I India paper – 2 of 1992, Final Population Totals : Brief Analysis of Primary Census Abstract, pp.198-200.

Appendix XXI

Bereday's Model of Comparative Study

Stage I

Description and Interpretation of the Pedagogical data

Historical Political Economic Social	Area A	Mizoram
Historical Political Economic Social	Area B	Nagaland

Stage II

Juxtaposition - Establishing Similarities and Difference

Criteria of Comparability

Area A Mizoram	Area B Nagaland

Hypothesis of Comparative Analysis

Stage III Comparison

Simultaneous Comparison

Area A Mizoram	Area B Nagaland

Conclusion

Conclusion will be leading to suggestions for further study.

Appendix XXII

Terms and Conditions of Schools Transferred to Autonomous District Councils in Mizoram.

**GOVERNMENT OF MIZORAM
EDUCATION & SOCIAL WELFARE DEPARTMENT**

NOTIFICATION

Dated Aizawl, the 9th September 1975

No. EPS. 4/74/53: The Lt. Governor (Administrator) of Mizoram is pleased to order that all the existing Government Lower Primary Schools within the area of Lakher District Council, as per details in Annexure "A" Stand transferred to the Lakher District Council as per terms and conditions detailed in Annexure "B" with immediate effect and until further orders

Sd/- G.N. Chatterjee
Secretary to the Govt. of Mizoram
Education and Social Welfare Department
Dated Aizawl, the 9th September, 1975.

Terms and conditions as accepted in the Meeting of the Chief Executive Members of Chhimtuipui District, which was held in the chamber of Chief Minister, Mizoram, on 21.7.1975 at 11 A.M.

1. All Govt. of L.P. Schools under the jurisdiction of the three District Councils shall stand transferred to the authorities of the District Councils shall stand transferred to the authorities of the District Councils with their buildings, furniture, teaching aids and equipments etc. with effect from the dates suiting their convenience. The schools so transferred shall be run by them under their management and will, with effect from the date of transfer, be deemed to be

recognised as non Government aided Primary Schools run under the management of the District Councils authorities who shall be bound to follow the general patterns of education in Primary Schools as laid down by the Government from time to time.

2. The services of the existing Government teachers in these transferred schools shall stand transferred as on deputation on foreign service without any deputation allowances with effect from the date of transfer until further order. During the period of their deputation they will be under the full administrative control of the concerned District Council Authorities. They will, however, continue to retain their status as Government servant with all the benefits attached to such status subject to the condition that in respect of grant of leave admissible to such transferred Government servants, their transfer and posting from one school to another in their respective jurisdictions and initiation of disciplinary proceedings against any of the transferred staff, the concerned District Council authorities shall have full powers. Release of recurring grant-in-aid to cover salaries and other admissible dues in respect of the teaching staff transferred to the District Council on deputation shall be made quarterly in advance by the Deputy Inspector of Schools, Chhimtuipui District to the District Council Authorities on production of proper utilization certificates in respect of all previous grants made on this account.

In case, the District Council authorities desire at any time to send back any of the staff transferred to their control, they will do so only by relinquishing the post against which the concerned staff is entertained.

They will also ensure that staff at present working in the existing schools in their respective jurisdictions with children belonging to minority communities therein, are not transferred there from without first making necessary alternative arrangement to meet their special need.

Any post vacated due to resignation, retirement, death, etc., of existing transferred teachers should be continued as a Government post. The concerned District Council authorities shall have the power to make thereon selection to fill up the vacancy and made appointment of the selected persons subject to approval of Director of Education.

3. They shall be eligible for all types of grants-in-aid both recurring and non-recurring as permissible under Grants-in-aid Rules for other non-Government aided Primary Schools.

4. The District Council as the managing agency of these non-Government schools, shall have to observe prevailing grants-in-aid and recognition rules and regulations and instructions of the

Education Department, Government of Mizoram.

5. The District Council authorities shall ensure regular disbursement of monthly salaries and other dues of the transferred teachers in their L.P. Schools from the funds made available to them by the Deputy Inspector of Schools for this purpose. In case, it is found by their Education Department that regular monthly payment of salaries and other dues to the transferred teachers is not being made, the Government shall have the right to order direct payment of salaries, etc. to the transferred teachers by the Deputy Inspector of Schools, Chhimtuipui District or any other Officer of the Education Department and to adjust the same against recurring grant-in-aid payable to the District Council authorities on this account.
6. The Education Department shall continue to be the appropriate authority for –
   (a) recognition of new Primary Schools in the District Council Areas
   (b) prescription of academic and training qualifications of teachers in the Primary Schools in the District Council areas
   (c) approval of syllabi, curriculums and textbooks in the recognised L.P. Schools in the District Council areas;
   (d) approval of class promotion rules and conduct of scholarship examinations;
   (e) inspection of the L.P. Schools in the District Council areas. In addition, the District Council authorities may also have their own Inspecting Staff for the L.P. Schools in their respective areas. Copies of Inspection reports from Government Inspecting Staff should be endorsed to the respective District Council for their appraisal and appropriate action. Similarly, copies of Inspection Reports of Inspecting Staff of the District Councils shall also be endorsed by them to the Deputy Inspector of Schools, Chhimtuipui District.
7. Future maintenance of the transferred schools, furniture, equipments etc. therein shall be the responsibility of the District Council Authorities

Sd/ G.N. Chatterjee
Secretary to the Government of Mizoram
Education and Social Welfare Department

Appendix XXIII

Rules of Discipline for the Management and Control of School Education in the Lai Autonomous District Council

CIRCULAR, 20TH APRIL, 1995

In view of the deterioration of the qualities and standard of Education within Lai Autonomous District the Executive Committee of the Lai Autonomous District Council is pleased to make Rules of discipline for the purpose of uplifting and promoting the standard and qualities of Education by encouraging and stimulating the Teachers to motivate the pupils by Oiling them and by building up their character to achieve qualities and excellence in their studies as well as in their performance.

1. Responsibilities of Teachers

It is the responsibilities of the Teachers to guide and inspire their pupils, to enrich their discipline and to inculcate values which are in consonance with our cultural heritage and our social objectives. They are the sole responsible for moulding and building up the pupils' character. As a result, they have to be bound by some sets of Rules and duties as follows:-

(a) **Punctuality:** Punctuality is regarded as one of the sources of success. All teachers should be punctual in their daily duties, especially, Head of the School concerned has to keep the proper/right time.

(b) **Regularity:** Regularity is one of the sources of powers for controlling the pupils to improve the standard of schools. As such all teachers should be regular in their duties as far as possible to achieve excellence and competence in their professions.

(c) **Grant of Casual Leave:** Casual leave is not a recognised form of leave and not to be treated as absence from duty.

Due to unavoidable circumstances compelled or if a situation so demands to avail Casual Leave from amongst any working staff, the Head of the School is authorised to grant Casual Leave for a period of 3 days at a time for which he/she should submit to the authority concerned for further record.

(d) **Class Room Management:** The role of the teacher is vital and central to the whole process of learning and teaching. As such the system of teaching should be organised on a systematic basis so as to motivate the pupils by drawing their attention to the subject which is taught. The teacher should have command over their pupils inside the class room. So as to make the pupils to respect their teachers. Teachers should try to explain the subject what they are teaching to the pupils in a simple language so as to make them understand what they learnt.

(e) **Cleanliness:** All teachers should wear a respectable dress so as to draw the attention of the pupils to make them proper, clean and tidy as this is the first step for controlling and disciplining the pupils.

(f) **Prohibition of Intoxicating Drinks etc:** If teachers are found practising intoxicating drinks, drugs, tobacco, gambling etc. Inside the school complex, a severe action should be taken against the defaulters by the authority concerned up to the termination from service.

(g) **Absence form duty/station:** It is known that some teaches are found absent from their duty/station without the prior permission of the authority concerned. If they are found absent from duty/station without the prior permission of the authority concerned, or if they are found negligent or loose in their daily duties, a disciplinary action should be taken against such teachers by the authority concerned as per conduct rules, as amended from time to time. All cases of unauthorised absence from duty or in continuation of leave will render the employees liable to disciplinary action treating it misconduct.

(h) **Staff Meeting:** Staff meeting in the school itself should be conducted at least once in a month for the purpose of maintaining co-operation between Head Master/Head Teacher and the staff.

(i) **Withdrawal of the Monthly Pay:** It is found that most of the Teachers left their station to draw their salary which drastically cut short the teaching period. In this matter, Headmaster/Head Teacher of each school is authorised to draw the salary of his/her staff, or in case, if the Headmaster/Head Teacher is not in a position to leave the station by that time he/she should send one representative to draw the salary of all. If some teachers who are not entrusted to draw the salary of the staff are found in the office of the authority concerned. The salary of such teachers should be withheld by the authority concerned.

(j) **Submission of Monthly Report:** Monthly report should be submitted to the Office of the authority concerned by the Headmaster/Head Teacher of each school regularly. If the monthly report is not submitted before 25th of every month, salary of staff of the school concerned should be withheld.

(k) **Office Manner (for the Teacher):** All teachers are instructed once again to keep up manners and etiquette in the office of the authority concerned, they have not to approach their concerned E.M/Superior Officers directly or if they want to meet them, they have to approach them according to the proper channel.

(l) **School Supply material:** All the materials which is supplied for the school should be utilized properly, or for the specific purpose.

2. Responsibilities of the Pupils

(i) All pupils should obey and respect their teachers, and they should wish them whenever they meet them.

(ii) All pupils should not practise drinking, smoking, gambling etc. inside the classroom.

(iii) Manners and etiquette should be adopted inside and outside the classroom.

Provided that if any pupil who fails observing the rules quoted above may be expelled from the school concerned or a fine of Rupees 50/- should be imposed against the defaulters.

3. Relationship between Teachers and Parents

There should be good relationship between parents and teachers in order to motivate the pupils. Teachers are expected to contact the parents of their pupils as much as possible to discuss the problems of their pupils with their parents. Regarding children's addiction to drugs, alcohol, tobacco and smoking etc. teachers and parents are the sole responsible. For this reason, all schools are encouraged to organize Seminar/ Conference at least once in a year, including Village Board Member's/ Parents.

4. Relationship between Teachers and Village Board of School Education

Good relationship between the teachers and the Village Board of School Education should be made for the Welfare of the School Education. All teachers are expected to obey and respect the proposal or suggestion made by the Village Board of School Education for their schools for building up of their pupils' character and conduct in their social and academic life as far as possible.

Whenever there is a report from the members of the Village Board regarding the undesirable activities of the teachers as well as the pupils, immediate action may be taken by the authority concerned.

Appendix XXIV

Rules for the Constitution of Village Board of Education in the Lai Autonomous District

Circular dated 10th March 1995

Whereas it is expedient to make rules for the purpose of promoting the qualities and standard of Education which is fast deteriorating year by year in the Lai District. The executive committee of the Lai Autonomous District Council is therefore pleased to constitute a village level school board namely 'Village Board of School Education' with functions for dealing with running system of schools.

1. **Constitution:** (a) A Board shall be constituted in every village in the Lai Autonomous District and shall consist of three to six members according to the size and population of the village as may be determined by the Executive Committee of the Lai Autonomous District Council including the V.C.P. of the village concerned who shall act as Chairman of the Board and other members shall be nominated by local church/churches. For among members of the church including members of any voluntary organization except those exclusively belonging to any political body.

   Secretary of the Board shall be elected by the members of the Board from among themselves and he shall function as member Secretary of the Board.

   (b) The life of the Board members shall be two years counting from the 1st date of the first month in the Calendar year.

2. **Meeting of the Board:** The Board shall meet 3 (three) times at an interval of 3 to 4 months a year and may even have more than 3 times in case of emergency. Each meeting shall be convened and presided over by the Chairman at any place selected by him. The proceedings of the meeting shall be recorded by the members Secretary and be maintained in the Office of the Board.

3. **Functioning of the Board:** The Board shall be provided with the functions as given below:-

(a) The Board shall function purely on voluntary basis without claiming any right for receiving financial benefits in the form of contracts, remuneration etc. and shall confine itself mainly in activity concerning the welfare of schools and school education.

(b) It shall keep a close watch of the working system of teaching staff relating particularly to activities, maintenance of discipline, regularity of attendance of teachers, etc. and shall associate in matters of giving advise or suggestions to those teachers for improvement of system of teaching in schools.

(c) The Board shall hold itself responsible for submitting reports of their findings about the nature and conduct of teachers who in its opinion are indulging in activities undesirable and also unbecoming of teachers who after receiving advices/warning from the Board but still in violation of total negligence of such advices or warning are found continuing to get on doing to competent authority for necessary action.

(d) The Board shall give to all teachers from time to time some proposals, suggestions etc. to be implemented or executed by them for building up pupil's characters and conduct in their social and academic life and also keeping strict discipline in their study.

(e) It shall also hold responsible for motivating and encouraging parents of pupils to make themselves ready to cooperate teachers in carrying on their duties for building up the characters of their children towards the betterment in every sphere of life by occasionally organising meeting with parents and teachers by exchanging ideas and for good understanding.

(f) The Board in discharge of its functions be given honour by the controlling authority and any proposal made thereon be given place of the importance while considering such plans for actions.

(g) The Board shall have power of recommendation for the approval of E.O.L. for the period of six months of a time to those teachers who are negligence of duty and irregular in attending the school. The authority should grant notice to such teachers as recommended by the concerned Board.

Appendix XXV

1. **CONSULTATION OF VILLAGE EDUCATION COMMITTEE OF KOHIMA**
   (a) The committee will have a minimum of five members of which one third will be women.
   (b) The civil administration officer of the area will be the Chairman of the Village Education Committee.
   (c) All its members will be selected by the respective village council and should be approved by the chairman, district planning board.
   (d) The committee should have representatives of various Khels and tribes of the village.
   (e) The Secretary of the committee will be the teacher-in-charge of the L.P. School and when they are more than one L.P. Schools in the village this post will be held in rotation.
   (f) The committee may include retired Government servant/ educationist residing in the village as its member.
   (g) The tenure of the village committee may be initially for five years.

2. **THE FUNCTION OF THE VILLAGE EDUCATION COMMITTEE WILL BE AS FOLLOWS**
   (a) The committee will ensure that schools starts only 8 in the morning and adhere to four hours teaching for Class I-IV/V and two hours for primary classes on each working day excluding half an hours recess.
   (b) The committee will be responsible to organise the educational functions including sport meets in the village.
   (c) It will recommend to the DPE/SDPP for upgradation of schools/ classes in conformity with existing policy of the department.
   (d) All developmental activities of the school/schools will be recommended/ supervised by the committee.
   (e) It will arrange accommodation for teacher coming from other village whenever Government accommodation is not available.
   (f) Maintenance of school compound/building, safe custody of Government property will be responsibility of the committee/ school authority.

(g) The committee will supervise the regular attendance of teachers in schools and its chairman should sign the necessary certificates for release of pay of L.P. School teachers under its jurisdiction on the basis of actual attendance and performance of duty.

(h) The committee will assists enrolling the children in L.P. Schools as soon as they attend the school-going age and the retention till they attend the terminal stage.

(i) It will assists the enrolling of illiterates into Adult Education centres and drop out with non-formal education centres in the village.

(j) The committee will serve as a watchdog to ensure proper use of L.P. Schools and the equipments supplied to them.

(k) It will be committee's responsibility to make available land for setting up a new L.P. School in the village.

3. The Village Education Committee will be set up in all the villages in the State of Nagaland.
4. It will have jurisdiction over all the L.P. Schools in the same village and will replace the existing management board/boards.
5. Relevant portion of the education manual stands amended to give effect to the Village Education Committee in place of school managing board.

Sd/-Z. Obed
Chief Secretary, to the Government of Nagaland.

NO. EDS/128/87/ //dt. Kohima, the 13th January 1989.

Copy to :-

1. The Chief Secretary, to the Govt. of Nagaland.
2. The Commissioner, Nagaland, Kohima.
3. The Home Commissioner, Nagaland, Kohima.
4. All Secretaries/Jt. Secretaries.
5. The Director of School Education, Nagaland, Kohima.
6. All Deputy Commissioner/Additional Deputy Commissioners.
7. All Heads of Departments.
8. All Departments/Branches in Secretariat
9. All Inspector/Deputy Inspector of School/DAEO's.
10. All S.D.O. (Civil) EACs.
11. The Publisher, Nagaland Gazette for publication.

Sd/- P. TALITEMJEN
Secretary to the Govt. of Nagaland.

Bibliography

Primary

Government o India, *Census 1961*, New Delhi, 1961.

Government of Arunachal Pradesh, *Statistical Abstract of Arunachal Pradesh*, Itanagar, 1989.

Government of India "Progress and Problems of Educational Development in the States and, the UTS of North Eastern Region", mimeo, Planning Commission. New Delhi, 1985-86.

Government of India, *Census 1971*, New Delhi, 1971.

Government of India, *Census 1981 Series 31, Mizoram*, District Census Hand Book, Chhimtuipui District, 1981.

Government of India, *Census 1981*, New Delhi 1981.

Government of India, *Census 1981, Part XC, Series 31* Mizoram, *Survey Report on the Restudy of Village Lawngtlai*, 1988.

Government of India, *Census 1981*, Tables Pertaining to Nagaland, New Delhi, 1981.

Government of India, *Census 1991*, New Delhi, 1991.

Government of India, *Census of India, 1961, Vol. III, Assam Part IA General Report*, New Delhi, 1961.

Government of India, *Census of India, 1981, Series – 31, Mizoram*, 1981.

Government of India, *Census of India, 1991, Series – 17, Mizoram, Provisional Population Totals*, 1991.

Government of India, Ministry of Education, *Committee on the Relationship between State Government and Local Bodies in the Administration of Primary Education, 1951*. New Delhi, Ministry of Education, 1954.

Government of India, Ministry of Education, *Education in India*, 1978-79 and

1985-86, New Delhi.

Government of India, Ministry of Home Affairs, *Basic Statistics of North Eastern Region 1995*. Shillong, North Eastern Council Secretariat, 1995.

Government of India, Ministry of Human Resource Development, Department of Education, *Cabe Committee on Decentralized Management of Education*, New Delhi, 1993.

Government of India, Ministry of Human Resource Development, *Annual Report, 1994-95*, Department of Education, New Delhi, 1995.

Government of India, Ministry of Human Resource Development, *Selected Educational Statistics 1993-94*, Department of Education, New Delhi, 1993-94.

Government of India, Planning Commission, Education Division, Progress and Problems of Education Development in the States and UTs of the North Eastern Region, mimeo, New Delhi, 1985-86.

Government of India, Planning Commission, Education Division, *Report of the Working Group on District Planning*, Vol. I, New Delhi, 1984.

Government of India, Planning Commission, *Report of the Working Group to Study the Selection and Implementation of the Development of Programmes with particular reference to Community Participation*, New Delhi, 1985.

Government of India, Series 31 Mizoram, *District Census Hand Book, Chhintuipui* District.

Government of Manipur, *Statistical Handbook of Manipur*, Imphal, 1983.

Government of Meghalaya, *Statistical Handbook of Meghalaya*, Shillong, 1989.

Government of Mizoram, *Annual Plan, 1994-95*, Planning and Programme Implementation Department, Aizawl, 1995.

Government of Mizoram, *Fifth All India Educaional Survey*, Aizawl, SCERT, Education and Human Resource Development, 1989.

Government of Mizoram, Lai Autonomous District Council Records, Office of the District Council Affairs, Aizawl, 1995.

Government of Mizoram, *Mizoram at a Glance*, Directorate of Economics and Statistics, Aizawl, 1983.

Government of Mizoram, *Mizoram School Statistics*, Directorate of School Education, Aizawl, 1995.

Government of Mizoram, *Mizoram School Statistics*, Statistical Wing, Directorate of School Education, Aizawl, Mizoram, 1993.

Government of Mizoram, *Sixth All India Survey*, Directorate of School Education, Aizawl, 1993.

Government of Nagaland, Department of School Education, *Draft Annual Plan*, Kohima, 1989-90.

Government of Nagaland, Directorate of Economics and Statistics, *Statistical Handbook of Nagaland*. Kohima. 1988.

Government of Nagaland, *Statistical Handbook of Nagaland*. Kohima. 1989.

Government of Nagaland, *Statistical Handbook of Nagaland*, Kohima, Directorate of Economics and Statistics, 1987.

Government of Tripura, *Some Basic Statistics of Tripura*, Directorate of Statistics, Agratala. 1985.

Jalali. Jayashree Roy, "Universalisation of Elementary Education in Nagaland : Status Problem and a Perspective", mimeo, New Delhi, 1990.

Kothari, D.S., *Report of the Education Commission, Education and National Development*, New Delhi, 1968.

National Council of Educational Research and Training, All India Educational Surveys, (First to Sixth 1957-1993), New Delhi, NCERT.

National Institute of Adult Education, *Statistical Database for Literacy*, New Delhi, NIAE, 1993.

North Eastern Council, *Basic Statistics of North Eastern Region*, Shillong, GOI, Ministry of Home Affairs, 1992.

North Eastern Council, *Plans and Programmes for Regional Development*, Shillong, GOI, Ministry of Home Affairs, 1990.

Secondary

Abbi, B.L., (ed) *Northeast Region: Problems and Prospects of Development*. Chandigarh: CRRID, 1984.

Adiseshsah, Malcalm. S., (ed) *Planning Perspectives for North Eastern and Eastern Zone*. New Delhi: IIC, 1992.

Agarwal, M.M., (ed), *Ethunicity, Culture and Nationalism in N.E. India*. New Delhi: Indus Publishing Company, 1996.

Anand, V.K., *Conflict in Nagaland*. New Delhi: Chanakya Publishers, 1980.

Banerjee, Amalesh, Kar, Biman. *Economic Planning and Development of North-Eastern States*. New Delhi: Kanishka Publishers, Distributors, 1999.

Bareh, H.M, (ed), *Encyclopaedia of North East India*. New Delhi: Mithal Publication, 2001.

Bareh, Hamlet, *Progress of Education in Meghalaya*. New Delhi: Cosmo Publication, 1997.

Barkataki, Meena Sharma, *British Administration in North East India (1826-1874) A Study of their Social Policy*. Delhi: Mithal Publications, 1985.

Baruah, S.L. *A Comprehensive Hisotry of Assam*. New Delhi: Munshiram Manoharlal Publishers Pvt. Ltd., 1985.

Basu, Sajal. *Regional Movement Publics of Language, Ethnicity – Identity*. Simla:

Institute of Advanced Studies, 1992.

Bereday, George Z.F., *Comparative Method in Education.* Oxford: Oxford University Press 1964.

Bhatnagar, S. *Rural Local Government of India.* New Delhi: Light and life Publishers, 1978.

Bhattacharjee, K.K. *North East India: Political and Administrative History.* New Delhi: Cosmo Publication, 1983.

Bose, J.K. *Glimpses of Tribal Life in North East India.* Calcutta: Institute of Social Research and Applied Anthropology, 1980.

Chakraborty, Saroj. *The Upheaval Years in North-East India.* Calcutta: Saroj Chakbraborty and Chakraborty, 1984, pp. 93-105, Epilogue – 205-224.

Chakravarty, Archana. *History of Education in Assam 1826-1919.* Delhi: Mithal Publications, 1989.

Chaube, Shibanikinkar. *Hill Politics in North-East India.* New Delhi: Orient Longman Revised edition, 1999.

Chib, Singh Sukhdev. *Caste Tribe and Cultue of India Vol. 8, North East India.* New Delhi: ESS ESS Publications, 1984.

Datta Ray, B. *North East 2000 A.D. Perspective for Futurology.* New Delhi: Deep & Deep Publications, 1987.

Debi, Renu. *Progress of Education in Assam.* Gauhati: Omsons Publications, 1987.

Dubey, M.S. *North East India: A Sociological Study.* Delhi: Concept Publishing Company, 1978.

Gassah, L.S. (ed) *The Autonomus District Councils.* New Delhi: Omsons Pubications, 1997.

Gopalakrishnan, R. *The North-East India Land, Economy and People.* New Delhi: Vikas Publishing House, Pvt. Ltd, 1991.

Gopalakrishnan, R. *Insur nt North-Eastern Region of India.* New Delhi: Vikas Publishing Ho: ; Pvt. Ltd., 1995.

Goswami, B.B. *The Mizo Unrest.* Jaipur: Aalekh Publishers, 1979.

Hans, N. *Comparative Education.* London: Routledge and Kegan Paul, Reprint. 1971.

Kandel, I.L. *New Era in Education : A Comparative Study.* Boston: Houghton Mifflin, 1955.

Kandel, I.L. *Studies in Comparative Education.* London: George Harrap, 1933.

Kumar, B.B. *Higher Education in North East India.* New Delhi: Omsons Publication, 1994.

Kumar, B.B. *Trends in Briish Annexation of North East India.* New Delhi: Omsons Publiations, 1994.

Kumar, B.B. *Tension and Conflict in North East India*. New Delhi: Cosmo Publications, 1995.

Kumar, Krishna. *Political Agenda of Education*. New Delhi: Sage Publications, 1991.

Laird, M.A. *Missionaries and Education in Bengal, 1793-1837*. London: Oxford University Press, 1972.

Lalchungnunga, *Mizoram Politics of Regionalism and National Integration*. New Delhi: Reliance Publishing House, 1994.

Laldena. *Christian Missions and Colonialism*. A Study of Missionary Movement in North East India with Particular Reference to Manipur and Lushai Hills 1897-1947, Shillong, Vendrame Institute, 1988.

Laskar, Bina. *Development in Women Education* (A Study of Assam). Guwahati: Omsons Publications, 1987.

Mackenzie, Alexander. *The North East Frontier of India*. Delhi: Mithal Publications, 1979.

Maheshwari, Shriram. *Local Government in India*. New Delhi: Orient Longman, 1976.

Maithani, B.P. (ed) *Local Self-Government System in North-East India : An Appraisal*. Hyderabad: NIRD, 1977.

Mallinson, Vernoon. *An Introduction to the Study of Comparative Education*. London: Meineman, 1975.

Mark, Tourist. "Issues Confronting the State of Universalization of Elementary Education", Shillong, Directorate of School Education, Government of Meghalaya, 1996.

Mathew, A. *Christian Missions, Education and Nationalism*. Delhi: Anamika Prakashan, 1988.

Mathew, Muttumama. *Christianity in Assam and Inter Faith Dialogue*. A Study on the Modern Religious Movements in North Eastern India. Indore: Satprakashan Sanchar Kendra, 1985.

McCall, A.G. *Lushai Chrysallis*. Aizawl, 1977, Reprinted.

Mishra, R.N. *Regionalism and State Politics in India*. New Delhi: Ashish Publishing House, 1984.

Moehlman, Arthur, B., Co-editor. *Comparative Education*. New York: Holt, Rinehart and Winston, 1951.

Ramakant (ed), Mohan Lal Sharma, *Regionalism in South Asia*. "Elite Conflicts, Regionalism and Compatibility: A Study of the Autonomy, Movements in North East India", Jaipur: Aakku Publishers, 1983, pp.47-91.

Nag, Sajal. *India and the North East India: Mind, Politics and the Process of Integration, 1946-1954*. New Delhi: Regency Publication, 1998.

Narulla, Syed, Naik, J.P. *Students History of Education in India (1800-1965)*.

Revised edition. Bombay: Macmillan and Co. Ltd. 1965.

Nayar, Usha. *Universal Primary Eduation of Rural Girls in India*. New Delhi: NCERT, 1991.

Nibedon, Nirmal. *Nagaland – The Night of the Guerillas*. New Delhi: Lancer Publishers, 1978.

Nibedon, Nirmal. *The Ethnic Explosion*. New Delhi: Lancers Publishers, 1981.

Pakem, B. *Coalition Politics in North-East India*. New Delhi: Regency Publications, 1999.

Pakem, B. *Insurgency in North East India*. New Delhi: Omsons Publications, 1997.

Prasad, R.N. *Government and Politics in Mizorram*. New Delhi: Northern Book Centre, 1987.

Prasad, R.N. *Public Administration in North-East India*. New Delhi: Vikas Publishing House Pvt. Ltd., 1998.

Rao, Amimesh. *Mizoram Dynamics of Change*. Calcutta: Pearl Publishers, 1982.

Rao, V. Venkata. *A Century of Tribal Politics in North East India 1874-1974*. New Delhi: S. Chand and Company, 1976.

Reid, Sir Robert. *History of the Frontier Areas Bordening Assam from 1883-1941*. Delhi: Eastern Publishing House, 1983.

Roy Chowdhury, P. *The North East : Roots of Insurgency*. Calcutta: Firma, KLM. 1986.

Roy, Burman, B.K. *Towards Poverty Allevialion in Manipur and Nagaland*. New Delhi: Mithal Publications, 1983.

Sareen, H.K. *Insurgency in North East India*. New Delhi: Sterling Publishers Pvt. Ltd. 1980

Sarin, V.I.K. *India's North-East in Flames*. New Delhi: Vikas Publishing House Pvt. Ltd., 1980.

Sema, Hokishe. *The Emergence of Nagaland, Socio-Economic and Political Transformation, and the Future*. New Delhi: Vikas Publishing House Pvt Ltd. 1986.

Seminar, 366. New Delhi, 1990, The North East – A Symposium on the Problem of neglected people and region.

Sen Gupta, K.P. *The Christian Missionaries in Bengal*. Calcutta: Firma K.L. Mukhopadhyay, 1971.

Sen, Sipra. *Tribes of Nagaland*. New Delhi: Mithal Publications, 1987.

Shukla, Bhanu Pratap. *What Ails India's North East*? New Delhi: Suruchi Sahitya, 1980.

Singh, K.S. *Economics of the Tribes and their Transformation*. New Delhi: Concept Publishing House, 1986.

Singh, Prakash. *Nagaland*. New Delhi: National Book Trust, 1972.

Singh, S.N. *Mizoram Historical Geographical Social Economic, Political and Administrative*. New Delhi: Mithal Publications, 1994.

Smith, B.C. *Decentralization: The Territorial Dimension of the State*. London: George Alen and Unwin, 1985.

Stracey, P.D. *Nagaland Nighmare*. Bombay: Allied Publishers Pvt. Ltd, 1968.

Tarapat, Phanjoubam. *Insurgency Movement in North-Eastern India*. New Delhi: Vikas Publishing House Pvt. Ltd., 1993.

Articles

Ahmad, Nasir, "Decentralization – A Case for Administrative Federalism", *Journal of Rural Development and Administration*, Vol. XXIII, No.2, Spring, 1999.

Bordolai, B.N. "Traditional Self-Governing Institutions in Hill Districts of Assam", mimeo, nd.

George, Jacob, "Local Self-Government Institution in Assam" in *Local Self-Government System in North-East India: An Appraisal*, ed. B.P. Mailtani. Hyderabad: NIRD, 1977.

Horam, M. "Problems of Understanding in North-East India" in *North East Region Problems and Prospects of Development*. ed. B.L. Abbi. Chandigarh: CRRID, 1984.

Hooja, Rakesh. *District Planning : Concept, Setting and State Level Application*. Jaipur: Aalekh Publishers, 1986.

Hussain, Monirul. "The Nationality Question", *Seminar*, 366, February 1990, New Delhi.

Jalali, Roy Jayashree. "Universalization of Elementary Education : Innovative Strategies in Asia", *Progressive Educational Herald*, Hyderabad, 1987.

Jalali, Jayahsree. "Universalization of Elementary Education : A Case Study of Mizoram" UNESCO sponsored National Workshop on Universal Primary Education Disadvantaged Areas, *Report*, New Delhi, NIEPA, 1988.

Jalali, Roy Jayashree. "Elementary Education in Meghalaya", *Third World Impact*. New Delhi, 1992.

Jalali, Jayashree. "An Approach to the Development of Educational Plan for the North Eastern Region", NIEPA, Mimeo, 1995.

Jena, A.C. "Local Self-Government Institutions in Arunachal Pradesh" in *Local Self- Government System in North-East India : An Appraisal* ed. B.P. Maithari. Hyderabad: NIRD, 1977.

Kumar, B.B. "Religional Political Parties in Nagaland" *Regional Political Parties in North Eastern India*, ed. L.S. Gassen. New Delhi: Omsons Publications, 1992.

Misra, S.N., "Property Rights and the State of Development of North Eastern Region", Mimeo, 1987.

Narain, Iqbal, "The Idea of Democratic Decentralization", *Indian Journal of Political Science*, April-June, 1960.

Omem, Deori. "Northeast – A Perspective" in *Northeast Region Problem and Prospects of Development*, ed. B.L. Abbi. Chandigarh: CRRID, 1984.

Roy Burman, B.K. "Issues in the Northeast: An Appraisal" in *Northeast Region Problem and Prospects of Development*, ed. B.L. Abbi. Chandigarh: CRRID, 1984.

Rao, Hanumantha M. "Decentralized Planning and Development – An Overview of Experience and Prospects" in *Man and Development*, Vol. XI No.3, September 1989.

Srivastava, S.C. "Local Self-Government Institutions n Manipur", in *Local Self-Government System in North East India : An Appraisal*, ed. B.P. Maithani. Hyderabad: NIRD, 1977.

Dissertations

Acharyya, Sudhir Chandra. "Pre-Primary and primary education in Tripura, and Cachar : Development and Problem:, Ph.D. Edu., Gauhati Univ., 1985.

Bhattacharjee, Rohini Nath. "Socio-economic strategies of education in Nagaland : A historical study", Ph.D. Edu., Gauhati University, 1983.

Borah, H.R. "Effectiveness of the Scheme of Upgradation of Primary and Middle Schools in Kohima District of Nagaland", New Delhi, DEPA dissertation, 1982.

Chakravorty, A. "History of education in Assam 1826-1919", Ph.D Arts, Gauhati Univ., 1971.

Darchhunga, "Problems of Implementation of Universalization of Elementary Education in Mizoram with special reference to Aibawk Circle". Dissertation, DEPA, NIEPA, 1986.

Das, R.C. "Administration of Elementary Education in relation to the Problem of Universalization", SIE, Assam, 1979.

Debi, Renu. "Progress of Education in Assam', 1882-1937", Ph.D. Edu., Gauhati Univ., 1971.

Debnath, N.B. "A Study of the Causes of Low Enrolment and High Drop-out of S.T. girls in Five Primary Schools of Jiramin Block", West Tripura District. DEPA, NIEPA, 1991.

Hluna, J.V. "Education in Mizoram 1894-1947: A historical study with special reference to the role of Christian Missions, Ph.D. History, Gauhati Univ., 1986.

Jacob, C.S. "Problem of Implementation of Universalisation of Elementary Education in Arunachal Pradesh with focus on Tawang District". Dissertation, DEPA, NIEPA, 1983.

James, Mingmayang A.S. "Role of Ukhrul Autonomous District Council of Manipur in Decentralizing Primary Education", DEPA, NIEPA, 1999.

Mahanta, Dayananda, "Non-governmental inputs in elementary education", Dissertation, DEPA, NIEPA, 1982.

Malakar, Sudhir. "Regional Development and Changing Situation in North East India (1901-1971)", M.Phil dissertation JNU, 1985.

Purkeyastha, R.B. "A Diagnostic Study of District Educational Administration of Nagaland – A Case Study of Kohima District", NIEPA, DEPA Dissertation 1988-89.

Ralte, Lalliani. "An analytical study of primary education in Mizoram during the post independence period", Ph.D. Edu. North-Eastern Hill Univ., 1990.

Saikia, Devika. *Sociology of Elementary Education in Khasi and Jaintia Hills*. Gauhati: Gauhati University, 1981.

Santam, A. "Inspection and Supervision of Elementary Schools in Tuensang District of Nagaland,' DEPA, New Delhi, NIEPA, 1996.

Shilu Ao, "Role of the Village Education Committee in Planning and Management of Primary Education – A Case Study of Kohima District of Nagaland", DEPA, New Delhi, NIEPA, 1995.

Sinha, Neelam. "Role of the Local Bodies in Primary Education in Meghalaya", Shillong NEHU, M.Ed. dissertation, 1977.

Tongpangshilu, "Constitution of Village Education Committee and its responsibilities for Promotion of Primary Education in Nagaland – A Study of Mokokchung District", DEPA, New Delhi, NIEPA, 1990.

Interviews

B. Langhranga, EM LADC.

B. Rualchhinga, Executive Member, In-charge of Education, Lai Autonomous District Council, Lawngtlai.

B. Thanchunga, Member LADC and Vice Chairman, Planning Board LADC.

B. Tinchunga, Primary School I Lawngtlai II Bazar.

C. Nunmawia, Head Teacher, Primary School I, Lawngtlai IV.

C. Thanghluna, Chief Executive Member, Lai Autonomous District Council, Laungtlai.

F. Lallura, Director School Education, Government of Mizoram.

F. Thangluala, Head Teacher, Primary School (College Veng) Lawngtlai VI.

H. Chhunkunga, Primary School I, Lawngtlai.

H. Ngunlala, Primary School I Laungtlai (AOC) – Headmaster.

H. Siami, Primary School II, Lawngtlai VI.

H. Thanghmuna, Primary I Laungtlai III.

H.C. Hungchara, Head Teacher, Primary School II Lawngtlai IV.

H.C. Lalnighinga, Education Officer. LADC.

Hrangthanga, Ex-Director School Education, Government of Mizoram and Chairman Mizo Board of Secondary Education.

J.C. Sengluaia, Deputy Secretary, Affairs of the District Council, Government of Mizoram, Aizawl.

Jack Sekose, Education Officer, State Council of Education Research and Training, (SCERT), Kohima.

K. Nitumi, Head Teacher, Primary School II Lawngtlai III.

K. Rohuna, Head Master, Govt. Chandmary High School, Lawngtlai, College Veng and Member District Primary Education Board LADC.

Laldunga Chinzah, Sub-Divisional Education Officer, Lawngtlai.

Laltaunga, Chairman, Mizo Board of School Education, and Principal, DIET, Aizawl.

M.C. Lalchinga, Education Officer.

N. Somohendro Singh, Ph.D., Research Student, JNU, New Delhi, Aizawl, 1995.

T. Darvunga, Head Teacher, Primary School III Lawngtlai IV.

T. Tumsanga, EM. LADC.

Talitsuba Ao, Ex Director of Education, Government of Nagaland, Kohima.

Tongpanshilu Ao. Officer on Special Duty, Directorate of School Education, Government of Nagaland, Kohima.

V. Vanthawanga, EM LAPC.

Zoranthanga, Chief Minister, Government of Mizoram.

Zungchena, EM, LADC.

Index

A

Agarwal, M.M., book. 35
Agricultural labour percentage-Mizoram, 37
All India Educational Survey (NCERT)
  First, 73
  Second, 73
  Third, 73
  Fourth, 75 - primary level, 74
  Fifth, 80
American Baptist Mission, 67
Ancillary Facilities,
  in schools, 80
  in Primary schools, 81
  in Upper Primary Schools, 82
Animistic beliefs, 56
Ao Nagas embracing of Christianity, 66
Arunachal Pradesh data on Primary schools having incentive schemes, 254
Assam education post 1961, 31
Autonomous District Council under Sixth Schedule, 147
Autonomy and infrastructural facilities, (Schools LHDC), 191

B

Backward Districts with low age specific enrolment ratio for girls in rural areas statewise, 115
Balwant Rai Mehta Committee, 138
Baptist Missionary Society. 20
Baptists dominations, 63
Bereday's Model of Comparative study, 266
British disinterest in hill administration, 47
Burdoloi Sub Committee, 43

C

Central Govt. aid to Schools, 67
Chieftainship (Mizoram) abolition, 43
Chinees and Naga agreement, 47
Coalition governments, 50
Chieftainship, 146
Chhimtuipui district, 170
Christian Missions Control of Schools, 67
Colonial Policy, 58
Colonial Rule North East territory, 138
Community Participation LHDC, 193
Constitutional provisions of formal division of power, 138
Constitutional Provisions post independence, 28, 71
Curricular Innovations LHDC, 188, 192
Curzon, Lord education improvement by, 25
Crown Colony of Eastern Agency, 42

D

Decentralisation meaning, 137
Demographic indicators

- Nagaland, 208
- Mizoram, 164

Democratic decentralization, 137
Despatch of 1859, 23, 141
Districts classification according to
  Total Literacy levels, 124
  Female literacy levels, 125
Districtwise Percentage of girls to total enrolment in class I-V in 1986-87 in SC/ST Categories, 127
District Council
  Powers and Functions, 139
  and State government, 140
  functioning, 140
Districts / Educational Blocks, Inhabited Villages,
  Naga, 209
  Mizo, 158
Draft Constitution of Mizoram, 43
Drop out rates, 1987-88 for SC - ST, 73

E

East India Company
  education during, 19
Eastern India Tribal Union (EITU), 39
Economic Classification of Populations, 110, 112
Economic Underdevelopment of region, 33
Education demand / Policy, 37
Educational Development Districtwise 1981, 1991 levels, 116, 119
Educational Facilities in Rural Habitations, 253
Elementary Education, 112
  Act of 1870, 141
  in Mizoram, 166
  in Nagaland, 211, 218
  Policy, 19th century, 1892, 18
Employment (Mizoram), 38
Enrolment in Mizoram
  Primary / Middle, 167
  By Management type sub-
    divisonwise, 171, 174
Enrolment Growth
  Primarty level, 129
  Middle level, 130
Enrolment / Dropout N.E. States,
  Primary, 131
  Middle Schools, 132
Ethnic Composition Nagaland, 207
Ethnic discontent, 40
Excluded Areas, 147
  in constitution, 38

F

Facilities of Schooling per sq. km.
  Mizoram, 168
Female education prejudice Assam, 30
Female literacy, 109
  state and district-wise position, 126
Female population percentage 1991, 109
Finance of Elementary education (1975-94), 97
  Arunachal Pradesh, 98
  Assam, 99
  Manipur, 94
  Meghalaya, 101
  Mizoram, 102
  Nagaland, 103
  Tripura, 104
  State-wise (1994-2002), 105
Financing of
  Primary education Mizoram, 170
  Elementary education Nagaland, 221
First FYP, 28, 72
Five Year Plans (FYPs) on education, 27
Furniture and mats for students/ teachers, 82-83

G

Geographical Homogeneity, 56
Girl Enrolment/Dropouts Elementary level, 129
Gokhale, G.K., Bill, 25

Government proposal for education 1992, 73
Government / Primary Middle Schools, Nagaland, 212
Government Primary Schools Teachers Qualification, 177
Growth Rate
  Primary / Upper Primary Level, 77
  Middle Schools, 78
  of Literacy statewise, 113

H

Hill / Valley administration separation, 147
Hindu Schools of learning, 18

I

Illiterate STs percentage Nagland, 201

Indian Education Commission 1882, 23
Indigenous Elementary Schools, 18-19, 24
    merits, 19
Industrial Sector, 36
Insurgency causes, 33
'Inner line' regulation during British, 146
Inspection /Supervision (LADC), 187
Insurgency roots, 38
Inter district disparity, 113
  in literacy 1981, 1991, 114
Isolation, 55

K

Kaito Sema (Naga Leader), 47
Kher Committee, 144
Kohima ST workers
  Marginal workers, 203
  Non-workers, 204
Kohima District
  development, 221
  enrolment, 222
  economic activities, 224
  population, 223
  study sample, 224

L

Lai Autonomous District Council (LADC) education Budget 1995-96, 178
  primary schools, 181
  facilities provided in schools, 182-83
  teaching
    staff, 184
    Aid used, 185
  Autonomy and infrastructural facilities, 191
Lai District Primary Education Board, 189
Laldenga, 35
Lals (tribes chieftians), 142
Lalthanwala, 50
Language/Languages
  problem, 34
  taught Mizoram, 172
Lawngtslai (Study sample), 172
  location, 176
Literate workers, main workers, ST Population in District Kohima, 206
Literacy
  North East, 56
  Indicators, 57
  Nagaland, 210-11
  Mizoram, 166
Local Authorities, Role in Primary Education, 141
Local bodies (North East)
  Education under, 145
  Groups, 145
  System, 145
Lushai Hills, 62
  as excluded area, 42
  inclusion in India, 43
  Dissolution , 147
  district incorporation in Constitution, 151

M

Macaulay. Lord on Western learning, 21
Main Workers in Cultivation
    % age in Mizoram. 161. 163
Manipur Hill Areas District Council Act, 1971, 149
Manipur State Peoples' Regulation of 1947, 153
Marginal Workers by Activity education level in Nagaland, 202
Matriarchal tribes and female education, 109
Missionaries
    activities, 58
    contribution, 20
    role in education, 59
    arrival—Mizoram, 158
    education principles and
        practices, 65
Mizoram
    word, 157
    post 1961, 31
    separatist movement, 34, 40
    clan distinction—absence, 41-42
    dialects, 42
    development, 44
    education, 162, 166
    history, 157-58
    ethnicity, 157
    physical features, 158-59
    economy, 160
    demographic features, 162
    demographic indicators, 164
    literacy rates, 165
        district wise breakup, 165
Mizo National Front (MNF), 35
    aim of Chin State, 159
    origin, 44
Morunges (Dormitories) Nagas, 65

N

'Naga Khats', 47
    insurgency, 48
        origin, 46
    separatist movement, 40-41
    clans, 41-42
    club foundation, 45
    boycott of elections 1952, 46
Naga National Democratic Party (NNDP), 49
Naga People's Conference (NPC), 49
Nagaland, 33
    Location / Infrastructure / schools,
        226
    Administrative aspects VEC, 228
    Study, 197
    history, 197
    inclusion as Indian State, 198
    population, 198-99
    educational development in
        districts, 199
    literacy districtwise break up, 200
    number of education institutions,
        215
    academic facilities, 227
Nagaland Mizoram differences, 218
National education growth, 26
Nehru on Hill autonomy, 45
New Testament in Khasi Language, 62
Nokama (Garos), 150
Non Formal
    education—introduce, 94
    education centres and enrolment
    1918, 95
    education in villages numbers, 95
    education enrolment
        - 1973, 95
        - 1993, 96
Non workers by Activity / Level of education in Nagaland, 203
North Eastern
    States / Region, 30, 55
    Literacy Rate,
        male literacy rate 1991, 233-34
        SC - ST, 235
North Eastern Frontier Tract/Agency, 32

O

Objectives of Study, 50
Operation Black Board, 84
Oriental
    education / orientalists, 21
    learning, 30

P

Panchayat System adoption of, 148
Panchayati Raj System, 150
Patel, Vithalbhai J., 26
People's Convention at Shillong, 47
Phizo, Zapa (Naga leader), 47
    British support, 47
Political Parties North East—origin, 34
Population
    Female, 109
    Economic Classification, 110
Positive / Nagative Developments LHDC, 194
Post Independence period and Primary education role, 27-28
Primary Schools having incentives Schemes, (data)
        Arunachal Pradesh, 254
        Assam, 255
        Manipur, 256
        Mizoram, 258
        Nagaland, 259
        Tripura, 260
Practical Work in Lushai Hills Schools, 64
Pre-British education, 71
Pres byterians establishment of, 62
Protected and Progressive village, 35
Provincial autonomy, 27
Purdah Schools, 30
Pupil Evaluation LHDC, 193

Q

Qualification of Teachers, 90
    Primary in % age 1993, 93
    Middle School, 93-94

R

Recognized Primary and Middle Schools in North East, 78
Ripon's Local self Govt. Act, 142
Rural Habitation with and without Primary Section in North East, 236
Rural Habitation with / without
    Primary Schools / Sections in
        North East,
            -1973, 237
            -1978, 239
            -1986, 241
            -1993, 243, 250
    Middle Schools/Sections, 245
        -1973, 245
        -1978, 247
        -1986, 249

S

Sailo, Brigadier, 50
Salvatarian Mission, 67
Sanskrit Literature (Ahoms), 61
Schools Transferred to Autonomous District Councils in Mizoram
        Terms and Conditions, 267
School Completions Mizoram Primary, 167
School Education Mizoram Structure/ Administration, 169
School Buildings 1986, 1993
    Primary Schools State-wise, 79
    Middle Schools State-wise, 80
SC - ST- Non SC- ST population (North East) 1981-91, 265
SC - ST Literacy 1991, 2001, 128
Structure / Administration of School Education in Nagaland, 219
Scott, David Oriental Learning, 30
Secessionist Movements, 40
Sema, Hoksia Nagaland CM, 35
State Regulation Committee, 39
State Percentage of Rural Population with / without
    Primary School / Sections,
        251

Upper Primary Schools, 252

STs with 10,000 and above Population with 3 major languages excluding Assam, 261-64

T

Total workers main / marginal and their categories N.E. states, 111

Tea Garden and Salvatarian Mission of Italy, 67

Teachers in Primary / Middle Schools Mizoram by Mgmt. / Trng. / Sex Sub-divsion-wise, 173-175

Teachers
- growth rate, 85
  - primary, 86-87
  - middle, 87-88
  - upper primary, 87-88
- in position (percentage)
  - in primary Schools, 1986, 1993, 90
- Accountability LHDC, 193
- Pupil Ratio district-wise
- Nagaland, 214
- Training Nagaland, 213
- Mizoram (Nos, Trained Ratio), 168
- by Institution types (Numbers)
  - Nagaland, 216-17

Tripura types of local self Govt., 152

U

UFN (United Front of Nagaland), 49

Universalization of Elementary Education, 17

V

Victorian era
- (1854-1902) features, 23-24
- (1902-21), 24

Villages with centres of Non Formal Education, 95

Villages Councils, 146

Villages Department Boards (VDBs) Nagaland, 152

Village Education Committee (VEC)
- Nagaland, 225
- duties, 225
- academic aspects, 228
- finance, 229
- facilities, 227

Trained Teachers / Primary/Middle Schools, 91

Tripura Tribal Area Autonomous District Councils (TTAADC), 153

W

Wellesley, Lord on missionary work, 61

Welsh Revival movement, 63

Wokha missionaries at, 66

Work force in Nagaland Sector-wise distributions, 201

Woods Despatch, 22

Wardha Scheme of Basic Education (Gandhi's), 26

Y

Young Mizo Association, 36